Dornford Yates is th   cer.
Born into a middle-cl   ped
together enough mon   of a
solicitor, he qualified fo   our
of his great passion for   ion
and experience, Yates' books feature the genteel life, a nostalgic
glimpse at Edwardian decadence and a number of swindling
solicitors. In his heyday and as a testament to the fine writing
in his novels, Dornford Yates' work was placed in the bestseller
list. Indeed, 'Berry' is one of the great comic creations of
twentieth-century fiction, and 'Chandos' titles were successfully
adapted for television.

Finding the English climate utterly unbearable, Yates chose
to live in the French Pyrénées for eighteen years before moving
on to Rhodesia where he died in 1960.

G000150939

201479611

Adèle and Co.
And Berry Came Too
As Berry and I Were Saying
B-Berry and I Look Back
Berry and Co.
Blind Corner
Blood Royal
The Brother of Daphne
Cost Price
The Courts of Idleness
An Eye For a Tooth
Fire Below
Gale Warning
The House That Berry Built
Jonah and Co.
Ne'er Do Well
Perishable Goods
Red in the Morning
She Fell Among Thieves
She Painted Her Face

DORNFORD YATES

THE BERRY SCENE

HOUSE OF
STRATUS

This edition published in 2001 by House of Stratus, an imprint of Stratus Books Ltd, 21 Beeching Park, Kelly Bray, Cornwall, PL17 8QS, UK.

www.houseofstratus.com

Typeset, printed and bound by House of Stratus.

A catalogue record for this book is available from the British Library and the Library of Congress.

ISBN 1-84232-966-9

To those who have done me the honour to ask
me to write this book.

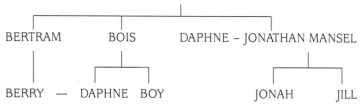

BERTRAM PLEYDELL
(of White Ladies, in the County of Hampshire)

BERTRAM   BOIS   DAPHNE – JONATHAN MANSEL

BERRY — DAPHNE BOY   JONAH   JILL

Contents

Prologue

At the beginning of his last term but one, Berry was removed to the Lower Sixth. Throughout his five years at Harrow, his interest in a classical education had not been marked, and of his new form-master and himself, I do not know which was the more surprised at his promotion.

After three days –

"Pleydell," said the former, "until recently this form-room was tenanted by the Lower Shell. You're sure you're not under the impression that that lease is still running?"

"No, sir," said Berry, sadly. "I'm afraid there's no doubt about it."

"About what?"

"That my dignity, sir, has been served at the expense of yours."

From that moment, the two became friends.

His form-master was a man of the rarest wit, and, while Berry sat at his feet, the exchanges between the two were frequently worth hearing.

One morning Berry, who had been requested to translate a passage from Juvenal, stumbled through a line and a half and then stopped dead.

"Go on, Pleydell."

Berry looked up apologetically.

"I'm sorry, sir, but the English equivalent of the next phrase has for the moment escaped me."

"Can you construe?"

"I – I don't believe I shall do the satirist justice this morning, sir. Tomorrow, perhaps…"

"The artistic temperament?"

"You're very understanding, sir."

"I am. You hoped for the best."

"I still do, sir."

"Optimist. Write it out twice."

"Very good, sir."

"And I know your cousin's writing."

Berry sighed.

" 'Put out the light,' " he murmured, " 'and then put out the light.' "

(The School had been addressed on *Shakespeare* the week before.)

"For that rejoinder, your punishment is – halved."

"You're very good, sir."

"No. Only just. 'And other fell on good ground.' "

On another occasion –

"You force me to the conclusion, Pleydell, that Plautus is not among your favourites."

"I feel, sir, that he loses by, er, translation."

"I see. Endeavour to subdue that emotion by writing out, instead of memorizing, the construe for tomorrow."

"Yes, sir. A, er, free translation?"

"I must be able to recognize the passage. And you may add a short comparison of the audiences for which Plautus wrote and – What theatres do you patronize?"

"I've heard of the Gaiety, sir."

" – and the audiences for which you have reason to believe that Mr George Edwardes caters."

"Very good, sir."

"And don't underrate the intelligence of the former."

"Nor its taste, sir?"

"No. But this is not a licence to submit an obscene libel."

"Certainly not, sir. Only…"

"Only what?"

"Were *débutantes* admitted to Plautus' plays, sir? I mean, I believe they go to the Gaiety."

There was a little silence. Then –

"I feel," said the form-master, "that this comparison had better not be drawn. The possibilities are too grave. Let's play for safety and have a hundred lines of Virgil, instead."

Once, when Berry's written translation of the death of Patroclus proved disappointing –

"There is a saying, Pleydell, that Homer sometimes nods."

"Yes, sir."

"I have yet to hear it suggested that some of his work was done when he was in his cups. Yet, that is the inference to be drawn from your handiwork."

"I must admit, sir, that I found this particular passage a little less straightforward than usual."

"Don't spare him. Say incoherent, and have done with it."

"I hesitate to presume, sir. I mean…"

"Go on."

"I've always understood that he was a great master, sir."

"Well, you've shown him up today, haven't you?"

"Not him, sir. Myself."

"That's better. When you perceive a mote in Homer's eye, look immediately for the beam in your own. It'll save time – and labour."

An agonized look leapt into Berry's eyes.

"I won't fail to remember that, sir."

"You'll make a mental note of it?"

"I have, sir."

"Good. But I feel that such a note should be reinforced."

"With respect, sir, I believe that to be unnecessary."

"Do you, indeed? Well, I'll back your belief: but I warn you that, should it prove to be ill founded, the belated reinforcement will be a work of some magnitude."

"Thank you, sir."

"Not at all. I've made my bet safe."

One day we were desired to draw from memory a map of the Mediterranean. When our efforts had been examined –

"Pleydell."

"Sir?"

"I said 'A map of the Mediterranean.' "

"Yes, sir."

"Are you of the impressionist school?"

"Er – yes, sir."

"Then it's my fault. I should have made it clear that I wanted an old-fashioned map. Do me one this afternoon – in colour."

"Very good, sir. Any colours I like?"

"Except scarlet. And you might show the voyages of St Paul. That will remind you of the existence of an island called Malta."

"Of course, sir. That was where the snake did it on him."

"That's right. And he did it on the snake. As a matter of fact, The Authorized Version puts it rather better. You might make two copies of the verses in question and add them to the map. Any more reminiscences?"

"No, sir."

And once again –

"It would be idle to pretend, Pleydell, that the memorizing of Greek verse was your strong point."

"I respectfully agree, sir."

"What are we going to do about it?"

"May I suggest, sir, that I should be permitted to perform some other labour, instead?"

"Such as?"

"Anything, sir. I'd cheerfully pick oakum."

"That would be premature. Besides, we must stick more or less to the curriculum."

"A series of articles, sir, on the less obvious advantages of a classical education?"

"So be it. But be careful. Scurrility will meet with a very short shrift. You must render unto Caesar the things that are Caesar's."

"It shall be done, sir."

After a week –

"I find this article a little equivocal, Pleydell. You must beat down Satan under your feet."

"Believe me, I'm scourging myself, sir."

"You don't believe all you say?"

"Not all, sir."

"Lay on more heartily. Help thou thine unbelief. Hang it, man. A classical education has been commended by my betters for hundreds of years. We can't all be wrong."

Berry looked at his form-master.

"That's very true, sir."

After another week –

"This rings more true, Pleydell."

"I, er, hoped it would, sir."

"Good. You're beginning to focus the picture?"

"By standing back, sir. I – oughtn't to come too close."

"A respectful distance?"

"Very respectful, sir."

"That's all I ask."

To this day, Berry will commend a grounding in polite letters with all his might.

1

In Which I Drive Daphne to Brooch on Midsummer Day, and Berry Gives Evidence

The day was Midsummer Day – and fairly deserved its name.

Breakfast had been served upon the terrace, for all the winds were still; and the meal refreshed the spirit as well as the flesh. This was natural. The cool, sweet air was laced with the scent of flowers: still overlaid with dew, the lawn was quick with magic – a sparkling acre of velvet that filled the eye: full-dressed, the peerage of timber stood still as statuary: and the great sun was in his dominion, arraying all foliage with splendour, gilding clipped yew and warming chiselled stone, and lending the lovely distance the delicate shimmer of heat.

As I watched, the spell was broken. A woodpecker fluttered to the lawn, and the boughs of a chestnut dipped to the swing of a squirrel at play.

My sister tilted her head and raised her voice.

"Do hurry up, darling. There's a letter for you from Jonah. We want to see what it says."

Berry's voice floated down from the bedroom above.

"I know. So do I. I am devoured by curiosity. But I'm going to tread it under. Instead, I'm going to concentrate upon the suspension of my half-hose. Two confections confront me – one in smouldering amber and one in reseda green. Now, if my trousers come down – "

"If you don't come down in two minutes…"

The protasis went unanswered; but fifty seconds later Berry appeared upon the terrace, perfectly groomed.

"Do be quick," said Daphne.

Her husband frowned.

"The empty stomach," he said, "must always take pride of place. Once the pangs of hunger have been assuaged – "

"By your leave," said I…

I gave the letter to Daphne, who opened and read it aloud.

23rd June, 1907.

Dear Berry,

I've arranged for a car, with a chauffeur, for us to try. Hired the two for one month. If the vehicle suits us, we order a similar car. If it doesn't, we don't.

We shall, of course, be unpopular. Sir Anthony will denounce our decision and will declare that we are letting the neighbourhood down. But he'll have a car himself in two years' time. You see. Speed has a convenience which nobody can deny: and cars don't have to be cared for, as horses have. Of course they are going to kill the romance of the road, rather as gunpowder killed the romance of the battlefield. But that is the price of progress.

Well, there we are. I feel at once ashamed and excited. It is going to be a remarkable experience – taking familiar roads at forty-five miles an hour.

Expect me, then, on Monday, complete with car. I shall hope to arrive for lunch, but we may be delayed.

Yours ever,
Jonah.

There was a guilty silence.

Then –

"There you are," said Berry. "What did I say? That long-nosed viper left here on the strict understanding that he was surreptitiously to investigate the possibilities of good and evil which might result from our acquisition of an automobile. He was then to return to this mansion and submit his report. Does he observe those crystal-clear instructions? No. And now we're all in the swill-tub up to the waist."

"I feel quite frightened," said Daphne. "What ever will everyone say?"

Berry continued his complaint.

" 'Forty-five miles an hour!' And the day before yesterday I subscribed to the imposition of substantial fines upon no less than five motorists for covering a measured mile in less than three minutes of time."

(Berry had lately been appointed a Justice of the Peace.)

"That's all right," said my sister. "You can ask where the traps are, and we can give them a miss."

"And supposing we're caught outside our area?"

"You won't be summoned," said I. "Unless you propose to drive."

"Oh, nor I shall," said Berry. "Then that's all right. And if they take my name, I shall say I was being abducted. All the same, it's going to be awkward. On the Bench, I mean, as soon as the news gets round. The Colonel's nose will increase in crimson and purpure. He may even foam at the ears – I mean, the mouth."

"Let him," said Daphne boldly. "Why shouldn't we have a car?"

"Oh, I know that bit," said Berry. "But you haven't got to consort with the bigoted fool. He says it's a breach of one's duty towards one's neighbour. And when you remember the dust, I'm not sure he isn't right."

There was another silence.

"We must use the thing early," said Daphne. "Before other people are up. It's light at five now."

Berry pushed away his plate and covered his eyes.

"I wish you wouldn't say these things," he said. "I know it's just thoughtlessness, but idle words like those are bad for my heart. Fancy rising at four in the morning for the privilege of raving about a cheerless countryside, through lifeless villages, past promising pubs that are straitly shut and barred, with a herd of indignant milch-cows round every bend. Oh, no. We've done it now – or, rather, Jonah has. We shall have to brazen it out."

"We can't tell the Dean," said I. "He'd turn us out of the house."

Always, on Midsummer Day, we lunched at the Deanery, Brooch – a very pleasant engagement, which we were happy to keep. The Dean was a human prelate and, though very much older, a distant cousin of ours. He was also intensely conservative.

Berry addressed his wife.

"Which reminds me, if you must have the mail-phaeton, then Boy can drive. I've split three new pairs of gloves, holding those greys. And my arms were half out of their sockets on Monday night. I'll take the dog-cart – Rainbow was properly mouthed."

"The greys," said I, "are short of exercise."

"Well, I'm not," said Berry, passing his cup. "And when I am, I'll take it – in some conventional way. Bowls, for instance. But I won't be dismembered." Daphne's hand flew to her mouth. "Yes, you may laugh, you siren. You just sit still and radiate sex-appeal: but I have to hold the swine."

"I'm s-sorry, darling," wailed Daphne. "But, Boy, if you could hear him. He talks to the greys just as if they were naughty children, and on the way home he told them a fairytale."

"I was seeking to divert them," said Berry: "in the hope of saving our lives. They've only got one idea – that is to out-strip the phaeton. And they did seem to listen – till Order noticed a haystack a couple of fields away. Oh, and who called them Law and Order. If he'd called them Battle and Murder, he'd have been nearer the mark. Anyway, I've got to see Merton. So I'll go by Dimity Green and be there as soon as you."

My sister regarded her wristwatch.

"I should like," she said, "to leave here at half-past ten. I want to give an order at Wilson's before we drive to the Close."

"Make it eleven," said I. "We're bound to be there in less than an hour and a half."

"Half-past ten," said Daphne. "I love having time to spare."

Berry was right about the greys. Before eleven o'clock I had split my left-hand glove. I was glad when we came to the foot of Hunchback Hill. Here was a long ascent, and, as we approached its head, I saw a brewer's dray at rest by the side of the road. The driver was breathing his cattle after the climb.

As I turned my head, to give the fellow good day –

"It's Curly," shrieked Daphne. "Stop, Boy, stop. Curly, Curly, how good to see you again!"

I pulled the greys in to the hedgerow, and William, sitting behind us, slipped down and ran to their heads. I gave the reins to my sister and left my seat. As I gained the road, the mighty drayman came forward, cap in hand.

"It's my day out, Master Boy."

"And ours, Curly." I shook his enormous fist. "Come and – meet Mrs Pleydell."

The fine old waggoner stepped to the side of the phaeton, touched his forelock and made my sister a bow.

"Your servant, ma'am."

"How dare you, Curly? Shake hands and call me 'Miss Daphne', just as you always have. How many times have you put me up on Yorick? But what does this mean? You've not come back to the road?"

"For two months only, Miss Daphne. Two of our drivers are sick, an' I was glad of a chance to help the firm. They've been very good to me; and in summertime, you know, I'm as good as I was."

5

For five or six minutes we spoke of bygone days, for Curly Jordan was one of our childhood's friends. Then the three of us went to make much of his 'unicorn'. Three fine shire horses they were, with bells on their collars and plaited manes and tails. The leader was outstanding – a benevolent giant that blew upon Daphne's face and then stood on his dignity.

"They do you great credit, Curly."

"One does one's best, Miss Daphne. An' now that I'm back, you know, I feel I want to go on."

"I'm sure you do. So should I. But I hope you won't. The winter weather, Curly, would bring you down."

"Maybe you're right, Miss Daphne. I'm rising seventy-four."

Then we all strolled back to the phaeton, and Curly stood beside it, while I put Daphne up and then climbed back to my seat.

He was smiling gravely as he stood there, still a magnificent figure, his humble apron of sackcloth about his waist. But as my eyes met his, I read their long farewell, and I knew I was looking my last upon a great-hearted man. And Curly knew it, too.

My sister leaned forward.

"Come round to my side, Curly."

When the waggoner did her bidding, she put out her hand for his.

"D'you remember you used to say that I was the light of your eyes?"

Curly bent his grey head.

"Ay, Miss Daphne," he said. "I used to make that bold."

"I'm so proud to remember it, Curly. I always shall be proud that such a famous waggoner said such a thing of me."

She stooped and kissed his rough cheek.

As Curly stood back, glowing, I nodded my head to William, whose eyes were upon my face.

He sprang aside and I touched the greys with the whip...

Two miles had bowled by before Daphne lifted her voice.

Then –

"We're going down, Boy," she said. "We don't breed men like Curly Jordan today."

"I'm afraid you're right," said I. "Now, don't be silly, Law – that's only a five-barred gate."

The way from White Ladies to Brooch is still a lovely way, but now there is much more traffic, and pretty roads that were crooked have been made straight. And the tarmac has swallowed verges, amid time-honoured trees have been felled. But on that midsummer morning the way was as it had been before my father was born.

Three miles I well remember as being the fairest of all. Here Nature and Husbandry seemed to go hand in hand: wild rose and honeysuckle tricked out the wayside hedge, elms guarded lovers' stiles, and oak and ash and chestnut held up a ragged canopy for passers-by. Now and again an aged, five-barred gate hung like a window-sill, to offer such a landscape as Thomson sang and Constable loved to paint, and once the road curled down to a little ford, where the stream ran clear upon gravel, murmuring out of a thicket and into a meadow's arms, and turning sweetness to fragrance down all its length.

There I pulled up the greys that morning, for the day was hot and the water was good for their legs, and the spot was one which from childhood my sister and I had loved.

So we rested for five or six minutes…

As we were leaving the water, a gig came slowly towards us, drawn by a strawberry roan.

"Mary Anne," said Daphne.

Mary Anne was the roan.

I checked the greys, and the farmer driving pulled up and took off his hat.

"Good morning, Mr Ightham."

"The sweet of the morning to you, ma'am." His eye ran over the greys. "You've a handful there, Mas'r Boy."

I laughed.

"My arms'll be stiff tomorrow. Mrs Ightham quite well?"

"In wonderful trim, sir, thank you."

"And Bridget?" said my sister. "I thought she was coming to me."

"So she hopes, ma'am. She wrote her letter last night. But don't you spoil her, Miss Daphne. Her mother came out of White Ladies, and Bridget's going to you to learn how to make a good wife."

"I'll bear that in mind, Mr Ightham. Her mother's name is still a household word."

"Like mistress, like maid, Miss Daphne. An' Mas'r Berry? I hope he's keeping well."

"In splendid form, Mr Ightham. You know he's a magistrate now?"

"That's as it should be, Miss Daphne. I reckon he'll put them motorcars where they belong."

"He'll, er, do his best, Mr Ightham. Give Mrs Ightham my love."

"Thank you kindly, ma'am."

We bade him goodbye and drove on.

As the phaeton swung up the hill –

" 'Them motorcars,' " breathed my sister. "We're going to lose half our friends."

"For the time being only," said I. "I quite agree with Jonah – that very soon our neighbours will follow suit."

I saw a car in the distance, as we were entering Brooch. Before Law and Order had seen it, I turned to the left. It was no good asking for trouble. But when I had fetched a compass, to enter the square of St Giles, there was another car fuming some fifteen paces away.

Happily the square was not crowded, for the greys, with one consent, proposed to mount the pavement, if not to enter some shop.

I spoke over my shoulder to William.

"Ask the chauffeur to stop his engine. Be very polite."

With the tail of my eye I saw my orders obeyed, but the chauffeur only laughed and let in his clutch.

There was only one thing to be done.

As the car moved forward towards us, I stood up, lashed Law and Order and let them go. Oblivious of all but the pain, the greys leaped forward, flung past the moving car and down the length of the square.

To this day I do not know how we entered Bellman Lane, but I managed to pull them up before we had reached its end.

William came running, white-faced.

"All's well," I said, "but stand to their heads a minute."

When he was there, I gave the reins to Daphne and went to their heads myself. I did my best to repair the wrong I had done them, soothing and making much of the handsome pair. Then I turned to the groom, who clearly had news to tell.

"Yes, William. What do you know?"

"It was just beginning, sir. Joe Chinnock had got the chauffeur, and Mr Bertram was there."

"Then we'll hear all about it later. They're all right now, I think; so we'll get along."

But I felt better already. Joe Chinnock came out of our village and plied a blacksmith's trade.

Half an hour had gone by, and we were in the Deanery garden, taking a glass of sherry before we sat down to lunch.

"Act Two," said Berry, "was most enjoyable. Let me say at once that I shouldn't have enjoyed it so much, if I had had the faintest idea that you and my only wife had been on in Act One. But the phaeton was out of sight when I drove into the square.

"The first thing I saw was Joe Chinnock holding a wallah up by the scruff of his neck. Then he swung him into the horse-trough and let him lie.

"Now there was no constable present, and I felt that, if worse was coming, it might be my bounden duty to interfere. Not physically, of course. A dirty look, or something – you know what I mean.

"In some uneasiness, therefore, I trotted up to the scene.

"By the time I was there, the car, deprived of its helmsman, had ravaged a barrow of strawberries and butted the nearest lamp-post, which it had snapped in two. The top, complete with lantern, had fallen into the front or driver's seat; but the bottom had held the car, whose engine had stopped.

"You never saw such a mess. Cast iron sticking out of the windscreen, glass all over the cushions, and the whole of the car's off forehand plastered with the succulent mush to which the slightest pressure reduces our scarlet fruit.

"The chauffeur had emerged from the horse-trough and was standing, streaming with water and trying in vain to unbutton his uniform: and a man, not unlike a gorilla, had erupted from the back of the car and, using most regrettable language, was declining the hawker's invitation to view what had once been a barrow, but now bore no resemblance to that commodity.

"I had just told George to take Rainbow, when Constable Rowe appeared. This, of course, absolved me; so, as I had a good seat, I sat still where I was.

"Now Rowe never saw the chauffeur. But he saw the gorilla and the hawker, engaged in mutual abuse: he saw the strawberries and the lamp-post, clearly the prey of the car; and he jumped to the natural conclusion that the gorilla had been driving the car and had done first the barrow and then the lamp-post in.

"So the stage was set for confusion.

"After the opening chorus, which was taken very fast by the gorilla and the hawker and was consequently not so much incoherent as distracting, Rowe cursed the two into silence and took out his book. Then he turned to the gorilla.

" 'Well, if you wasn't drivin', who was?'

" 'Nobody was,' cries Gorilla. 'I tell you – '

" 'Then that's 'ow it 'appened,' says Rowe, beginning to write and reading his entry aloud. *'Car left unattended.'*

" 'It wasn't unattended,' yells Gorilla. 'My chauffeur – '

" 'If no one was drivin' – '

" 'I was drivin',' says the chauffeur, who had come up unobserved.

" 'No, you weren't,' screams Gorilla. 'Nobody was.'

" 'Well, I should 'ave been,' says the chauffeur, 'if – '

" 'Ah,' says Rowe, staring upon him. 'You should 'ave been, but you weren't.'

" 'No, *no, NO,* ' screams Gorilla. 'You've got it all wrong. The man was dragged out of his seat.'

" 'Just as well,' says Rowe, regarding the front of the car. ' 'Ooever done it probably saved his life.'

" '*Saved his life?*' howls Gorilla. 'He damned near killed us all.'

" 'Then he *was* drivin',' says Rowe. 'Why couldn't you say so at first?'

" 'Of course the man was driving, until he was dragged from the car.'

"Rowe makes another entry.

" '*Chauffeur was driving – damned near killed us all.*'

"Till now, to my mind, the crowd had been very restrained; but, before this new rise of the tide of misunderstanding, all within earshot broke down. Pent-up emotion, so to speak, burst its banks. There was a roar of laughter to which even the hawker subscribed, and when, with a scream of rage, the gorilla seized Rowe's notebook and flung it down upon the ground and then launched himself at the hawker, so that the two fell together into the billow of fruit, I frankly confess that the tears ran down my cheeks.

"And there I left the scene – for the police-station, where I saw the Inspector on duty and asked him to send a sergeant to help Rowe out.

"I imagine action will be taken; but if Joe Chinnock is summoned, by Heaven, I'll see him through. If only I had been there…"

"I'm so thankful you weren't," said Daphne.

"That's almost unkind," said Berry.

The Dean put in his oar.

"The relish with which you have reported the discomfiture of the wicked convinces us that, had you witnessed Act One, your reluctance to interfere would have been less marked."

"D'you blame me, sir?"

"Not in the least. I hope you'd have sent for me to bail you out. But I do share Daphne's relief."

Berry regarded his wife.

"I expect you're right," he said. "But she's still as good as new, and I don't want her bent."

Two hours and a half had gone by, and we were about to be gone.

Daphne was taking her leave of Mrs Dean, but the Dean, who was still a fine whip, came out and into the Close, to have a look at the greys.

His inspection over, he motioned to Berry and me and strolled across to the sward.

As we fell in beside him –

"You'll have to give them up," he said quietly. "Next time whoever is driving mayn't be so fortunate."

"We can't amble about, sir," said I, "behind a couple of slugs."

"No," said the Dean, "you can't. Youth must be served. Still, I value your lives. So I think you had better consider acquiring an automobile."

As we drove back to White Ladies, my feelings were mixed.

The Dean's approval apart, we now had a perfect excuse for acquiring a car: but I could not lose sight of the fact that sentence had been passed upon our stable and that its execution was now but a matter of time. And the horse was part of our lives. The pleasant smell of stabling, the rhythm of hooves upon the road, the creak of leather, the brush of a velvet nose – these things were familiar to us as the gurgle of the rain in the down-pipes and the afternoon sunshine that badged the library shelves. And now the end of that chapter was drawing near. Never again could we take the greys to Brooch. To Merry Down – yes: for a while we could use them to cover the countryside. But not for long. If, instead of a gig that morning, a car had come down to the ford... And the equipage would be superseded. Who, if he had a car, would take a carriage and pair to drive twelve miles to a dance – and twelve miles back...at three o'clock of a bitter winter morning? And what of the staff? Of Peters and George and William, sitting behind me now?

I thrust the nightmare away and pointed to a kingdom of barley, rippling under the touch of some zephyr we could not feel.

"You used to love that, darling."

"I know," said Daphne gravely. "I love it still. I think it beats falling water. It's really a miracle – a rustle that you can see. What did Berry say about this business?"

"Summonses are to be issued. Joe Chinnock is to be summoned – of course for assault. The gorilla, whose name is Slober, is to be summoned twice – once for assaulting the hawker and once for obstructing the police. The cases will probably be heard on Monday week. Berry has instructed Mason on Joe's behalf."

"What will happen?"

"I've no idea. They'll probably be taken together, and if Mr Slober is wise, he won't press the case against Joe. I mean, if they send Joe down, they're not going to let Slober off."

"Will you have to give evidence?"

"I don't know. But William will."

My sister raised her voice.

"Do you hear that, William? You'll have to go to Court and bear witness for Joe."

"I'll be happy to do that, ma'am. He only done his duty."

"I entirely agree," said I. "And so, I hope, will the Bench. Hullo, who's this coming? First time I have seen that pair."

"It's Mrs de Lisle, sir," said William. "She's sold the bays."

The landau approached us slowly. As we were drawing abreast, I checked the greys.

My sister leaned forward.

"How d'you do, Mrs de Lisle?"

"Good evening, my dear. Boy, where's your button-hole?"

With a glance at my empty lapel –

"I'm afraid I forgot it," said I.

Mrs de Lisle frowned.

"When driving a lady, you should be properly dressed. Never mind, you're both in the country – which most young things of your age now seem to abhor. Did you lunch in Barchester?"

"Yes – with the Dean," said Daphne. "We always do, you know, on Midsummer Day."

"A pretty habit, my dear. And the Dean is the best of the bunch. The Close is well named. Most of their minds are as narrow as their hats are high. Because a man takes orders, he shouldn't let orders take him. But the Dean is aware of the strangers without his gates."

"And Mrs Dean's very charming."

"So she is. I was her bridesmaid a good many years ago. And a dashing young lady she was. But the odour of sanctity's drugged her. The charm is there, but the mettle has disappeared. Never mind. Come to lunch on Tuesday and tell me the news. Withyham may be there – but I hope he won't."

"Oh, dear," said Daphne.

(Lord Withyham was our *bête noir*).

Mrs de Lisle smiled.

"Very well. Come on Friday instead. And Berry, of course. And I quite agree with you – Withyham doesn't go with weather like this."

"We'll love to."

"I'm not so sure: but I'm selfish. And you and Berry and Boy will do me good." The lady raised her voice. "Drive on, Weston."

We cried our farewells, as the carriage moved leisurely on, and the greys, impatient for their stable, snatched at their bits.

One more encounter we had that Midsummer Day, and that was with General Stukely – a man among men.

The four-wheeled dog-cart was still, drawn up by a gap in the hedgerow on Steeple Ridge. From his seat beside his coachman, the General was viewing the acres which had stood in the name of Stukely for more than three hundred years. And soon another would claim them, for he was ninety-two and the last of his line.

It was not a great estate – less than a hundred acres, when all was in: but love and pride had made it a specimen piece. There was the rose-red manor, neighboured by timber so lovely it seemed unreal. Horses were grazing in a paddock, and cows were standing, musing, under a parcel of elms. The purest woodland embraced the pretty picture – oak and beech and chestnut, in splendid heart: and here, in the foreground, a magnificent crop of oats was spreading an apron of promise, to fill a farmer's eye.

As we drew alongside the dog-cart –

"Good evening, General," cried Daphne.

"Good evening, my dear. You look so fresh and so eager, you might be going to market, instead of coming back."

"You always say nice things to me, General."

"An old man's privilege, Daphne – one of the many we have. Boy, you've your father's style – and there's a compliment."

"Thank you, sir." I pointed with my whip to the oats. "You maintain the standard, General, which the Manor has always set."

"They look very well, don't they? The soil is good, you know, and I do my best." He returned to my sister. "And how is Berry, my dear?"

"Very well, thank you. He took the dog-cart today. We've been to the Deanery to lunch."

"You keep good company, Daphne. The Dean and his lady adorn the office he holds. Will you come and take tea at the Manor one of these days?"

"May we come next Friday, General?"

"It will give me great pleasure, my dear. Whom may I ask to meet you?"

"Mayn't we come alone?" said my sister. "And then we can over-eat and I can pour out the tea."

The General smiled.

"You give the right answers, Daphne. You always did. And your lady mother before you, bless her soul. And now I'll delay you no longer. White Ladies should have its mistress before the sun goes down. Goodbye, my dear. My kind regards to Berry. And I shall look for your coming on Friday next."

We left him there, by the edge of his fair demesne, and five minutes later we crossed the verge of the forest to which White Ladies belongs.

Here Nature came into her own.

The sun was low and was lacing the beauty about us with golden light. Majestic oaks rose from a quilt of bracken that might have been cloth of gold: birches laid heads together, so that their lovely tresses made up one golden shower: a watch of firs became a gleaming cohort: and a glorious company of beeches, their shapely boles flood-lit with golden magic – an order of pillars holding the shadows up, spoke to enchanted forests and all the lovely lore of fairy-tales.

So, for the last four miles, our progress was royal – the dark-blue phaeton skimming the yellow roads, and the constant flicker of the sunshine caparisoning the equipage, now badging Order's shoulder, now making the panels flash, now leaping up from the splash-board, to magnify the beauty for which my sister was known.

Ears pricked to catch a whisper, obedient to some presence we could not feel, the greys sped through the forest – a model pair. When a gypsy rose out of some bushes, to brandish a broom, they took no notice at all: the two might have been bewitched – I think they were.

So we came back to White Ladies in the evening of Midsummer Day.

Three hours had gone by, and a precious silence reigned in the library.

Daphne was reading a novel, Berry was at his table and I was nodding over *The Morning Post*.

"How are your arms?" said Berry.

"Not too good," said I.

"You wait till tomorrow," said Berry. "You won't be able to dress."

Daphne put out a hand and touched my hair.

"I don't think I thanked you, darling, for saving my neck."

"Don't put it too high," I said. "I chose the lesser evil and brought it off. If Bellman Lane had been blocked…"

"D'you mind not discussing it?" said Berry. "It sends the b-blood to my head. Oh, and what do you do with these pens? Clean your nose – nails with them?"

"You filthy brute," said his wife.

"Well, the nibs are done in," said Berry: "and that, as the obvious result of having been used for some purpose other than that for which they were bought and sold. Where's your typewriter?"

"No, you don't," said I. "That cost me twenty-five pounds. Where's your fountain-pen?"

Berry made no reply.

After a moment Daphne raised her voice.

"Why don't you use it, darling? The new one you had sent down and that wrote so well?"

Berry swung round.

"Look here," he said. "I don't want that pen mentioned. I don't want any reference, direct or indirect, veiled or manifest, made in my hearing to what are called fountain-pens. 'Fountain-pens.' Sounds so romantic, doesn't it? Suggestive of nymphs and groves and shepherds' pipes. No one, of course, would buy them, if they were called pocket-skunks."

"What ever d'you mean?" said his wife.

Berry expired. Then –

"Deluded," he said, "by a pictorial advertisement, as, of course, I was meant to be – as have been thousands of other innocent lieges of His Majesty, I wrote for a fountain-pen, enclosing a cheque in favour of a firm which, I have every reason to hope and, indeed, expect, will shortly be eaten of worms. According to the prospectus, the implement was super-fine. It could neither leak nor blot: it could be replenished in the dark: it liked being dropped and carried upside down: I'm not sure it couldn't spell – according to the prospectus. Best of all, it was 'of vest-pocket size'." He paused to cover his eyes. "When I think that I filled the swine – with the finest blue-black ink… Oh, it wrote all right. The words slid out of its mouth. I wrote three letters in triumph. Then I put it into my pocket and lay down upon the sofa, to take a short nap. That was on Sunday last, at three o'clock."

"My God," said Daphne. "Not your new, grey suit?"

"My new, grey suit," said Berry, between his teeth. "The tares were sown, while I slept. Waistcoat, coat and shirt utterly and completely destroyed. Soaked, steeped and saturated with the finest blue-black ink." He shrugged his shoulders. "The thing was undoubtedly capacious – the stain on the coat must be quite six inches by four. And I never knew it, till I saw myself in a glass. Went to wash my hands, and, as I was turning away, I saw this – this devastation outlined upon my trunk. In shape, it was not unlike the Iberian Peninsular.

"At first I thought it was a shadow – I couldn't believe it was true. As in a dream, I touched it... And then, in one hideous flash, I saw the pit that had been digged, into which *I had paid* to jump. Those filthy, black-gutted lepers had sworn that it couldn't leak. But they never swore it couldn't break... Screaming with agony, I plucked first one half and then the other out of the sodden pouch which, half an hour before, had been an elegant pocket in a gentleman's vest.

"Well, there you are. Adding things up, the, er, souvenir has proved expensive. The pen was twelve shillings, and the suit – '

"You must have lain on it," said Daphne.

"I never lay on it," screamed Berry. "I never subjected it to any strain, stress, tax, pressure or other kind of violence. The swine had no shadow of excuse. I put it into my pocket, as I was incited to do. It had every comfort and convenience – and every opportunity to do its filthy work. I tell you, it was a snare – a treacherous snare, set by verminous blackguards for honest men. And now what about a restorative? Or would that be out of place?"

"I'm dreadfully sorry, darling. Besides, I liked that suit. By the way, have you written to Jonah?"

"I have. I've told him to cancel the car and leave the country."

"Don't be absurd," said Daphne. "We've got to have the thing now. Besides, I'm all excited."

As Berry passed the sofa, he laid his manuscript in my sister's lap.

"Let the blots," he said, "speak to my emotion. Few could compose such periods: fewer still could cover two pages with a nib which resembled a miniature grappling-iron. Not that your brother is not to dredge his no-nails; but what's his hoof-pick done?"

I read the letter over my sister's shoulder.

Dear Brother,

Your letter caused me much pain. Indeed, for some hours after its perusal I was afflicted with griping of the guts, a malady which, if we may believe the ancient registers, was prevalent in the seventeenth century. But, then, look at their habits.

It was, of course, distinctly understood that you were to take no action beyond the spending of certain moneys upon the intoxication of some of your less reputable friends. You were then to worm out of them the secrets of the motor-car trade: I think you called it 'spilling the beans' – a coarse and vulgar metaphor, the origin of which I am glad to find obscure. Instead, if I read your letter aright, you have gone so far as to engage or hire a self-propelled vehicle, together with its conductor, for the space of one calendar month.

As I read those last words again, a host of unanswerable questions, like bulls of Bashan, gape upon me with their mouths. Where is the swine to be put? Don't say 'In a coach-house', for the greys might hear you. I mean, they're not mad about cars. And what about liability? Supposing some poultry misjudge their distance, or an assertive heifer decides to sit on her horns to spite her base. Oh, and what do we do if one of the tires is punctured? Suck the wound?

It is within your knowledge that inconsideration is my portion and disregard my cross. It might have been thought that, in these circumstances, a near relative would have hesitated further to offend one whose qualities are so clearly enumerated by the Beatitudes. But of such is my present incarnation. Oh, for the good old days when I was Artaxerxes' favourite wife! The fun we used to have in the sherbert slimming-pool! And how our husband laughed when we put a scorpion into the Chamberlain's slacks. Jujube, he used to call me. Ah, well…

Till Monday, then.

I yearn upon you with my large intestine.
Berry

"You might," said Daphne, "have told him what the Dean said."

"My sweet," said Berry, "if he does these things in the green-room, what will he do in the flies? If be knew what the Dean had said, he'd order a portable garage and two more cars."

Monday came at last, and my cousin with it.

Precisely at a quarter to one, a long, low, open car came to rest in the drive. At least, it seemed low then. It was blue and was built to take seven – and so it did. The back seat was extremely comfortable. The tonneau was very roomy. This was as well, for my cousin had brought twelve tires and fifteen tubes – on sale or return. The chauffeur was a pleasant-faced man, whose name was Fitch.

While Jonah expounded its virtues, we moved about the vehicle, marking its points.

"It's very nice-looking," said Daphne. "How fast can it go?"

"Just over fifty," said Jonah. "But thirty-five is her pace: she's smoothest then."

"What about twenty?" said Berry.

"She won't do twenty in top. At twenty-two or three you have to change down."

"Forgive my ignorance," said Berry, "but which of the gears do you most often employ?"

Jonah shrugged his shoulders.

"Well, the great idea," he said, "is to keep her in top. If you see a hill coming, you rush it – if you possibly can."

"I see," said Berry. "In other words, one's main object is to maintain an unlawful speed – to do anything rather than sink to the level prescribed by law."

"That's what it amounts to," said Jonah. "But twenty-five is nothing. After a mile or two you seem to be crawling along."

"I see," said Berry thoughtfully. "Well, before we go out, we'd better inquire which way the Colonel's gone. My learned brother, Colonel Buckshot. I mean, I'm sitting on Thursday:

and if on Wednesday we met him, when we were rushing a hill…"

"He's got to get used to it," said Jonah.

"Yes, I wasn't thinking of him," said Berry. "If I'm to violate the law one day and administer it the next, I'd just as soon not ram this elegant inconsistency down the Colonel's throat. It's just possible it might stick in his gullet. Oh, and talk about not letting your right hand know what your left hand doeth…"

We handed Fitch over to Peters and went to lunch.

Two days later we put the car to the test. In a word, we went out for the day – to Sacradown and back. This was a great adventure, for Sacradown was seventy miles away.

The day was brilliant, and distance faded into a haze of heat. Fleeting the well-known ways was an enchanting exercise. Jonah was driving, with Fitch in the seat by his side. Behind them, Daphne, Berry and I sat in excited silence, tasting the joy of speed.

It was not quite ten o'clock and we were twelve miles from White Ladies, when one of the hind tires burst.

Jonah steadied the car and brought her, going short, to the side of the road.

For a moment nobody spoke.

Then –

"I suppose the thing's broken," said Berry. "I thought it was too good to be true. Oh, and where's the Red Cross outfit? I've slipped my spinal cord."

The chauffeur left his seat and my sister opened her eyes.

"Does it often do this?" she said.

Jonah spoke over his shoulder.

"The day is hot," he said, "and although you won't believe it, we were doing fifty-one. Under such conditions tires sometimes lose their temper."

"The wages of sin," said Berry. He looked round comfortably. "At least, it's a pleasant spot, and I'm ripe for a nap. I didn't have a good night. Daphne had eaten something, and – "

"You wicked liar," said his wife.

"D'you mean to say I dreamed it? It was remarkably vivid. Never mind. Can repairs be effected? Or must you walk back to Cleric and hire an equipage? I shouldn't call at the Grange. Its occupant might be unresponsive."

(Colonel Buckshot lived at the Grange.)

"Nothing doing," said Jonah, alighting. "In the first place, the tools we need are beneath your seat; in the second, your services will be required."

"In what way?" said Berry, staring.

"As a relief," said I. "Changing a tire is exhausting."

Berry moistened his lips.

"I'd better not," he said. "I – I might break something."

"We'll risk that," said Jonah. "And I don't think you'll break the pump."

With an awful look, Berry followed my sister out of the car, to take his seat on the bank by the side of the road...

The wheels were not detachable, and the jack was much less efficient than those of today. To place the jack was very difficult: to upset it, when placed, was very easy: to operate it was just possible. And tires could be most refractory. By the time the new cover was on, Jonah and Fitch and I were ready to rest.

Jonah looked at Berry and wrung the sweat from his brow.

"You shall inflate it," he said. "That'll give us a chance to cool down."

With that, he and I sat down by my sister's side.

Fitch attached the pump, showed Berry the action required and then moved round the car, to open the bonnet upon the opposite side.

With starting eyes, Berry took off his coat and laid hold of the pump...

After two minutes, he took off his collar and tie.

After five minutes he felt the tire, laid the pump carefully down, took his seat on the step and closed his eyes.

"What's the matter?" said Jonah.

"The pump's not working," said Berry. "I'm damned near killing myself, but inflation is not taking place."

"Yes, it is," said Jonah. "Another quarter of an hour and you'll see what I mean."

"From on high, perhaps," said Berry. "I shan't be alive. No man born of woman – "

Here Fitch reappeared, to pick up the pump.

After five more minutes, Berry again took charge.

"You see?" said Jonah.

Berry looked round.

"If I told you what I saw," he said, "you'd be afraid to die."

After fifty strokes, he once again felt the tire.

"I'd better not do it any more," he said. "We don't want to burst this one."

"Another hundred," said I, "and then I'll go on."

In a loud voice, Berry began to count...

He had reached 'Seventy-nine', when I saw a dog-cart approaching, taking the way we had come. But Berry's back was towards it. Besides, he was occupied.

When the dog-cart was fifty yards off, I recognized the shape of Colonel Buckshot's grey hat.

"Ninety-four," raved Berry: and then, with a frightful effort, Ninety-five."

Daphne, sitting beside me, began to shake with laughter...

The dog-cart was very near, and the Colonel's eyes were fast upon Berry's back, when the latter screeched "*One hundred*", dropped the pump, staggered up to the step and sat himself down with a violence that shook the car.

Then he looked up, to meet the Colonel's glare.

For a moment the two regarded one another.

Then –

"The price of devotion," said Berry, and wiped his throat.

At the third attempt –

"The price of what, sir?" snapped the Colonel, whose face was red.

"Devotion to duty," said Berry. "I'd meant to keep it a secret; but now you've found out."

"What the devil d'you mean, sir?"

"Observe my state," said Berry. "D'you think I'm enjoying myself?"

The Colonel started, and Berry went quietly on.

"For some time now, it has been apparent to me that the hand of the Riding Hood Bench would be immensely strengthened, if one of its members knew something of motoring. Week after week, we have to listen to excuses by motorists which we believe to be lies, but which we cannot ignore, because we lack the experience which motorists have. I, therefore, decided that, as the youngest of the Justices, it was my duty to acquire a degree of expert knowledge which none of us have. I've already found out a great deal. In the first place, twenty miles an hour is excessive. Fifteen is quite enough. Then, again – "

"I've always said so," cried the Colonel. "But those blasted fools of politicians – "

"Exactly," said Berry. "And why? Because, when that limit was fixed, not two per cent, of the House had cars of their own."

"I've no doubt you're right, sir," said the Colonel. He smiled a grim smile. "And something else you've found out – that the stinking machines break down."

"And this is nothing," said Berry. "A common occurrence, I'm told. The chauffeur's worn out, and so I've been lending a hand. I don't like to ask my cousins, because it's really my fault."

Here the Colonel turned and saw us and raised his hat.

"How d'you do, Mrs Pleydell. How d'you do, you two." His brows drew into a frown. "Nothing to do with me, but I should have thought that Pleydell had done enough." He returned to Berry. "I can't send you help, can I?"

"No, thank you, Colonel. Another half-hour, and we shall be under way. Experience is always costly: but after a week or so, I think I ought to be able to be of some help."

"Very public-spirited of you, Pleydell. I'm sure the Chairman will think so. He's dining with me tonight." Again he raised his hat. "Goodbye, Mrs Pleydell. Don't let him wear himself out."

Ignoring Jonah and me, he touched the grey with his whip…

As the dog-cart swung round a bend, Berry crossed the road and lay down on his back.

"You heard what he said," he said unctuously.

Ten minutes later, we all re-entered the car…

As my cousin let in the clutch –

"Now for God's sake be careful," said Berry. "The moment you see the dog-cart, slow down and turn off. I've sown the zephyr, but I'm not reaping any whirlwinds. After two miles of our dust, he might revise his opinion of my self-sacrifice."

"And if there's no turning," said Jonah, changing gear.

"Then we must wait," said Berry. "Once we're past the old fool, cry Havoc! and let her rip. But I will not have my winnings cast into the draught."

Here a sinister jarring declared that a tire was flat – the tire we had just put on.

"You needn't worry," said Jonah. "By the time we've done it again, he'll be out of the way."

With that, once again he brought the car to rest.

As Fitch left his seat –

" 'Done it again?' " screamed Berry. "Oh, give me strength. And what's the matter with the swine? We've only gone half a mile."

"It's a puncture," said I. "Not a burst. We shan't have to change the tire."

"Shall we have to inflate it?"

"Of course. The air you put in has escaped."

Berry covered his face.

"Come on," said Daphne. "They want to get at the tools."

As Berry left the car –

"This, I may say," said Jonah, "is pure misfortune."

"Is it, indeed?" said Berry. "Well, if this is pure, I hope we shan't meet some obscene."

"What I mean is that it's unusual. When we came down on Monday we had no trouble at all."

Berry sat down in the grass and took off his hat.

"Must be the weight," he said. Here Fitch began to take out the tools. "Oh, there's the pump. How nice to see it again. I'd almost forgotten what it looked like. It must be nearly ten minutes since we put it away."

"We'll ring the changes," said I. "This time you shall jack her up."

"I will – next time," said Berry. "I'd like to. But I think if I watched you once more – "

"Take your choice," said I. "It's the pump or the jack."

In a pregnant silence, Berry began to disrobe…

I showed him where the jack must be placed.

After a long look –

"Of course," he said, "if I was eight inches high and my arms were six feet long, it would be quite easy, wouldn't it?"

"It would simplify matters," said I.

"Quite so. I do hope I shan't hurt the nether parts of the car."

"I hope not," said I. "Go on."

The next three minutes were crowded.

In that short space of time, Berry thrice placed and thrice overturned the jack, split his shirt, hit his head upon a joint which was discharging heavy oil, screamed, called "St Scum and all slow-bellies" to witness that he was "without spot or blemish in a naughty world", protruded his tongue farther than I would have believed possible and was with difficulty prevented from hurling the jack-lever into the middle distance.

Needless to say, Daphne, Jonah and I could hardly stand up, and tears of mirth were running on Fitch's cheeks.

Gravely Berry regarded us.

Then –

"In the last few moments," he said, "the shortest era on record has come to a violent end. Never again will I defile my body or prostitute my brain by subscribing to the maintenance of any self-propelled vehicle. I won't seek to raise it from the ground, I won't introduce God's air into its filthy wheels, I won't add petrol to its maw or oil to its intestines. I'll bruise its seat, but I'm damned if it shall bruise my soul."

With that, he smoothed his hair, inspected his palm, laughed like a maniac, threw himself down on the bank and tore the grass with his teeth.

It was Daphne who cleaned his head with petrol, while Jonah and Fitch and I made good the damage which a two-inch nail had caused.

We had no further trouble, the roads were not too bad, and the way was a handsome way. Sacradown was won at a quarter to two. By the time we had sighted its chimneys, old rose against powder blue, we remembered no more our misfortunes for our joy in the fifty-eight miles which we had covered at twenty-three to the hour.

"Splendid," cried the old squire, from the head of the steps. "If it means we shall see our friends, I accept the automobile. It'll be a mixed blessing, of course. But omelets or eggs, you know. You can't have them both. And to think that you'll dine at White Ladies this very night!"

"That's right," said Berry. "We may be a few hours late, but dinner will eventually be served."

"Rot," said Daphne. "And I think we came awfully well."

"We didn't fare badly," said Jonah: "and that's the truth, If we do as well going back…"

We did not do as well going back.

We had one burst and three punctures: and then, ten miles from White Ladies, the petrol-pipe became choked. Still, we sat down at half-past nine – after a memorable day. Breakdowns or no, the car was a great success. Not even Berry denied it. The exhilaration of speed, the swoop at a sudden valley and the lift at the hill to come, above all, the reduction of distance and the breaking of ground that was new – these things had taken us by storm. When I say 'new ground', I mean it. Twice we had passed through Poke Abbas that afternoon. Poke Abbas is a famous beauty, a washpot of History, over which Tradition has cast out her shoe. But, because it lay sixty miles off and was served by another line, till that day we had never seen it, except from the train.

To say that the proceedings against Joe Chinnock and Mr Slober assumed the proportions of a *cause célèbre* would be to understate the case.

There was a full Bench and the police-court at Brooch was crammed, while a crowd, quite a hundred strong, was gathered without the doors.

Geoffrey Mason, Solicitor, appeared on behalf of the smith. Mr Slober had engaged Counsel – an unattractive man, rude and overbearing, contemptuous of the Court. How fine was his practice in London, I do not know; but he made it clear at once that, while, as a matter of form, the Justices sat upon the Bench, their function was that of a jury, but his was that of a Judge.

The summonses were taken together – this, by consent.

The first witness was Constable Rowe: and, as might have been expected, Counsel 'knocked him about'. But this the Bench did not like, for Rowe was an honest man.

The chauffeur followed Rowe, and was carefully led by Mason to put his case too high.

"You say you did not understand the groom's request?

"That's right."

"You recognized him as a groom?"

"Yes."

"As the groom belonging to the phaeton?"

"I –might 'ave."

"What request did you think he was making?"

"I'd no idea."

"You knew he was making a request?"

"I can't say I did."

"Why did you think he was addressing you?"

"I didn't know."

"Did you care?"

"I 'ad to get on."

"You saw the greys were frightened?"

"I saw there was somethin' goin' on."

"You didn't associate their fright with the presence of your car?"

"Never entered my head."

"Not even when their groom addressed you?"

"No."

"You know that horses are frightened by cars?"

"I've heard so."

Amid an indignant murmur, Mason sat down.

William followed and really did very well. Counsel attacked him fiercely, but William hit back. He described how the greys had bolted.

"But that was due to the driver's thrashing them?"

"If he hadn't o' done it, the mistress would 'ave been killed."

"How d'you make that out?"

William leaned forward.

"The car was movin'. Another six feet, an' the greys would of *swung round* an' bolted…on to the pavement…tryin' to scrape their way by. An' the phaeton crushed to matchwood against the wall. An' the mistress was on the near side."

"That's so much fancy. In this Court we deal with facts – at least, I hope we do."

"More like a nightmare," said William.

"Wasn't the bolting a nightmare? The bolting your master caused?"

"It was – but not 'alf such a bad one. You see, he's a lovely whip, an' it give him a chance."

"A lovely whip, is he? Wouldn't a lovely whip have turned his horses round?"

"What, across the bows o' the car? Oh, good night, Nurse."

There was a roar of laughter, and Counsel sat angrily down.

William was followed by the hawker, who was not particularly helpful, but made us all laugh very much.

It was natural that Berry, who followed, should give his evidence well. What is more to the point, he was the only witness who had observed what was happening, but taken no part. Such testimony is of value. Counsel saw this as clearly as did the Court. And something else he saw. That was that, unless he could 'crack' Berry, his cake was dough.

He rose to cross-examine, with a menacing air.

"I believe you're a Magistrate?"

Your belief," said Berry, "is correct."

Counsel's head, which had been turned away, came round with a jerk.

After a long look at Berry –

"What Petty Sessional Court do you adorn?"

"I attend that of Riding Hood."

"And there you dispense justice?"

"I subscribe to its administration."

"You're sure it *is* justice?"

"We do our best."

"I see. Now with regard to this disgraceful business on the twenty-fourth of June… As being present, as being a Justice of the Peace, why didn't you take some action?"

"Because it is not my practice to interfere with police-officers in the execution of their duty."

Counsel leaned forward.

31

"Wasn't it because it was your wife's horses that had taken fright at the car?"

"That fact," said Berry, "did not affect my outlook."

"D'you expect the Court to believe that?"

"I do."

"Don't you value your wife's well-being?"

"To be irrelevant," said Berry, "it is not necessary to be offensive."

There was more than a murmur of applause, and Counsel grew slowly red.

"This isn't Riding Hood, Mr Pleydell."

"Yes, I'd realized that," said Berry. "The dock's much bigger for one thing, and the court-room's a different shape."

There was a roar of laughter.

Counsel's eyes narrowed, and a hand went up to his mouth. When order had been restored –

"Mrs Pleydell might have been injured?"

"She might," said Berry, "have been killed."

"Exactly. Yet you solemnly declare that that fact did not influence your conduct?"

"I do," said Berry. "You see, I didn't know it."

"What d'you mean – 'didn't know it'?"

Berry shrugged his shoulders.

"It was not," he said, "within my knowledge. That being so, for it to affect my outlook was quite impossible."

"You didn't know that Mrs Pleydell had been involved?"

"That is the impression," said Berry, "which I am endeavouring to convey."

"Don't you know your own carriage, when you see it?"

"When I see it – yes. But not when it's round two corners and a quarter of a mile away."

Everyone was waiting for this, and the burst of laughter which followed shook the room. Counsel turned and rent his solicitor. Though no one could hear his voice, his manner was eloquent. Then he straightened his back and faced his prey.

"Let me get this clear. When did you appear upon the scene?'

"About fifteen seconds before the constable."

"Did you see the chauffeur dragged from the car?"

"No. The one had been taken, and the other left."

"I suppose you realize that no accident would have happened, if he had remained at the wheel?"

"I realize nothing of the kind."

"What d'you mean, sir?"

"This. When he was at the wheel, the chauffeur put in peril four valuable lives. Left to itself, the car was less exacting."

"Are you seriously suggesting that, if the chauffeur had not been removed, the barrow would have been upset and the lamp-post destroyed?"

"No. But I am suggesting that, had he not been removed he might well be standing here or elsewhere on a charge of manslaughter."

"A curious point of view – for a Magistrate. Because a chauffeur misunderstands a request, he is to be branded as a potential murderer."

"I do not believe that he misunderstood the request."

"He has sworn so."

"I know. I don't believe him."

"Pray, why not?"

Berry leaned forward.

"Because he has not misunderstood one single one of the questions asked him today."

That was a kidney punch, and the rustle that ran round the Court showed that everyone present was well aware of its worth.

Counsel's face was working.

"Try to remember," he rasped, "that you are not on the Bench."

"May I respectfully offer the same advice?"

In a pregnant silence, the two men regarded each other. Then Counsel returned to his brief.

"When you arrived upon the scene, where was the chauffeur?"

"In the trough," said Berry.

"And Mr Slober?"

"Standing beside the car."

"And the hawker?"

"Was importuning Mr Slober, who seemed preoccupied."

"Preoccupied?"

"Yes. He was, er, soliloquizing upon what had occurred."

"Soliloquizing?"

"Yes, in blank prose."

When the gust of laughter had passed –

"And the hawker had hold of his arm?"

"No. The hawker never touched him from first to last."

Counsel wagged a menacing finger.

"I put it to you that he did."

"You can put it," said Berry, "where you like, but – "

In the roar of delight at this answer, the rest of the sentence was lost.

But Counsel stuck to his guns.

"The defendant will swear, Mr Pleydell, that the hawker took hold of his arm."

"That will confirm the opinion I formed at the time."

"What opinion was that?"

"That the defendant was beside himself. Didn't know what he was doing or what was being done. If he didn't know then, he can't remember now."

"His evidence should be ruled out?"

"That is a matter for the Court."

"Of course. But you would advise them to disregard it?"

"I should not presume to advise them on any point."

"But you're a Justice of the Peace."

"Yes," said Berry, "I am. I'm also a member of the MCC and the Army and Navy Stores. But at the present moment I'm a witness."

34

As the laughter died down –

"When you are, er, enthroned at Riding Hood, do you frequently reject evidence on the ground that the witness was temporarily insane?"

"No."

"Yet you're asking this Court to do so."

"I am doing no such thing."

"What are you doing?"

"I was under the impression that I was giving evidence."

"Which you ask the Court to accept?"

"That, I think, is the privilege of the advocate."

"Are you trying to teach me my business?"

"No," said Berry, "I'm not. My ability is, er, limited."

Counsel glared.

Then –

"You saw the constable arrive?"

"I did."

"And proceed to take particulars?"

"Yes."

"He produced the traditional note-book?"

"Naturally."

"Would it be fair to say that he was officious?"

"It would not."

"And obtuse?"

"No."

"What was he?"

"Dutiful."

"Thank you. He hasn't said that Mr Slober was out of his mind?"

"Neither have I. My words were 'beside himself'."

"What is the difference?"

"Well, I'm not a lexicographer," said Berry, "but I believe 'out of his mind' to be the more serious condition of the two."

"He didn't even say 'beside himself'?"

Berry shrugged his shoulders.

"The phrase may not have occurred to him. He said 'labouring under excitement'."

"Do you agree with that statement?"

"Fully."

"He had had enough to excite him?"

"More than enough. A chauffeur in a horse-trough, and a car doing a lamp-post to the bushel – well, it's like a bad dream."

I am glad to record that Counsel contrived to smile.

"The arrival of the constable did not improve matters?"

"I don't agree."

"Can you deny that after his arrival the situation deteriorated?"

"That was not the officer's fault."

"Whose fault was it?"

"If it was anyone's, it was Mr Slober's."

"How do you make that out?"

"The constable's confusion provoked him to violence; but it was his own incoherence that confused the constable."

"Incoherence?"

"That," said Berry, "was the word I used."

"I am aware of that, sir. Of what did his incoherence consist?"

"Of an inability to give intelligible replies."

"Give me an instance."

"The constable asked him who was driving the car. Mr Slober replied, 'Nobody.' Well, that wasn't very helpful."

Counsel leaned forward.

"It happened to be the truth?"

"No doubt. It would have been equally true *and* misleading to say that his chauffeur had gone to have a bath."

There was a roar of laughter.

As it died down –

"Mr Slober is charged with obstruction. Honestly, Mr Pleydell, can you substantiate that charge?"

"To this extent – that I saw him snatch the note-book out of the constable's hand."

"I suggest that the constable dropped it."

Berry shook his head.

"I'm sorry. I saw the, er, rape of the book."

"And the alleged assault?"

"Just naughty temper," said Berry. "The hawker's laughter provoked him and so he went for the man."

"You saw that, too?"

"I did."

"Is there anything you didn't see?"

"Oh, quite a lot," said Berry. "I didn't see the accident happen. I didn't see any reason to interfere. I didn't see the hawker pull Mr Slober's nose."

"Did he?" – excitedly.

"Not that I know of," said Berry. "That's probably why I didn't see it."

There was a howl of delight.

Counsel was trembling with anger.

"My point, sir, is that you are suspiciously well informed."

Berry shrugged his shoulders.

"Sitting up in a dog-cart, I could see more than some."

"On a Bench of your own?" sneered Counsel.

"No," said Berry, "I had a box-seat put in. They're really more comfortable."

Another burst of laughter shook the room.

"And you, a Justice of the Peace, sat there at your ease, watching one assault after another?"

"That," said Berry, "is a perversion of the truth."

"Aren't you a Justice of the Peace?"

"That's right," said Berry excitedly. "Of Riding Hood. If you remember, you asked me if I dispensed liquor – I mean, Justice, and I said – "

"Didn't you watch two assaults?"

"No. I saw them committed."

"What is the difference?"

"What you want," said Berry, "is a grammar – not a witness."

"Never mind what I want, sir," raged Counsel. "Answer the question. What is the difference between watching an assault and seeing it committed?"

Berry took a deep breath.

"Watching suggests anticipation. I *watch* you heading for a cesspool: I *see* you…"

The rest of the sentence was rather naturally lost.

"Tell me this, Mr Pleydell. Is it fair to say that if a pair of horses had not taken fright, this Court would not be hearing two summonses today?"

"That," said Berry, "is undeniable."

"And the lady behind those horses happened to be your wife?"

"That is equally true."

"Bearing those things in mind, would you be human if you did not hope for Mr Slober's conviction?"

"To be perfectly honest," said Berry, "I don't care a hoot. So far as I am concerned, he and his chauffeur have paid their respective debts. He's had his car done in and the chauffeur was ducked. And I'll lay they stop their engine next time they're asked."

There was a burst of applause.

"Are you posing as Solomon?"

"No," said Berry. "As Job."

The retort was deservedly acclaimed.

Counsel played his last card.

"It is easy to see that you're not a motorist."

Berry raised his eyebrows.

"My car's outside," he said simply. "I always leave it outside – it's too big to…"

The rest of the sentence was lost, and Counsel sat down.

As Jonah later observed, the case was over when Berry stepped out of the box. Mr Slober was certainly called, but

Berry had queered his pitch: and when Mason declined to cross. examine, the impression that his evidence was worthless was driven home.

After a short consultation, the Chairman announced the decision of the Bench.

"We understand that Mr Slober is prepared to compensate the hawker and to pay for the damage to the lamp-post. In these circumstances, the Bench is satisfied that justice will be done if, on the summons for assault, he is bound over in his own recognizances to keep the peace for six months. The summons for obstruction will be dismissed on payment of costs. With regard to the other defendant, the Bench feels that it would be unfair to deny to him the clemency shown to Mr Slober: while he had no shadow of right to take the law into his own hands, we cannot lose sight of the fact that, if the chauffeur had acceded to the groom's request – "

"Which he misunderstood," said Counsel violently.

The Chairman looked at him.

"The Bench," he said coldly, "does not accept the chauffeur's evidence on that point. As I was saying, had the chauffeur acceded to the groom's request, no lives would have been put in peril, no damage would have been done and the Bench would not have been hearing these summonses today. Joseph Chinnock will, therefore, be bound over in his own recognizances to keep the peace for six months."

"Scandalous," said Counsel; but the word was nearly drowned in the tide of applause.

When I left the court, he and his client were still engaged in a furious altercation, regarding, I imagine, his conduct of the case.

An hour had gone by, and we were in the Deanery garden, where we had had a late tea.

"As no doubt you realize," said the Dean, "the *deus ex machina*, from whom, of course, all credit has been withheld, was the lamp-post. Had the lamp-post not stopped the car, Joe Chinnock might well have faced a much more serious charge. Had the lamp-post not damaged the car, Berry could not have submitted that Slober had been punished enough. Still, Joe Chinnock's been saved, and we can throw up our hats – though I have an uneasy feeling that Counsel's final comment was not altogether undeserved. Mark you, had I been on the Bench, I should have let him off, too. But I fear I should have been wrong. Rough justice is as attractive as going to sleep in Church: but it is equally indefensible."

"Yet, if he'd been sent down, sir, justice would not have been done."

"That's a good point," said the Dean. " '*Their justice* rooted in *injustice* stood.' Any way, to mark my gratification at Joe Chinnock's deliverance, kindly instruct Mr Mason to send me his bill of costs."

2

In Which Withyham Pays the Piper, But Berry Calls the Tune

Six weeks had gone by, and the car which we had ordered was overdue. We were, of course, keeping the hireling, until our own car should come.

On the whole, our fall from grace had been well received. A few eyebrows had been raised: Mrs de Lisle had been caustic: Withyham had been rude. But our farmer friends were amused and the village was proud.

"That's a fact," said the Vicar. "Bilberry's one up on Cleric – I heard the taunt hurled myself. 'We've got an auto, we 'ave.' "

"I confess I'm a convert," said Daphne.

"Not a convert," said Berry. "A complacent heretic."

"So," said my sister, "are you. You never stop abusing the thing, but, if anyone took it away, you'd go off the deep end."

"I'll say it's convenient," said Berry.

"No more than that?" said I.

"No more than that."

"Then don't you come tomorrow. We're only going to lunch with a friend of mine."

Berry regarded the Vicar.

"There's a viper," he said. "Just because I decline to vomit a lot of slush about – "

"You disgusting brute," said Daphne.

"There you are," said Berry. "That's what I have to put up with. I sometimes think I shall take orders. You don't want a curate, do you?"

As soon as the Vicar could speak –

"I have a feeling," he said, "that, even if you were available, I should look somewhere else. But I'll give you this – I think the church would be crammed when you were going to preach. By the way, have you heard the latest? Lord Withyham has closed the Roman Lane."

"But he can't," cried everyone.

"He's done it," said the Vicar. "He's put up a five-barred gate – and the gate is locked."

"And here's trouble," said Berry. "There's been a right of way there for years and years."

"So I'm told," said the Vicar. "D'you think you could see him about it?"

Berry shook his head.

"We've never got on," he said. "He'd take it better from you."

"He won't listen to me," said the Vicar. "But something will have to be done. If I know the parish, feeling will run very high."

"And there you're right," said Jonah. "The neighbourhood won't stand it – and that's the truth, With us, the right of way is the Ark of the Covenant."

There was an uneasy silence.

Then –

"We must avoid violence," said the Vicar. "If the matter must go to the Courts, to the Courts it must go. But there must be no violence."

"I don't know about violence," said Berry. "But, once the murder is out, that gate will be short of its hinges within the hour."

"More," said I. "Old Chalk's to be buried on Wednesday."

"Oh, dear," said Daphne.

The Vicar looked round, wide-eyed.

"But what of that?" he said.

"There's an old belief," said Berry, "that where a funeral has passed, there for ever will be a right of way. In fact, it's bad in law; but such beliefs die hard. 1 think it more than likely that an attempt will be made to take Old Chalk to the churchyard by way of Romany Lane. And Withyham may try to stop it."

The Vicar covered his eyes. "This is dreadful," he said.

"Why d'you think," said Daphne, "Lord Withyham won't listen to you?"

The Vicar frowned.

"We had words last year," he said. "The Scouts spent week at Bluecoat – camping, you know. The weather was very fine, and they were abroad all day: but their camp was in the meadow. I know it's close to the house, but they did behave very well and they made no noise. But Lord Withyham resented their presence. He wouldn't even give them water. And when I protested, I'm sorry to say he ordered me out of the house."

"Outrageous," said Daphne. "And if that was how he felt, why did he let them come?"

"He didn't," cried the Vicar. "It was Ightham's meadow – not his."

"But you said it was at Bluecoat."

"So it is. But that meadow belongs to Ightham."

The three of us stared at him.

"Well, I thought I knew Bluecoat," said Berry: "but this is a new one on me."

"I must be right," said the Vicar. "If the meadow had been Lord Withyham's, he would have turned them out."

"Well, I don't understand it," said I. "But it's perfectly clear that you can't go to the man." I looked at Berry. "You and I'd better beard him tomorrow. On our way to Hammercloth – we have to go by his gates."

"You're very good," said the Vicar, and got to his feet.

"Don't speak too soon," said Berry.

The Vicar smiled.

"I'm not speaking too soon. Whether you fail or succeed cannot alter the fact – that you are very good to do so distasteful a duty on my behalf."

"My dear, good sir," said Berry, taking his arm. "For you and the village, we'd do far more than this. That is what White Ladies is for. She has always done what she could to be Bilberry's rod and staff. Our reluctance to interfere here was dictated by one thing alone – the fear that with Withyham, White Ladies will cut no ice."

We all came to the door, to see the good man off.

The Reverend John Chisholm had been with us nearly three years. A gentle fellow of Oxford, he was a man of peace. On four Sundays out of five, he lunched with us, and we were glad at his coming and sorry to see him go.

The first Lord Withyham had been a riveter when he was seventeen. He had risen by sheer merit, to become the honoured Chairman of one of the shipping lines. Never was a peerage more deservedly bestowed. And then he died, and his son, the present Withyham, reigned in his stead. But his was a spirit of another sort. It was said that his mother had spoiled him. Be that as it may, he was not even a shadow of what his father had been. The man was proud of his title, ashamed of his birth. He set no store by work, but much by his dignity. His father had never had time for a country place. Withyham repaired the omission the moment the Will was proved. The Ferrers had lived at Bluecoat for more than two hundred years, but the last of the line was poor, and the place was for sale. Withyham bought it as it stood... And there you are. I fear that Withyham disliked us, because, though Bluecoat was lovely, White Ladies took pride of place.

As we returned to the terrace –

"The man must be mad," said Daphne. "Romany Lane has always been a short cut. It goes through his land, of course."

"That doesn't matter," said Berry. "No doubt, many years ago, it was a private road. But the Ferrers were lax or kindly and failed to close it once in twenty-one years. And so the public acquired a right of way. I can't go back so far, but plenty of people can."

"What exactly d'you mean?" said his wife.

"Well, if it comes to a show-down – a fight in the Courts – people will have to be found who can swear that the lane's been open for twenty-one years. Prove that, and Withyham's sunk."

"That'll cost money," said Jonah. "That's what he's banking on – that no one will put up the money to fight the case."

"We'll put it up," said Daphne. "if we have to re-let Cholmondeley Street."

She spoke for us all.

Number Thirty-eight Cholmondeley Street had always been our home, when we were in Town. Seven years ago the house had been let on lease. But now that lease was up, and the house was being decorated against our return. But better that we let it again than that Romany Lane should be closed.

"That's all right," said I, "so far as it goes. But don't forget this – with the Law, you never know. No case is ever cast-iron. I'd say that the odds against Withyham were about five to one. Well, that's good enough. But I must remind you that there's a Court of Appeal...and the House of Lords... If Withyham took us up to the House of Lords, and there we lost, the costs we should have to pay would probably be between six and eight thousand pounds."

"Oh, hell," said everyone.

"Exactly. We cannot afford to stake eight thousand pounds. But Withyham can. So, if we can possibly avoid it, the case must not go to the Courts. We cannot *afford* a row. If the parish gets his goat, Withyham will force our hand."

"Well, what do we do?" said Berry.

I raised my eyebrows.

"We'd better put Peters wise and tell him to learn what he can at *The Rose* tonight. And tomorrow we call on Withyham."

"Yes, that's going to be a genial interview, isn't it? You must take what he says in shorthand, behind your back."

"Oh, my dears," said Daphne, "I am so sorry for you. Yes, Falcon?"

The butler approached.

"I think you would like to know, madam, that Mrs Ightham is here."

"Oh, splendid," said Daphne. "She's come to see Bridget?"

"Yes, Madam."

"Ask her to come to the Blue Room in ten minutes' time."

"Very good, Madam."

"Falcon," said Berry, "is Mr Ightham here?"

"Yes, sir. He drove her over."

"Where is he now? With Peters?"

"Yes, sir."

"All right. I'll go and see him."

"Shall I tell him, sir?"

"If you please."

Falcon bowed and withdrew. Berry raised his eyebrows.

"May as well get the low-down, what ever it is."

Ten minutes later Ightham declared the truth.

"No wonder you're beaten, sir; it's a curious case. Our land marches with Bluecoat, as well you know. A hundred years ago, the Ferrers o' that day wanted to buy the acres we call the Dale. My great-grandfather, George – he wouldn't sell. 'But I'll tell you what, sir,' he says, 'I'll give you a lease.' An' that's what he did. A ninety-nine years' lease. Well, that was near enough freehold... An' if you ask me the truth, I think the Ferrers forgot. An' then, two years ago, just after his lordship buys it, the lease falls in. Now if it had been Mr Ferrers, he should have had the Dale. Ninety-nine years is a lifetime – an' more than that. I'd have let 'is lordship have it, if only he'd spoken me fair. But he couldn't do that. We're only farmer stock, and he's a lord. But he's a stranger, sir, and we've been here for a hundred and fifty years. An' he talked to me as if I was one of his gardeners... 'I'm buying those meadows,' he says. 'I don't want another lease. I'm telling my lawyers so, and you'll hear from them.' Well, that's not neighbourly, sir. An' when his lawyers wrote, I said they was not for sale. An' then he writes to me, an' talks about 'impertinent conduct'. So I put the Boy Scouts there... An' now he shuts Romany Lane... He don't know behaviour, sir, and that's the truth."

"What on earth's he playing at – shutting the lane? I mean, he must know he can't do it."

"That he can't," said Ightham, "and so he'll find. To my knowledge that lane's been open for forty-five years. And there's others older than me."

"Then why's he done it?" said Berry. "He must know the law."

"It's a try-on, sir. He's having a very big house-party next weekend. Some foreign royalties is coming – a German prince an' princess. That's what Jack Belcher told me – he's acting as bailiff now. Jack told him he couldn't do it: but his lordship shouts him down. Says his guests' privacy's got to be respected, he says. 'You carry out your orders,' he shouts."

"A temporary measure?" said I.

Ightham shrugged his shoulders.

"The gate's there, sir. I've seen it. An' now it's there, I can't see him taking it down." He laughed abruptly. "A stranger shouldn't do that."

"What d'you know, Mr Ightham?"

The farmer looked round.

Then –

"I'm told, sir, Old Chalk'll open it Wednesday next."

We called at Bluecoat the next day, precisely at ten o'clock.

"His lordship in?" said Berry.

"He is, sir."

"Ask him if he'll give me ten minutes."

"Certainly, sir. Will you please to come this way?"

We entered a chamber which I had known as a child.

One minute later the peer strode into the room.

"Morning, Withyham," said Berry. "Forgive us for calling so early, but, if we hadn't come now, we couldn't have come today."

"Is it so urgent, Pleydell?"

"Yes," said Berry, "it is. The thing is this. I know your respect for tradition. Of that respect you chose Bluecoat, and of that respect you maintain it, as Bluecoat should be maintained. For that reason, I venture to ask you to reopen Romany Lane. I know – "

"If I'd had – "

"Bear with me for a moment." Lord Withyham bit his lip. "I know it's a temporary measure, but – "

"And there you're wrong," said Withyham. "Romany Lane is mine."

"Of course it's yours," said Berry. "But everybody has used it for many years."

"And now they think it's theirs."

"They don't, indeed," said Berry. "And there is no reason at all why you shouldn't put up a gate. But you've put a chain on the gate – and that is what upsets them. You see, they feel – "

"They think they've a right of way. Is that what you're trying to say?

"They do," said Berry. "And country people are jealous of rights of way."

"Well, I don't think – I know. Prescription doesn't apply in a case like this."

"I don't agree," said Berry, "but that's beside the point. You don't want to cross your neighbours – I'm sure of that. Yet, you want to close Romany Lane for the next weekend. Now, if you put a card on the gate – "

"Very clever," sneered Withyham. "A card requesting their indulgence. And then, when it comes to Court, that card's produced against me."

Berry frowned.

"I hope," he said quietly, "I hope it won't come to Court."

"I know. You're trying to bluff me. You and that snivelling priest – "

"Really, Withyham, you must not talk like that. John Chisholm's a better man than you or I. And – "

"What are you here for, Pleydell? To tell me how to behave?"

Berry raised his eyebrows.

"I wish you'd see reason," he said. "Today the public is ready to perceive the mote of oppression in every great man's eye. And you are offering them a beam. You really are. Giving them something to get hold of. And that's – unfortunate, Withyham. Class hatred's a dreadful thing. It's been deliberately fostered for some years now – by certain politicians, to gain their ends. But it's never touched our parish – we've always been happy here. And there's no reason why it should: for there's nothing for it to breed on. But if you shut Romany Lane – "

"I asked what you were here for."

"We are here," said Berry quietly, "to ask you to open that gate. I'm told you don't want the lane used during the next weekend. If you will take off that chain, I will guarantee that nobody uses that lane on Saturday, Sunday and Monday next."

"You will, will you? And what about after that?"

"Your guests will be gone, Withyham."

"I shan't be gone, Pleydell."

"Look here," said Berry. "We both of us know the law. If a private road is not closed for twenty-one years, the right to close it is lost and all His Majesty's subjects may use it whenever they please. In this case, before you bought Bluecoat, the right to close Romany Lane was lost for good. That right, you cannot revive. And if you seek to revive it, by closing the lane, the parish won't stand it, Withyham – and that's the truth."

"What you mean is *you* won't stand it?"

"No, I don't," said Berry. "But sides will have to be taken, and we shall take that of the parish, because you are doing something which you have no right to do."

"We'll see about that," said Withyham. "You'd better get out your hat. It costs quite a lot to go to the House of Lords."

Berry looked out of the window and fingered his chin.

"Bad show, Withyham," he said.

"What the devil d'you mean?"

"What I say. You know you've no case: but you know you've got the money – which we have not. And you're counting upon your money to weight us out of the race."

At the third attempt –

"Have you anything more to say?"

"Any amount," said Berry. "But we've got to be getting on." I turned, to open the door. "Funny thing, you know. The last time I was in this chamber, Jim Ferrers was speaking of you. 'He *should* be all right,' he said. Well, there we are. Don't bother to see us out."

As the car slid down the drive –

"Was it too awful?" said Daphne.

"Well, it wasn't very pleasant," said Berry. "The impulse to offer him violence was very strong."

"My darling," said I, "I give your husband best. His manner was as fair as Withyham's was foul."

"Let me put it like this," said Berry. "The man is a vulgar sweep. When he spoke of the vicar, he called him 'that snivelling priest'."

"He didn't!" – incredulously.

"He did, indeed. He gave offence every time he opened his mouth. I don't wonder he mucks in with Germans – they'd just about suit his book. Indeed, I can hardly believe that he is his father's son."

"What's the matter with him?" said Daphne.

"God knows. He's just aggressive. Can't live and let live. Basil, Baron Withyham, would be improved by death."

"Can't he see that he's cutting his throat by taking this line?"

"I don't know that he is. Very few people have him more than once. And now let's dismiss the matter."

"In a moment," said I. "Daphne's a right to hear your Parthian shaft."

"Ah," said Berry. "I think I got back there."

When I told Daphne, she put her hands to her mouth.

"He'll never forgive you," she said.

"I can think of few things more gorge-raising," said Berry, "than to be forgiven by Withyham." He lifted his voice. "Stop at the next pub, Jonah. I want to clean my teeth."

Lunch was nearly over, and fruit was being served, when the butler brought in a parrot and set him upon the table by Geoffrey Majoribanks' side.

"Let me present," said Geoffrey, "The Evil One. He always comes into dessert, and he likes it very much when strangers are here."

Daphne looked at her hostess.

"Why the misnomer?" she said.

"Because of his eye," said Diana. "He's really as good as gold, but he looks a rogue."

The Evil One surveyed the company.

"There you are," said Berry. "He's seeking whom he may devour."

The Evil One looked at the speaker. Then, with deliberate steps, he rounded a dish of plums and, avoiding a silver cream-jug, made for where Berry sat.

Diana Majoribanks began to shake with laughter.

"He's quite all right," said Geoffrey.

"Oh, I'm sure of that," said Berry. "Beautiful beak he's got, hasn't he? Well, Lucifer, what d'you know?"

The parrot regarded him straitly.

Then –

"Damn your eyes," it said.

As soon as Berry could speak –

"You wicked bird," he said. "And on a Monday, too. You – you ought to be ashamed of yourself."

The Evil One laughed heartily.

"Of course, you're abandoned," said Berry. "Old in sin. How's Proserpine?"

The Evil One appeared to digest this.

Then –

"You're a one," it observed.

Berry swallowed.

"The trouble with you," he said, "is that you don't know your catechism. What about ordering yourself lowly and reverently to all your betters?"

"Shut your face," said the parrot shortly.

Berry moistened his lips.

"I'm not surprised," he said, "at the name you bear. Here am I, only too ready to converse – "

"Give paw," said The Evil One.

Berry looked at Diana.

"He means it," she said, wiping the tears from her eyes. "He's taken a fancy to you. Put your hand on the table."

Berry laid his hand on the table, beside his plate.

Carefully The Evil One inspected it. Then he stepped on to Berry's palm and began to move up his arm.

We watched his progress breathlessly.

When he had reached Berry's shoulder, he whispered in Berry's ear.

"No, not really?" said Berry. "Did you see them?"

He laughed – and the parrot with him, as though enjoying some scandal, unfit for our ears.

Before this absurd communion, we all broke down.

As soon as she could speak –

"I can't bear to interrupt you," said Diana, "but there's a wasp on your collar – going up."

"Well, get it off, someone," said Berry. "I – I'm deeply engaged. My movement might be misconstrued. Besides, I don't know where it is."

"Quite still," said Jonah, rising. "It's passing on to your neck."

"Oh, hell," said Berry. "I can feel it."

"No, you don't," said the parrot.

"What d'you mean," said Berry, " – 'No, you don't'? A BF – that's what you are. Why don't you do it in?"

Bent double with laughter, Jonah was unable to help, and the wasp crawled doggedly forward, towards Berry's ear,

"My God," said Berry, "for the milk of human kindness, will nobody intervene?"

By a superhuman effort, my cousin straightened his back; but, as he approached his finger, to flick the insect away, the parrot read into his gesture a coming assault. With hackles raised, The Evil One rose in his wrath and aimed such a blow at his hand that, had it 'connected', would have cut the flesh to the bone.

"It's all right, old fellow," said Jonah, "I'm – "

"It isn't all right," raged Berry. "Why the devil don't you – "

"He can't," shrieked Daphne. "The parrot – "

"Damn the parrot," roared Berry. "I'm talking about the wasp."

"But the parrot won't let him."

"Won't let who?" yelled Berry.

"He's a drunken swab," said The Evil One.

"So he is," said Berry, unconsciously turning his head. The movement was fatal – he was immediately stung.

With a squeal of pain, he started up to his feet: but for this, the parrot was unready, and, to save itself, it laid hold of Berry's collar with all its might.

"A-a-ah, there's another," roared Berry. "I feel the swine. I tell you, I'm swarming with them. Why the devil doesn't somebody – "

"It's qui-quite all right," wailed Diana. "It's only – "

"All right?" screeched Berry. "There's one down my neck – I can feel it. Am I to stand here and be murdered before your eyes?"

With that, he inserted his finger beneath the parrot's beak...

Could we have helped, we would have: but we were so weak with laughter that we could not stand up; and when Berry, feeling the beak, believed it to be a stag-beetle, and, presenting his neck to Diana, implored her to pick it off, the vials of mirth were poured out.

And then the inevitable happened.

Sick of Berry's efforts to take from him what hold he had, The Evil One lodged the only protest he knew…

Staunching the wound with his napkin, Berry resumed his seat.

Gravely he looked round the table.

"Oh, very funny," he said. "Very funny, indeed. Couldn't tell me, could you? Couldn't indicate that I was unwittingly provoking a dangerous swine?" Then he spoke over his shoulder. "Sorry, old fellow. I didn't know it was you."

Thus reassured, the parrot released its hold and retraced its steps. Once more upon the table, it looked Berry up and down.

"You're a one," it declared.

Berry sat back.

"Let me say at once," he said, "that I suspect your use of that innocent substantive. I am by no means sure that, if you were capable of defining it, I should be satisfied with your definition. And now, if you'll forgive me, I must receive medical attention. This gash apart, thanks to your indifference, the poison recently injected into my nape is causing me considerable pain."

The parrot was convulsed with laughter.

Nearly three hours had gone by.

Berry had slept off his *malaise* on the famous Hammercloth lawns, Diana and Geoffrey Majoribanks had proved the car, and we were on our way home, when one of our tires gave out by the village of Shepherd's Pipe.

As Fitch began to take off his coat –

"That's the worst of them things," said a voice.

We looked up to see a fat man on the farther side of a gate. His arms were resting on this and he had a straw in his mouth. Though he looked the picture of health, he was wearing a mournful air; and he made me think of a jester, short of a job. His overalls suggested that he had to do with machines.

"I admit it's a fault," said Daphne. "But I think it's the only one."

The other nodded.

"They get you about, don't they? My brother-in-law's a chauffeur. 'E took me out one day. Course 'is bloke didn't know, but we 'ad a lovely ride."

"Where did you go?" said Daphne.

"Round about 'Ind'ead, lady. Course I know all the roads – I told 'im the way to go. But it's funny the way the country seems to slip by. I quite enjoyed it, I did."

"You travel the roads?" said my sister.

"That's right, lady. Born in a circus, I was. But that's no life. I've 'ad me own merry-go-round for twenty years."

"And you go from fair to fair?"

"An' private jobs. You soon get used to the noise."

"Oh, yours has an organ, has it?"

"I'll say it 'as," said the man. "You can 'ear it two miles off. That's what I meant about the noise. *'Oby's Steam Round-Abouts* – once 'eard, never forgot. It's a paraffin-engine reely – works a treat." He jerked his thumb over his shoulder. "I got it 'ere – in this field. But it's not set up. I'm wot they call 'restin' ', lady. Nobody loves me now. But I open at Brooch again on Saturday week."

"It's like that, is it?" said Daphne. "Up and down."

"That's right," said Mr Hoby. "More up than down, you know. I can't complain. But I 'aven't the private practice I 'ad two years ago. Still, I got a lot o' good frien's. 'Ere I am in this meadow – four 'orses grazin' their 'eads off, an' nothin' to pay. They draws the stuff on the road."

"All over England?" said Daphne.

"South and West, lady. I never did fancy the North. You can 'ave the Yorkshire dales."

"May I interrupt?" said Berry.

"If you must," said Daphne. "This is my husband, Mr Hoby, and that's my brother, there. We're all called Pleydell."

"Pleydell," said Mr Hoby. "I know that name. Don't you come out of the Forest?"

"That's right. White Ladies."

"Gaw bless my soul – I often bin by White Ladies. An' fancy it bein' you." He turned to Berry. "And wot was you goin' to say, sir?"

"From here to our village," said Berry, "is just about forty-five miles. How long would it take you to get there?"

"Three days," said Mr Hoby. "Is this a job?"

"It might be," said Berry slowly. The three of us looked at him. "If it was, it'd be…rather special."

"Special," said Mr Hoby. "And what would you mean by that?"

"Good money," said Berry, "long hours, collaboration and not a word to a soul."

Mr Hoby looked into the distance.

"Col-collabberation with 'oo?"

"With us."

"An' 'good money'?"

"A quid for each working hour – twenty-five hours guaranteed."

Mr Hoby started forward, so far as the gate would allow.

"Wot, twenty-five quid? I'm on."

"Wait a minute. What about working for twenty-four hours on end?"

"Seventy-two on end – for a quid an hour. You'd 'ave to help o' course. I might fall asleep."

"I think twenty-four should do it. Of course, I'm assuming you really can hear the thing."

" 'Ear it?" said Mr Hoby. "I've been offered five quid to stop it – by a bloke what was livin' over a mile away. It was *Daisy Bell* got 'im down; but I got four toons."

I began to see daylight. Twenty-four hours on end of *Daisy Bell*, rendered by a steam-organ a furlong away, would make Bluecoat untenable. As for the reactions of a house-party...

My admiration for Berry rose very high.

"Mr Hoby, I think you're my man. But first you must know what you're in for. Will you give me your word to keep this thing to yourself?"

"Strike me dead."

"Then listen to me," said Berry.

Quietly, he explained the position, naming no names.

"We saw him this morning," he concluded, "my brother-in-law and I. And he is plainly determined to use his riches to do this unjust thing. You see what I mean. Whichever side loses before the House of Lords will have to pay the whole of the costs from first to last. And they might well amount to six or eight thousand pounds. Well, we can't afford such a sum: but this fellow can."

"The dirty dog," said Mr Hoby.

"So, in fact, we're denied the help which the Law might give. Very well. Wash out the Law. 'Music hath charms', they say. Let's see what music can do."

"That's right," said Mr Hoby. "When will the nobs arrive?"

"I must find that out," said Berry. "I imagine on Saturday morning, in time for lunch."

"Say you're right. We start 'er on Friday evenin' and run her right through the night. On Saturday morning 'e'll be on 'is bended knees. 'Alf a mo. Wot about an injunction?"

"He won't have time," said Berry. "He might get it by Saturday night, but that's too late."

"Jam," said Mr Hoby. "You'll 'ave 'im cold."

"He may put up a fight," said Berry. "We shall be there, of course, but – "

"Let 'im," said Mr Hoby. He clenched an enormous fist. "Jus' let 'im put up a fight."

"Well, there we are," said Berry. "I'll see the farmer this evening and get his permission for you to enter the Dale. I'll also find out when the guests are due to arrive. Tomorrow morning the chauffeur will bring you a note, telling you where to meet us and at what time. By the way, you're not alone?"

"I got two lads, but they just does what they're told."

Here Jonah joined us, wiping the dirt from his hands.

"My cousin, Mr Mansel – Mr Hoby."

" 'Ow do," said Mr Hoby. "Is 'e in this?"

"He will be – up to the neck. He's half an engineer."

Mr Hoby beamed.

"Gawd, wot a team! I'm lookin' forward to this. An' if you 'adn't broke down 'ere…"

Berry nodded.

"Fate is behind us," he said. "No doubt about that."

That evening, behind closed doors, we put the farmer wise. Ightham was not given to laughter, but, when Berry gave him the details, he shook with mirth. And Saturday, he said, was the day. The Germans were due to arrive by the midday train,

"And Old Chalk's funeral," said Berry. "Can you fix that?"

"I can fix that," said Ightham. "They'll listen to me. Oh, an' by the way, Mas'r Berry, I was thinking of tarring that fence."

"Between the Dale and Bluecoat? How long will it take?"

"About four hours – a good coat."

"Superb," said Berry. "Do it on Friday morning. His lordship may take a little, so mind you lay it on thick." He got to his feet. "Five o'clock, then, on Friday. And Mrs Pleydell may spend the night at the farm?"

"Proud to have her, sir. An' the kitchen'll be at your service all night long."

A note went to Hoby next morning at nine o'clock.

At a quarter-past six on Friday, *Hoby's Steam Round-Abouts* came to rest in the Dale.

It was a lovely evening, and Bluecoat, a furlong away, was looking its best. On the terrace and in the gardens, men were at work, installing fairy lights.

No one, I think, would have recognized Jonah or me. No one, I know, would ever have recognized Berry. As a filthy, slouching mechanic, my cousin would have passed in something much less than a crowd: as a broken-down ring-master, even Mrs Ightham took me for what I seemed. And Berry was a clown, off duty. Above the most awful suit I have ever seen, beneath a dilapidated bowler, his daubed face and crimson nose peered like some sordid nightmare, to shock the world.

Disguise was, of course, essential, if we were to be on the spot: and we had to be on the spot, if we were to win the game.

So far as I saw, we did not attract much attention till the round-about was set up, and the lads had left with the horses for Ightham's farm. Indeed, it was half-past eight, and Berry and I were hanging from the canopy the strips of tin upon which the legend appeared, when I saw a commotion on the terrace and then a servant hastening over the turf.

Disliking the look of the tar, he stopped short of the fence.

Then he put his hands to his mouth and shouted.

Engaged in adjusting the saddle of an enormous duck, Hoby looked round.

"No show till tomorrer," he bawled. "Only re'earsal tonight. Open tomorrer midday. *'Oby's Steam Round-Abouts.*"

"You'll have to move," yelled the footman.

" 'Ave to wot?" bawled Hoby.

"Move," howled the other. "*Move.*"

"You buzz off," roared Hoby, "and 'and the srimps. I've work to do, I 'ave. Be up all night."

With that, he returned to the duck, and after a moment's hesitation, the man hastened back to the house.

"There's Withyham," said Berry. "See him waving his arms? And the footman's trying to tell him about the tar."

After a violent consultation, the butler descended the steps.

Then the peer glanced at his watch and called him back.

"Dinner first," said Berry.

I think he was right, for the servants re-entered the house, and, after perhaps two minutes, Withyham followed them in.

"Let him have his soup," said Berry, "and we'll come in with the fish."

The light was failing now, and the precious silence which sundown had ushered in had spread her ancient mantle over the countryside. Jonah had been lighting the lanterns, and when, under Hoby's direction, Berry and I had fitted them into their proper slots, Hoby withdrew to the engine and started her up. He let her run for five minutes. Then he engaged the gear...

There is a noise which is made by a gramophone. It may be heard, when the power, which has failed, is restored, if the tune is not yet done and the needle is still on the disc. It is not an agreeable noise. But conceive it magnified beyond all comprehension, and you will have some idea of the introductory movement to *Daisy Bell*. So for some five or six seconds... Then the organ was under way, and the well-known melody ranged, like a beast enlarged, the sleeping neighbourhood.

> *Daisy, Daisy,*
> *Give me your answer – do...*

I despair of describing the uproar. Daphne said it was frightening, and she was a mile away. The veil of silence was not so much rent as savaged – when *Hoby's Steam Round-Abouts* laid their simple oblation upon the altar of fun.

What was the effect upon Withyham, I cannot pretend to say, but the windows of the terrace were lighted, and we could see the flicker of figures against the gleams.

Hoby's mouth was close to my ear.

"Good enough, mister?" he blared.

" 'The half was not told me,' " I yelled.

"Here he comes," roared Berry, pointing.

A lantern was jerking its way towards the fence.

Hoby had lighted two flares, one upon either side of the rickety mounting-stair. Between them, he took his stand, while we withdrew to the shadows, to watch what befell.

The tar did not stop Withyham – all things considered, I doubt if it would have stopped me. Be that as it may, the peer arrived, panting, with tar all over his hands and, I am ready to swear, all over his clothes.

"Stop this blasted row," he yelled.

"Wot row?" said Hoby.

"This row," howled Withyham. "This fiendish tune."

"Change in a minute," said Hoby. With his words, *Daisy Bell* gave way to *The Washington Post*. "There you are. Wot did I tell you?"

"Stop the machine," screamed Withyham.

"Can't do that," said Hoby. "Can't disappoint the public."

"Damn the public," roared Withyham. "I've people staying with me in that house over there – decent, god-fearing people, and they're half out of their minds."

"Can't 'elp that," said Hoby. "I got to open tomorrer at twelve o'clock. An' I got to adjus' the orgin. It ain't no pleasure to me to work all night."

"*All night?*" screeched Withyham. "You can't. It's against the law."

"No, it ain't. Not if I'm not takin' money. Tomorrer's different – can't go on after midnight."

Forgetful of the tar, Withyham clapped his hands to his face...

For a moment he stamped to and fro, cursing Ightham with a fury that warmed my heart. Then he returned to the charge.

"I give you five minutes," he mouthed. "Five minutes to stop the swine. If it's still going by the time I'm back at the house, I send a man for the police and give you in charge."

"Wot for?" said Hoby.

"Everything," screamed the other. "You're committing every known crime. What about incitement to murder?"

"That's all right," said Hoby, clapping him on the back. "You go an' 'ave a lay-down."

"Lay-down be – " yelled Withyham. "For the last time I require you – "

"Now look 'ere," said Hoby. "I got my public, I 'ave – *'Oby's Steam Round-Abouts*. An' I'm proud o' my reputation. I tell you she's not runnin' true: an' I got to open tomorrer at twelve o'clock. Well, I got to get 'er right. Once she's right, I'm stoppin': but not before. An' then you'll be able to 'ear 'er."

Withyham's eyes bulged from his head.

"You mean it's going to be louder."

"This ain't nothin'," said Hoby. "A – whisper to wot she ort to do. I tell you, at noon tomorrer…"

Before this revelation, Withyham looked ready to drop. Then be stared wildly round. It was, I am sure, the organ's sudden reversion to *Daisy Bell* that pricked him to one more attempt.

"Stop it yourself," he raved, "or have it stopped. When I tell the police, they'll impound the blasted thing."

"I'd like to see 'em," said Hoby.

"And I'll get an injunction – that's what the Courts are for."

"Don' talk silly," said Hoby. "I shan't be 'ere that long. Finish on Toosday. Got to get ready for Brooch."

"You finish now," screamed Withyham. "If you don't, I'll send my men to break the thing up. I've people staying with me – and others coming tomorrow, for peace and quiet. How d'you think they can sleep – with this poisonous row? Sleep? They can't even think. And you talk about Tuesday! You must be out of your mind. If you think we're going to stand this… No one on earth could stand it – not even a maniac. It isn't human, man."

"Wot isn't 'uman?" said Berry.

Withyham looked round, saw Berry's appalling visage three inches from his, made a noise like a cat and jumped nearly out of his skin.

"Oh, my God," he said weakly, fingers to lip.

I pulled my signal-cord, and the music slowed down and stopped.

"Gawd 'elp," said Hoby, and leapt for the stairs.

Withyham had Berry by the arm.

"What's wrong?" he said.

" 'Ands orf," said Berry. "I don't 'old wiv bloodsuckers."

"Don't be a fool," said Withyham. "Why has the damned thing stopped?"

"Slipped out o' gear. She does it once an' again. There's a lug falls out. 'E's gone to shove it back."

"Listen. I want that lug. It's worth a fiver to me. If you – "

"I don' want bloodsuckers' money."

"I'm not a bloodsucker, you idiot."

"Yes, you are. They tole me up at the inn. I come from these parts, I do. An' wot price Romany Lane?"

"Blast Romany Lane. I'll give you ten pounds for that lug."

Berry stared upon Withyham, poking his head.

"Did you say ten quid?"

"That's right. Ten golden sovereigns."

Berry appeared to reflect.

Then he shook his head.

"I don't take bloodsuckers' money."

As Withyham stamped with impatience, I pulled the signal-cord...

As, when the organ had stopped, the utter silence seemed precious as never before, so, after the blessed respite, the brutal onslaught of Uproar seemed harder than ever to bear.

"Oh, my God," screeched Withyham, clasping his head. Then he turned upon Berry. "Be down at the fence," he blared, "in ten minutes' time."

And then he was gone – to where the lantern was waiting, some twenty-five paces away...

"Anythin' doin'?" said Hoby.

"We're off all right," said Berry, and told him what had occurred.

"We're 'alf-way 'ome," said Hoby, watching the lantern move.

"He's hooked," said I; "but we've got to land him yet."

"Hoby's right," said Berry. "We're half-way home. Picture the depression at Bluecoat. When the damned thing stopped, they assumed he'd done the trick. And while they were praising God, it starts again. Talk about disappointment... His guests'll be ripe for murder, when he gets back."

"Shall we try a noo toon?" said Hoby.

"No," said Berry. "Even *The Washington Post* affords a faint relief. But *Daisy Bell* recurring would break a rhinoceros down. And now let's rehearse the interview."

We kept Withyham waiting five minutes. Then Hoby picked up a lantern and made his way down to the fence, and I moved down behind him, to hear what befell.

Hoby threw his light downwards, until he was only three paces from where the man stood. Then he turned it upon his own face.

There was a stifled exclamation.

Then –

"Oh, er, it's – it's you, is it?" stammered Withyham.

Turning his light upon the speaker –

"What's all this," said Hoby, "about my lug?"

Withyham looked ready to burst.

Hoby continued deliberately.

"You're a good one, you are, to talk about breakin' the law. Wot price bribery an' corruption? Offerin' Joey a tenner, to do a poor bloke down... Bears out wot 'e says about you."

There was an ugly silence – except, of course, for the blare of *Daisy Bell*.

"Couldn' come ter me, could yer?" Withyham started forward, new hope in his eyes. "An' that's where you slipped up. Joey's my partner, 'e is – 'e's got a share in the show."

Withyham swallowed excitedly.

"I'll – I'll make it twenty," he said hoarsely. "Ten pounds apiece."

"Wot, twenty thick 'uns?" said Hoby.

"Twenty, er, thick 'uns," said Withyham. "I've got 'em here." Hoby fingered his chin.

"That's a tidy sum," he said slowly. "But wot about my public? I'm undertook to open – tomorrer at noon."

"That's all right," said Withyham. "They'll, er, understand. Say the thing's not working. It won't be able to work if you give me that lug."

"Gurn," said Hoby. "Think I 'aven't got any spares?"

"Well, say it's broken," cried Withyham. "Damn it, man, you won't take twenty pounds here."

"P'raps I won't: but I never disappointed my public."

"Then move," yelped Withyham. "Move to another pitch."

"Too late now," said Hoby. "I sent the 'orses away."

"Well, get them back, man," cried Withyham, waving his arms.

Hoby shook his head.

"I don' want to kill 'em all at once. They've 'ad three 'ard days' work, an' they got to rest."

Withyham stamped to and fro.

Then –

"Say it's postponed," he mouthed. "And open on Monday night."

"Can' do that," said Hoby. "I got to get on to Brooch. Doo to open at Brooch on – " With a howl of frustration, Withyham clasped his head in his hands. "An' wot's the matter now? Face-ache?"

"Everything," yelled Withyham. "Face-ache, ear-ache, head-ache and general agony. Why the devil can't you stop that tune? There must be some way out, but how the hell can I find it with that filthy, hag-ridden racket splitting my brain?"

"This ain't nothin'," said Hoby, "to wot she ort to do. Besides, you soon get used to it. Why – "

"Used to it?" screamed Withyham. "Used to Hell?" He pulled himself together. "Look here." He slapped his pocket. "Here's twenty pounds in gold. If you can't see your way to earning twenty pounds by taking a weekend off..."

"Orright, orright," said Hoby. "Gimme a chance. I'll 'ave a word with Joey. You wait 'ere."

"Oh, – Joey," said Withyham, as I began to withdraw.

"Now then, naughty," said Hoby. "An' you ain't got no call to talk about Joey like that. 'E's a better man than you are. 'Sides, 'e's my partner, 'e is. 'E's got to agree."

With that, he turned on his heel and walked back to the round-about.

"Yes?" said Berry. "Is the sheep in the shambles?"

" 'E's all washed up," said Hoby. "An' twenty quid in his pocket, a-burnin' a 'ole in his leg. But I said it was up to you. I'm up 'ere now, a-tryin' to bring you round. From the way 'e spoke of you, 'e don't fency that."

Berry smiled a grim smile.

"I'll give him something to fancy, before I'm through."

"It's up to you," said Hoby. " 'Ow long shall we keep 'im waitin'?"

"Half an hour," said Berry.

" 'Alf an hour?" cried Hoby. "Why, 'e won't be 'ardly 'uman in 'alf an hour."

"So much the better," said Berry. "I'll learn the brute. And now let's have some supper.'

With a veal-and-ham pie and some beer, we did very well. Then Jonah raised the speed of the round-about, and, since the organ conformed, at least a cubit was added to the stature of *Daisy Bell*. A rogue elephant, possessed by devils, might have made some such noise, say, once or twice in the hour. But this never stopped. I shall never know how we stood it, and that is the truth.

But Hoby was enchanted.

"Wunnerful, ain't she?" he said. "An' this after seven years."

"And now for the strong stuff," said Berry. "Off you go."

Once again Hoby advanced, and I followed him down to the fence.

Withyham was squatting on the ground, with his fingers stopping his ears.

As he approached the fence –

"Joey won't 'ave it," cried Hoby. "I done my best, but you got acrost 'im some'ow, an' 'e says 'e won't come in. Goo' night, mister. She's runnin' better now."

As we turned to go back, Withyham flung himself at the fence...

"Stop," he screamed. "Wait a moment." We hung on our heel, and he stumbled up to our side. "What the hell d'you mean – 'won't have it'?"

"Well, there's nothin' doin'," said Hoby. "I'm on – I'll give you that. Twenty quid's twenty quid. But Joey's my partner, and 'e won't give 'is consen'. 'E don' fency your money, mister. They've tole 'im some tale or other up at the inn."

"But, if you're willing – "

"Nothin' doin'," said Hoby, lifting a hand. " 'E's always bin square wiv me, an' – "

"Where is he?" cried Withyham. "I'll knock this blasted nonsense out of his head."

His boast was vain. Berry was very quiet, but very firm. He played the part to perfection – the part of the broken-down clown, that cracks his jokes for the fair, but is, in private, a simple, sad-faced being, whose zest for life is gone. And something more. A man of memories, to whom his childhood is precious, because he was happy then.

"Many a time I've bin down Romany Lane, a-pickin' the blackberries there with my sister, Mary Kate. An' once Squire Ferrems comes by – on a great bay 'orse. An' a belted groom be'ind 'im, like wot 'e always 'ad. An' Mary Kate, she curtseys, and Squire, 'e offs with 'is 'at. 'E was gentleman, he was. An' then 'e gives 'em a bob for 'em pretty face. Ah, them were the days... An' now 'e's gone, you'd go fer to shut it up."

Withyham could not shake him – but Withyham would not give way. He swore that the thing was nonsense, that he had not the slightest intention of closing Romany Lane, that he valued the rights of the people as much as any man. But he would not admit that there was a right of way – and we were afraid to press him, lest he should perceive the truth. Besides, we must have it in writing...

For more than forty minutes, the play went on – Withyham shouting and raving, Hoby urging his partner to throw in his hand and Berry quietly rejecting all offers made. And all the time the round-about roared on its way, and *Daisy Bell* went raving into the night.

And then another figure thrust its way on to the stage.

The Prussian officer was never a sight for sore eyes: but take off his uniform and put him, instead, into ill-cut evening dress, and he looked the vulgar bully he always was.

No one had seen him approaching, and the first thing the four of us knew was that a guttural voice was taking Withyham to task.

Then we looked up and round, to see a repulsive figure, some five feet eight by three, with a head indecently shaven and a neck that bulged over his collar, as a tire that is down bulges over the rim of its wheel.

"Den thousan' tevils, Baron, vot vas this mean? If you gannot make cease this hell, order a garriage that I shall drive into Brooch."

Withyham was all to pieces.

"Major, I beg you – "

"Be zilent. Because I vas His Highness' Gomptroller, I gome to your house to be sure that all vas fit for the Brince and Brincess to stay. And here is this goddam organ to blast the brains from their heads. An' you 'ave declare it was over an hour and a half ago." He dragged a watch from his pocket and dabbed at the dial. "Vive minutes I give you to cease it. Then I shall be driven to Brooch, to send a telegram. I gannot bermit that their Highnesses suffer the bains of Hell."

His eyes fast upon the Prussian, Berry jerked his head at Withyham, black in the face.

" 'E won't see reason," he said. "But you're a gentleman."

Withyham's face was a study, but Major von Blodgenbruck beamed.

"The beasant vos discerning," he purred. "Stob your organ, my vriend, and ye vill dalk."

As Berry nodded to Hoby –

"The man's not normal," cried Withyham. "I tell you. Major – "

The other lifted a hand.

"Be zilent, blease. As His Highness' Gomptroller – " The music stopped. "Observe. Before I vas here dwo minutes, the organ has ceased."

"Yes, but you're a gentleman," said Berry. "You wouldn' take advantage of blokes because they was poor."

"No, my vriend," smiled the Major. "That vas not my gountry's way. I do not know who are your blokes, but all the boor of my gountry were so happy because the rich were so good."

"Ah," said Berry. He looked at Withyham, by now the prey of emotions too deep for words. "But 'e's a bloodsucker. An' I don' want bloodsuckers' money."

"A bloodsucker?" said the Major.

"That's right," said Berry. "Grinds the faces of the poor. 'E's offered me twenty quid, but I wouldn' take fifty from 'im 'Coz why? 'Coz 'e's a bloodsucker. But you're a gentleman." Leering with pleasure, the Major patted his arm. As though he was touched by an attention he had never been shown before, the hideous ghost of smile stole into Berry's face. " 'Spect, if the troof were known, you've a bigger estate than this."

The other swelled.

"That vas so, my vriend. The Von Blodgenbrucks' estates in Schwerin are many times larger than this: an' all the beasants

69

are so happy, because their dear master and mistress love them so much."

"That's the style," said Berry. "Live an' let live."

"That vas my great gountry's moddo."

"Itch Deen," said Berry, and touched his hat – and von Blodgenbruck beamed and bowed, as though he were of the blood royal.

"I can talk to you," said Berry, " 'cause you're a gentleman."

"That vas why I am gome, my goot vriend. You vill say vot you blease."

"Well, now look 'ere," said Berry. "Supposin' acrost your estates there was a certing lane."

This was too much for Withyham.

As an unruly torrent, the words foamed out of his mouth.

"I protest against this, Major. The man's insane. For nearly an hour I've been trying – "

"Zilence!" barked the Major.

"As your host, I must request you to remember – "

"I vas here as His Highness' Gomptroller. As such you will blease to submit all arrangements to me. Their Highnesses did graciously consent tomorrow to come to your house. Until they shall go on Monday, I vas in charge. As such, I am to deal with this matter." He returned to Berry. "Go on, my goot vriend."

For a moment I thought that Withyham was going to fall down in a fit. Then he lurched to the crazy staircase, sat himself down on a step and put his head in his hands.

Berry reopened his case.

"Supposin' acrost your estates there was a certing lane."

"What sort of lane, my vriend?"

"A country lane, for 'orses an' carts an' cows. An' supposin' for fifty years poor blokes – wot you call peasan's – 'ad always used that lane... An' supposin' – jus' supposin' – one day you got tired o' your estates an' sold 'em to somebody else. Well, 'e wouldn' 'ave no right to shut up that lane."

"No, indeed, my vriend. If the neighbours – "

70

"That's right – neighbours."

"If the neighbours vere using that lane for, say, dwenty years, they would 'ave gain a servitude – I vas not know how you call it…"

"Right o' way," said Berry.

"That vas true. Right of way. They would 'ave gain a right of way to use it for always. That vas the law."

Berry pointed excitedly at Withyham.

"Well, that's wot 'e done. He's shut up Romany Lane. This ain't 'is property, reely. Not by rights. It belonged to Mr Ferrers – Ferrers of Bluecoat, 'e was. An' he was a gentleman, like you. An' all the neighbours always used Romany Lane. An' now 'e shuts up the lane, wot 'e ain't got no right to do. 'S a right o' way, an' 'e knows it. *An' if 'e'll put that in writin', I'll take 'is twenty quid.*"

"Vot vas he to write, my vriend?"

"The troof," cried Berry. "That's all. That 'e knows there's a right o' way down Romany Lane. I've pen an' ink 'ere, I 'ave; an' I bin a clurk in my time, an' I'll draw the paper out. An' if 'e'll sign it, I'll take 'is twenty quid an' we'll shut up shop."

"You vos say that if he will do this – sign your little baber, you vill not blay your organ till Monday noon?"

"That's right," said Berry. "Must 'ave it in writin'; because 'e's not like you. You're a gentleman, you are. But then you're a-goin' on Monday. We can stop our organ. But then, as soon as you're gone, 'e'll shut up the lane again. No, no. Gotter 'ave it in writin'."

"An' that is all that you ask?"

"*An'* twenty quid – golding sovereigns. 'E's promised that. Got 'em in his pocket, 'e says."

The Major patted Berry's shoulder.

"Write out your baber, my vriend, an' bring it to me."

Berry looked at Withyham.

"Name o' Mocket, ain't it? Basil Mocket, weren't you, afore they shoved you up?"

Ready to burst with indignation, Withyham made no reply, but averted his gaze.

As Berry shambled into the shadows –

"I'm damned if I'll sign it," said Withyham, and got to his feet.

"There you are," said Hoby, and turned and ran.

But before he could reach the machinery, Jonah engaged the gears.

The next few moments were crowded.

Von Blodgenbruck was storming at Withyham, and Withyham was storming back. I caught the words 'scrap of paper' and 'Court of Law'. Both were raving like madmen, while the round-about swirled beside them and *Daisy Bell* was trumpeted into the night.

Before the words 'insult to Royalty', Withyham broke down.

"All right, all right," he wailed. "Give me the blasted paper and stop this god-awful row."

As Hoby reappeared, I pulled the signal cord.

"The Baron vill zign," said the German. "Vere vas my vriend?"

Hoby went off for Berry, and host and guest stood waiting in a silence too big for words.

Presently Withyham looked round: but I was in the shadows and not to be seen.

"You will take charge of it," said Withyham.

"That vas mos' proper," said the other, closing one eye.

After another two minutes, Berry returned with his paper, and Hoby came after, bearing the pen and ink.

Von Blodgenbruck inspected the document, grunting at the end of a line.

"That vas in order," he said, and read it aloud.

Hoby took it from him, laid it down on a step and dipped the pen in the ink...

With bulging eyes, Withyham signed it, and Berry and Hoby subscribed their names as witnesses. Withyham made no attempt to read their signatures.

That sheet from an exercise-book is lying before me now. The shaky copper-plate writing is easy enough to read.

I, Basil Mocket, Baron Withyham, do hereby solemnly declare that to the best of my belief the British public has a right of way along Romany Lane, because, before ever I bought the Bluecoat estate, Romany Lane had never been closed for at least twenty-five years.

Withyham.
August, 1907.
Witnessed by:
Bertram Pleydell JP
Walter Hoby, Showman.

Hoby was looking at Withyham.

"Twenty quid, wasn't it?" he said.

In a thick voice, Withyham replied.

"I'll pay you on Monday," he said.

"No, you don't," said Hoby. " '*Oby's Steam Round-Abouts* always keeps its word."

Withyham hesitated.

"On the strict understanding," he said, "that you don't play that organ again before Tuesday next – "

"Strike me dead," said Hoby.

Withyham counted the gold into his palm.

Von Blodgenbruck put out his hand.

"And I shall charge myself with that baber. Give it to me, my vriend."

"Not on yer life," said Berry. He folded up the sheet and stowed it away. "I never did fency Germans. An' I seen your shape before – in a German band. Play the cornet – he used to. An' steal the pennies out of a blin' man's pail. They got 'im at las', red-'anded, an' down 'e goes for six months. You been in prison, ain't yer?"

"Me in prison?" screamed the Major, and Withyham let out a hoot.

"Look at yer 'ead," jeered Berry. "Yer can't fool me. 'The Caounty Crop', we call it… Estates in Swerring, I don't think. You go back to your band – an' try to run straight, like what the Magistrate said."

With that, he turned to the staircase, mounted the crazy steps, dived beneath a dragon and disappeared.

"There you are," shrieked Withyham. "That's what yot get for interfering. That's what *I* get for – "

But his guest had no ears to hear.

His eyes and arms upraised, in a loud and shaking voice, he dealt with all English peasants, root and branch. (He had abandoned English as now inadequate: but Jonah told us later all that he said.) He spoke of treachery and insult, of dogs and the wages of sin, and he vowed the most shocking vengeance when once *Der Tag* should dawn. Then he turned upon Withyham and rent him, and Withyham yelled "Speak English" and rent him back. Then he stamped off, shouting for a carriage, and, after a moment's hesitation, Withyham fell in behind.

I followed, to see them out, and so was made free of a tailpiece, which I should have been sorry to miss.

Because of his agitation, the German failed to remember that the fence had been tarred and had begun to climb it before its horrid condition reminded him of that fact. With screams of rage, he descended, to seek the spot at which he had climbed it before; for there he had hung a carpet, to save his hands and his clothes. As Withyham's lantern showed, the carpet which he had chosen was a very fine Persian rug, and, since he had laid this face downward upon the tar, it was fair to assume that much of its value was gone.

This typically German procedure was more than Withyham could bear.

With a choking scream, he caught the man by the arm.

"Face downward," he yelled. "And that's a museum piece."

"An' vot of my trousers?" roared the German. "Vot of my beautiful suit? I 'ave pay three pounds for this suit at the biggest store in Berlin."

He shook off Withyham's hand and turned to heave himself up.

His reply was, no doubt, the straw that broke the camel's back.

Offered a perfect target, careless of what might befall, Withyham thrust the top of his lantern against the German's seat...

To this day Daphne swears that she heard the yells from the farm: and the others came running, to see what the matter might be. I cannot pretend that it rivalled *Daisy Bell*, but I never would have believed that any one human being could make so fearful a noise.

Be that as it may, the Major rose into the air, and then fell heavily almost at Withyham's feet. And his host whipped over the fence and, taking the carpet with him, stumbled towards the house.

When we left him, the German, still roaring, was trying to crawl through the fence: but his bulk and the tar were against him, and I think that he would have done better to scale it at once.

Half an hour had gone by, and we were seated at supper at Ightham's farm.

Hoby's lads were now in charge of the silent round-about, and Ightham had sent his nephew to cut the padlock and chain from the gate which Withyham had set at the mouth of Romany Lane.

The fine, old kitchen was gleaming with copper and oak, and the Ighthams fussed about us, pressing viands upon us and keeping our glasses full.

My sister was regarding the paper.

"And this will sink him?" she said.

"It has sunk him," said I. "I'll lay you fifty pounds that the chain which George is undoing will never go back. If it does, our solicitors send him a copy of this. And when his solicitors see it, they will explain to him that he has no case."

"Can't he plead duress?"

"Not without the German to back him. And I hardly think he can count on Von Blodgenbruck's help. And even then he wouldn't get home. A man may make an admission, but he doesn't make an untrue admission because there's a barrel-organ a furlong away."

"Be fair," said Berry. "Call it a musical box."

"Be a Jew's 'arp, nex'," said Hoby.

As the laughter died down, Jonah lifted his glass.

"I look to Berry," he said. "First Withyham and then the German. He played them both to perfection. It looked so easy to start with. I mean, I thought Withyham was cracking quite early on. And then he stuck in his toes."

"And I couldn't push him," said Berry, "for fear he'd suspect a plant. You can't get away from the fact that Blood-and-Bunk pulled his weight."

" 'S a dirty dog," said Hoby. "All them love an' kisses. 'E meant to 'ave that paper an' tear it up."

"Without a doubt," said Berry. "And what's the betting their Grossnesses don't fetch up?"

"They probably will," said Jonah. "Withyham won't give him a carriage to go to Brooch."

(Ightham later reported that in fact they did arrive – to leave on Sunday morning, after a fearful scene. Their Comptroller accompanied them, crouching, because be dared not sit down. The next day Withyham left, and Bluecoat was shut for six months. Not so Romany Lane. In fact, when the gate disappeared, it was never replaced.)

Our farewells had been said, and we were all in the brougham, which was turning out of the gate, when a voice like a foghorn was lifted calling on the coachman to stop.

Hoby appeared at the window, cheque in hand.

" 'Ere, wot's this?" he demanded. "You've made it for twenty-five quid."

"That's what we arranged," said Berry.

"But I've 'ad twenty orf 'im. You only owes me five."

Berry leered out of the window.

"I don' take bloodsuckers' money."

Hoby took off his hat.

"I don' deserve it," he said. "You earned your corn tonight."

"Shove it into the show," said Berry. "Pin-money for *Daisy Bell*."

Hoby looked down at the ground.

"You tied me up, sir," he said. "I 'aven't got any words. Forty-five quid in one evenin' – you know, it ain't right."

Daphne put in her oar.

"From our point of view, Mr Hoby, this evening's been cheap at the price."

Hoby looked up.

"If you put it like that, lady…"

"I do, indeed. Mind you come and see us, next time you're by."

"You bet," said Mr Hoby.

The brougham rolled on.

Six days later a parcel, addressed to Daphne, arrived from Brooch. It contained a most beautiful rug, for use in the car. Attached to this was a card –

With the very respectful compliments of Hoby's Steam Round-Abouts.

3

In Which We Talk With Big James,
and Daphne Has Eyes to See

The handsome lease of August was nearly up: our car had been delivered: Fitch had entered our service; and Jonah had left for France, to bring his sister back from a chateau commanding the Loire.

Daphne and I were sitting over our breakfast: Berry was not yet down.

"What am I riding, Boy?"

"Gallant, this morning," said I. "Is that all right?"

My sister nodded.

"I'd like to come back by Blackstone. Falcon says that Margery's not too good."

Margery Kingcome had been our mother's nursemaid and our own nurse, and now she was living in retirement some nine miles off.

"Blackstone is damp," I sighed. "If only she'd stayed in the village, as we tried to make her do…"

"I know," said Daphne, "I know. But she is a miller's daughter, and Bilberry's got no mill. She'd rather live ten years at Blackstone than twenty at Bilberry." She glanced at her wrist. "What ever is Berry doing? It's twenty to ten."

With her words, her husband appeared.

As he helped himself from the sideboard –

"Last night," he said, "I had a most singular dream. I dreamt I was a mortgage on a fried-fish shop, which was situate in the precincts of Lambeth Palace itself. Weary of the perfume, the Church Militant sought to foreclose. I was unfolded, perused, dropped, used as a fly-swatter and finally spread before the Primate. Supposing me to be a dog-licence, His Grace signed me and I was sold for seven and six. No kidneys? What an outrage! Never mind, I'll get home on egg."

With a plate, charged after the manner of the Middle Ages, he took his seat.

"My darling," said Daphne, "you've cut yourself."

"Beloved," said Berry, helping himself to toast, "I cannot tell a lie. I did it – with my little hatchet. Elijah would have been ravished. The blood gushed out upon me."

"How dreadful."

"It was," said Berry, "a shocking spectacle. Had a police-officer entered the bathroom, I should have been arrested for attempted suicide. In my agitation, I also dropped the razor and cut myself on the foot. But I seem to be in good health. No shortage of red corpuscles, as far as I saw."

"But you did it only last week."

"My sweet," said Berry, attacking his scrambled eggs, "the copper-bottomed miracle is that I don't do it twice a day. Each time I uncover those weapons – one for each day in the week – I come all over of a tremble. The only trouble is, they don't seem to freeze the blood."

"Are you sure you strop them right?"

Berry shuddered.

"I don't want them any sharper, if that's what you mean The wonder is my jaw hasn't dropped."

"You must get a razor like Boy's."

Berry shook his head.

"I've tried his. It's the finest skin-eraser I know. I'd rather have a slice off the joint than erysipelas."

"I'm not sure you're not right," said I, caressing my chin. "What I go through every morning…"

"Jonah manages somehow."

"Jonah," said Berry, "has an abnormal skin. He could file his beard down every day, and it wouldn't leave any trace. If he was to have an injection, they'd have to send for a drill. Oh, no, there's nothing for it. My dressing-gown, by the way, had better go to Madame Tussaud's."

"What, not your new one?"

"The same," said Berry calmly. "It made me think of Omar Khayyám. You remember those deathless lines. 'The Moving *Razor cuts*; and, having *cut*, Moves on…' "

Calling her maid, Wilson, as fast as her habit would let her, my sister fled.

"Some years ago," said Berry, "when I was Caesar's wife, I used to shave with potsherds. It was most economical. When one got blunt, you dropped it, and then you had three or four. Of course you had to watch your step. There used to be a fresco at Pompeii of Julius using the bathroom after me. It was called *The night I overtrod the Ceramics*."

"I've sent for a new one," I said. "It's just come out. They say you can use it in the dark."

Berry laughed bitterly.

"I can use mine in the dark," he said, "But I'm not going to."

"Don't be a fool," I said. "The presumption – "

"All right," said Berry. "You try it. If, after one calendar month you look less like a gargoyle afflicted with the King's Evil – "

"That'll do, Heidelburg."

After a long look, Berry protruded his tongue.

I rose to my feet.

"Permit me to remind you," I said, "that the horses have been ordered for half-past ten."

Forty-five minutes later, we were riding over the forest to the pretty hamlet of Gamecock, which lay, seven miles from White Ladies, snug in a fold of the greenwood that kept it from curious eyes.

Our way was a lovely way – by heath and glade and water and gravel road; and the majesty of the timber, the sweetness of the prospects, the union of Husbandry and Nature – above all, the comfortable air of stability lifted up all our hearts. Progress or no, it was clear that this most goodly heritage could never be scathed; that, slowly but surely, Tradition had made it safe; that, wars or rumours of wars, this would endure – the same yesterday, today and for ever, the English countryside.

But for a milk-float, we had the world to ourselves, till we rounded Holy Brush, to see a gypsy encampment down in the dell below.

Our appearance occasioned a flurry.

Two children went flying, a giant of a man strode leisurely out of view, and a woman came lightly towards us, over the sward.

That she had been sent to delay us was perfectly clear.

Signing to Daphne to stay, Berry rode past the woman and up to the camp. And I, with him.

The man we had seen was standing in the mouth of a tent.

"Where's your pass?" said Berry.

"I need no pass," said the other, folding his arms. "I came last night and I am going today."

(Without a verderer's pass, no man, be he peer or ploughboy, might set up his camp in the forest for more than forty-eight hours.)

Berry looked round.

"You have been here at least three days. The ground shows that. And the traces which you will leave will remain for three months. All others are cleanly people, but whatever you touch, you foul. That is why you are made to move – that Nature may be able to repair the horrid damage you do."

His words were justified. The dell, which had been so lovely, was now a sordid place. Bushes were scorched and broken, old tins and filthy rags were choking the little rill, and a chain about a young beech-tree had bruised and broken the bark.

Berry continued slowly.

"Three weeks ago you stood before the Riding Hood Bench, The magistrates gave you the benefit of the doubt. It is clear that they made a mistake; for your action, when I appeared, was out that of an innocent man."

"I earn my living," said the other.

"You could, but you don't," said Berry. "You could earn an honest living with any man. But there's no health in you, Lewis, and that's the truth." He glanced at his watch. "It now eleven-fifteen, and I'll give you two hours' law. Then I shall tell the verderer what I have found."

"Curse your law," said the other.

"Very good," said Berry. "I'll tell him in a quarter of an hour."

He turned and rode back to my sister, with me behind.

"Morning, Mrs Lewis," he said. I saw the woman start. "You must try and make your husband see reason. He's a first-rate tinman, you know; and if he'd stick to his last, he'd do very well. But, if he will break the law – well, one day the law will break him."

After a long look, the woman returned to Daphne.

"His heart is honest," she said, "but he has not the eyes to see. But your sight is keen and pure as the wind on the top of a hill."

Daphne raised her eyebrows.

"My husband is very much wiser than you or I. You and your man would do well to hear what he says. What were you saying about my seeing the country?"

"I bade you lift up your eyes, because this day you shall see the countryside."

"That is all?"

"That is enough."

I held up a shilling.

"Tell all," said I, "to turn this to half a crown."

The woman covered her eyes.

Then –

"I will not lie," she said. "I can see no farther than that."

I put away the shilling and handed her half a crown.

"That for honesty."

She took the coin and bit it – a common fashion then, to be sure that the coin was real.

"You are good people," she said. "I wish you well."

She turned to go back to the dell, and we went on our way to Gamecock, taking another road.

"Hopeless," said Berry. "That man's a desperate poacher – in rather plainer language, a common thief. He could earn big money as a tinman, but he doesn't like work. But he does like the taste of pheasant. And he can see no reason why he should work and why he should not eat pheasant. In other words, he's an outlaw: and one of these days he'll do a keeper in."

(Berry was among the prophets: Lewis was hanged three years later, for shooting a keeper dead.)

"I'm sorry for the woman," said Daphne. "She has to do what she's told."

Ten minutes later, we rode into Gamecock's precincts and up to the forge.

The smith, Big James, was a very good friend of ours. More. He was a beautiful farrier, and had always shod our horses for twenty years. And the forge was the prettiest thing – with a mighty horse-shoe portal, and an aged wistaria hanging the beams with purple to show that the craft was royal.

Berry took Daphne down, and as George came up for the horses, Big James came out of the forge.

For a moment he stood, blinking.

Then –

"God bless my soul, it's Miss Daphne."

"Come to thank you, Big James, for shoeing the greys."

The fine fellow laughed.

"I'll allow they wanted humouring."

"I know how long it took you. And they were perfectly shod."

Big James coloured with pleasure.

"Thank you, ma'am. But it's nice to see you again. An' Mas'rs Berry an' Boy. It's like old days – when you used to blow the bellows, and Mas'r Berry would strike."

"Happy old days, Big James."

"So they was, Miss Daphne. An' Mas'r Jonathan?"

"Very well, thank you. He's bringing Miss Jill from France. How's Fanny?"

"Go you an' see her, Miss Daphne, an' she shall speak for herself." A whinny made him look round. "Why, Mermaid, lass, and Gallant…"

He stepped to make much of the horses; and the four of them squabbled for his favour – as rare a tribute as ever a man was paid.

That picture has stayed with me: it was matter for statuary. Big James, in his leather apron, lifting his valiant arms, and standing proud and square as an English oak; George, slim and spruce and belted, calling the horses to order and seeming small of stature beside the smith; and the four, fine heads together – two bays, a roan and a chestnut – eyes flashing, ears pricked, wide nostrils blowing sweet breath, rendering unto the master the things that were his.

As he turned away, towards us –

"Listen, Big James," said my sister. "Will you make me a garden gate?"

"That I will, Miss Daphne. You've only to draw it out."

"To hang in a wall," said Berry. "To close a decent gap that has never been closed before. It is to be purely obstructive. A wrought-iron nuisance, Big James. That's what the lady wants. Of course, if you could make it dangerous…"

The blacksmith laughed.

"It shall comfort the eye, Mas'r Berry. I'll lay to that. Wrought-iron in a wall, and the greenery showing through. That can be very pleasing, as madam knows." He pointed into the village. "There's one such at Mulberry Corner that's being sold up today. Round the back of the house, in an old brick wall. An' the green o' the woods beyond – it's a delicate sight. Walk down and view it, Mas'r Berry, before you go."

"He's only being tiresome," said Daphne. "I'll draw the design to scale, and I'll send you the measurements up."

"Keep it, Miss Daphne. An' I'll come over next Sunday and see the place for myself. An' then you shall give me the drawing – it's better so. But do you visit the cottage, to look at that gate. It's all corrupted now; but it's beauty, still."

"Where is it exactly, Big James?"

"Last house o' the village, ma'am. Old Miss Birchup, she died without makin' a will. Ninety-eight, she was, an' none of her people left. So the Crown takes all. They're selling the stuff today. Not that there's anything there, but it's got to be sold. I could have done with the chair, but Akers is after that."

"Who's Akers?" said I.

"He keeps *The Stag*, Mas'r Boy, an' he's money to burn. There's been some changes here in the last twelve months."

"We'll go and see Fanny," said Daphne, "and then we'll look at the gate."

"Who's that lad?" said Berry. "Can he give George a hand?"

"That he can," said the smith. He raised his voice. "Horses, Billy." The boy sprang up. "He's simple, sir, but the horses like him for that. Shall they have a little water?"

"A mouthful, please," said Berry. "We shan't be long."

We visited Big James' daughter, that kept his tiny home: and then we walked down to the cottage, to look at the gate.

A notice-board hung on the fence – SALE BY AUCTION THIS DAY AT TWO O'CLOCK, and doors and windows were open, although there was nobody there.

We passed through the tiny garden and round to the back of the house.

Big James was right – it had been a lovely gate, and how it had come to be hung there, I could not think. It might well have admitted to some Italian pleasance, for the design was noble and the workmanship very fine. But rust had done the evil that rust can do, and the gate had put on corruption before its time.

"And there's a pity," said Berry. "That was a work of art. And how in the world did it get here?"

Finger to lip –

"I suppose it's hopeless," said Daphne.

I touched the crumbling metal, to feel it give.

"You'd never get it down, my darling. It'll hang as it is for a while; but the moment you try to move it, it will collapse."

My sister nodded and turned, to lead the way back. Then she spoke over her shoulder.

"As we're here, shall we look at the house?"

"May as well," said Berry. "You never know."

The house was very small, and after the August sunshine, its rooms seemed dark.

We looked round the little kitchen, but there was nothing there. A fine old fireplace took up the whole of one wall: one door, which was just ajar, gave to a break-neck stair: another, which was wide open, gave to a second room. By this we passed, to enter the decent parlour, which gave the cottage the right to be called a house.

My sister was pointing.

"I'm not surprised," she said, "that Big James wants that chair."

Neither was I.

Its frame had been painted black, and the plush with which it had been covered was greasy and worn: but nothing could spoil its proportions or hide its beautiful lines. It was clearly the principal part of an old *chaise-longue*, that had been fashioned in France, when Louis Quatorze was king.

Berry tilted it sideways, to feel the weight.

"Period piece," he said. "No doubt about that. If you could get that paint off…"

But the chair was the only thing there.

The tall-case clock was hideous: a dark and dirty landscape loomed from a battered frame: a small, Victorian sideboard presented some dreadful shells; a horse-hair couch was repellent; the walnut overmantel, inlaid with scraps of mirror, was indefensible.

The three of us made the round, before we withdrew.

As we re-entered the kitchen, a figure appeared in the doorway by which we had entered the house.

"Good morning, ladies and gentlemen. Anything here you fancy?"

"Good morning," said Daphne. "Are you the auctioneer?"

"No, I'm the sexton, lady. I've kep' the keys. But if you don' wan' to attend, I can always bid for you."

"Thank you very much," said Daphne. "I'd like that chair. The one in the parlour, I mean, that's covered with plush."

"Certainly, ma'am. Fifteen shillings'll buy it, if you ask me."

"I'll go to two pounds ten." My sister looked at me. "Have you the money on you?"

"I haven't got half a sovereign. I've got three pounds."

"Make it three pounds," said Daphne.

The money passed.

"I'm to go to three pounds, then, lady?"

"That's right. And we'll be over tomorrow, to see what luck you've had."

"Very good, ma'am. I lives just two doors off."

We left the house and garden and turned to go back to the forge.

Daphne had us each by an arm.

"Show no surprise," she said, "but listen to what I say. That picture there is a Claude, and it's worth a thousand or more."

"What, that canvas in the parlour?"

"Yes."

"Oh, don't be silly," said Berry. "Until it's been cleaned, no expert could – "

"I don't care. It's got Claude's touch. Golden light in the middle, fading to blue, and the foreground green and strong."

"But you couldn't see it," cried Berry.

"Bear with me, darling," said Daphne. "I know I'm right. Besides, I could see it – really. Classical remains in a meadow, and hills beyond."

"Well, what do we do?" said Berry.

"Fitch must buy it," said Daphne. "He can drive over early, leave the car at the crossroads and walk the rest of the way. That's why I told the sexton to bid for that chair."

"I don't understand," I said, frowning.

"She's got it wrong," said Berry. "We leave the sexton at the crossroads and let Fitch bid for the car. Then we give Akers three pounds and walk the rest of the way."

"You really are dense," said Daphne. "In the sexton's eyes, we are experts – don't forget that. That was why he was eavesdropping."

"Eavesdropping?"

"Yes. I think he was on the staircase, when we came in. I heard his step in the kitchen when we were inspecting the chair. And of course he heard what we said. So I was frankness itself. I said I'd pay four times as much as he thought the chair would fetch. My innocence should disarm him. If it does, he will report that, except for the chair, there is nothing of value there. But in fact there's a Claude – a landscape by Claude Le Lorrain."

As soon as Berry could speak –

"You wicked, deceitful girl. You – "

"If you ask me," said Daphne, "I think it was rather quick. Of course we shan't get the chair, for Akers, who 'has money to burn', will know that he's on a good thing."

"Fitch can buy that, too," said I.

"So he can," said my sister. "Well done. I want Big James to have it. He picked it out."

"That's right," said Berry. "And let's give the Claude to the sexton. If he didn't suffer from corns, he'd have quite a nice face. Incidentally, the car will be stolen, while Fitch is attending the sale."

"I'll go with Fitch," said I, "and stay with the car. All the same, you're sure it's worth it? I mean, I'd arranged – "

"Worth it?" cried Daphne. "Wait till it's been restored and is hanging next to the Cuyp. And I've always wanted a Claude."

"My sweet," said Berry, "we're proud to humour your whim. But please don't ride so very straight for a fall. Thanks to our parents, we all know a bit about pictures – probably more than some. But we are, none of us, experts. And no expert that ever was foaled would be so – so definite."

"Sorry, old fellow," said Daphne. "I know I'm right. How much can we raise in cash?"

Berry uncovered and gave his head to the air.

"If nobody else desires it, you'll get it for four and six. But if somebody else has been gifted with second sight..."

I stopped in my tracks and put a hand to my head.

"She has been," I cried. "That's the answer. She saw what we couldn't see."

The others stared.

"Egg-bound," said Berry shortly. "It's that damned house. Perhaps the old dame was a witch Let's find some running water. I don't feel too good, myself."

"What d'you mean, Boy?" said my sister.

"That picture's a landscape," I said. "Well, what did the gypsy say? 'Lift up your eyes, and this day you shall see the countryside.' "

We all drove with Fitch to the crossroads: and there we waited, while he went off to the sale.

For fear of exciting suspicion, he was not to bid for the chair, unless, of course, it was offered after the Claude had been sold. He had twenty-six pounds in cash, which was all that we had in the house: but he had a blank cheque of Berry's, in case of accidents. He was not wearing his livery, and no one in Gamecock knew him for one of our men. If he secured the chair, he was to seek out Big James, ask him to keep his counsel and house it for us: but the Claude he was to bring to the cross roads, with all dispatch.

When an hour and a half had gone by, we began to grow uneasy. Gamecock was less than a mile from where we were, and we found it hard to believe that the contents which we had seen would take a full hour to sell.

"He's got to see Big James," said Berry. "And then. of course, they may start with the bedroom stuff."

Another half-hour dragged by.

"Oh, dear," said Daphne. "We ought to have gone ourselves. If we hadn't been so grasping – "

"No," said I. "You were right. The sexton thinks we rode over to see what there was in that house, and I'll lay any money you like we don't get that chair."

"Poor Big James," said Daphne. "Never mind. We'll have one made for him."

He damned well deserves it," said I. "But for him, we should never have gone to the house."

"And what of Mrs Lewis?" said Daphne.

"She's been paid," said Berry. "With all this fuss, I forgot to ring up Lyndhurst."

"Oh, I am glad," said Daphne.

Berry shook his head.

"I must do it tonight," he said. "Lewis must never believe that my threats are idle threats."

When another hour had gone by, we were much more than uneasy – we were alarmed. Indeed, we were on the point of driving to Gamecock, ourselves, when Fitch appeared in the distance, with a picture under his arm…

As we walked down the road to meet him –

"Well done, indeed," cried Daphne. "How much did you have to pay?"

"One and sixpence, madam. Mine was the only bid. But there's been some dirty work there. That sexton's a dealer's nark."

"Go on," said Berry. "Let's have it."

"Well, the moment I got there, sir, I saw there was something afoot. The auctioneer an' two others was whispering in the garden, as thick as thieves. One was the sexton, all right – I recognized him, an' the other turned out to be Akers, who keeps the inn. Well, they didn't start till just on twenty past two, and then they began with the bedrooms, which nobody seemed to expect. There was very little stuff there, and anyone could 'ave sold it in half an hour. But that auctioneer – an' then I realized that the fellow was going slow…

"That made me think. So I slipped down into the garden. Sure enough, the sexton was out in the road. An' then I knew they were holding things up for someone…

"Well, he took the kitchen next – as slow as he dared. Akers was in it, too – an' got landed two or three times, by tryin' to run things up. An' then he came to the parlour. By the grace o' God, he sold the picture first. He looked pretty 'ard at me when I said one and six, but he couldn't do nothing about it, an' there wasn't another bid. So I laid the money down and put it under my arm. But he wouldn't put up that chair…

"Slower an' slower he goes, always with his chin on his shoulder, watching Akers who's standing still in the kitchen watching the garden gate…

"An' then a trap drives up: and a moment later a little Jew fellow, all hot, comes into the room. And Akers and the sexton, behind.

"He gives the chair the once over. Then he takes out a penknife an' slits the cushion open, calm as you please. Inside it was kid – white kid, like a lady's gloves. An' then he nods, an' leans back against the wall.

"An' then, as bold as brass, the auctioneer puts up the chair...

"The sexton bids, as you told him, up to three pounds. You ought to 'ave seen people's faces. They couldn't 'ardly believe it. The biggest price made so far was one pound ten. An' that old chair...

" 'Guineas,' says the dealer.

"When I said 'Three poun's ten', his head come round with a jerk.

" 'Fifteen,' he says, defiant...

"Well, I took him up to six guineas, like what you said. And he got it for six fifteen, but I think he'd have given more.

"Well, that was that, an' I was walking out of the house, when, all of a sudden, I felt a tap on my arm.

"It was the dealer all right.

" 'Let me look at that picture,' he says.

"I held it out, an' he stands back an' shades his eyes. Then he outs with a glass an' goes all over it careful.

" 'No,' he says, 'it's a copy. All the same, I'll give you a fiver.'

" 'Make it fifty,' I said, 'an' then you're wrong.'

"He looked at me very hard.

"Then –

" 'What about a hundred?' he says, 'a hundred golden sovereigns.'

" 'Don' be silly,' I said. 'It's not for sale,'

"I walked off, but he followed me down the road... Wouldn't take no for an answer – you know the sort.

"At last –

"This is a do,' he says. 'You don't know nothin' of pictures.'

" 'Yes, you're a good one,' says I, 'to talk about does. Who had the sale held up – 'cause he wouldn't risk three quid on the sexton's tip? Serves you right,' I said, 'for usin' a man like that.'

"He stood quite still for a minute, staring straight at me and biting his thumb.

"Then –

" 'Holy snakes,' says he. 'If those two have double-crossed me…'

"Then he set off back to the village as hard as he could."

"Splendid," said Berry. "You've lighted the flare of suspicion. There'll be such a row at *The Stag* as never was heard. And now let's get back – with our bargain."

Daphne looked up from the canvas.

"Now we want a Turner," she said, "to hang on the other side."

"You should have told Fitch," said Berry. "Then he could have asked the dealer if he knew of any Turners that were going for half a crown."

We drove home by the hamlet of Blackstone, to visit our nurse; and I must confess, that when I stood in her garden, listening to the speech of the water and watching the flash of the mill-wheel between the leaves, the charm of the place was compelling and I could understand how Margery felt.

The old, familiar hand came to rest on my arm.

"You can't see him now, my dear, but when the leaves are gone, I can sit by the hour at my window and watch his bravery. The pictures I see in the papers of all these new machines – 'tis really wonderful: but no one can say they're pretty, and it can't be good for the men – shut up within bricks and mortar from morning to night. But the miller's duty is natural. The wheel belongs to the water, and when it's running it seems so pleased with life."

I stooped to kiss her cheek.

"If you go on like this, I shall come to live with you."

Margery laughed.

"You're not old enough yet, Master Boy. It's when you're tiny or when you're getting on that the simplest things taste sweetest and fill your life."

For all that, we got her to promise that she would go out in the car – to White Ladies and back, before September was old.

It was half-past six that evening before we were able, all three, to examine our prize. This we did on the terrace, by the light of the sinking sun.

That it was in truth from the brush of Claude Le Lorrain, we now had no shadow of doubt, though, how it had come to Gamecock, we could not tell. It needed restoring badly; and its frame, which had once been handsome, was only fit to be scrapped. We could not see the back of the canvas, for a sheet of brown paper had been pasted across the back of the frame; but, as we turned it about, the wedges which had slipped went sliding from side to side.

"Let's take off the paper," said Berry, opening his knife, "There may be a label or something…"

There was no label. But there was a small sheet of paper, folded to the shape of a note. This had been rudely sealed, as was the fashion before envelopes came into use.

Berry unfolded it gently…

The faded, spidery writing was not very hard to read.

Paris.

June, 1793.

You are a faithful servant, Birchup, and the thought of the little cottage in Hampshire is like a golden dream. With my chair, my favourite picture and you to care for me, what more should I want? You see, I am not without hope. An old man and the last of my line, I am not dangerous: beside my estates and my fortune, what is my life to them? So, my friend, I am not without hope that one day – perhaps very soon – you will have a pensioner. Be careful to keep the Claude from the summer sun.

Your affectionate master,
Montaugiron.

And the little gate, too, which Miladi loved so well. I shall – feel quite at home. A bientot, my good Birchup.

And underneath was written in a less educated hand:–

Put to death that month.

J B

"Poor old fellow," said Daphne. "Birchup must have been his valet. And Mulberry Corner was to have been his home. But those beasts wouldn't let him go. His chair, too. But for that rotten sexton, we'd have had that."

Berry nodded.

"At least, we'll care for his picture. I'll take it to Town myself."

And so he did – the next day.

He took it straight to the 'liners' who cared for what pictures we had – an old and honourable firm, well-known to Trafalgar Square. And, with their help, he chose a frame that was worthy of Claude's best work.

While he was gone, my sister and I drove to Gamecock – with Fitch at the wheel.

We did not leave the car, but the sexton came out of his cottage as soon as he saw my face.

I marked with pleasure that one of his eyes was black.

"Good morning, sir. I'm afraid we lost the chair. I did me best, but one of them dealers turned up an' took it out o' me mouth. As nasty a thievin' blackguard as ever I saw."

I put out my hand.

"Three pounds, wasn't it?"

The sexton counted two sovereigns and then a pound in silver into my palm.

As I put the money away –

"We didn' say nothin' o' my commission, sir."

"I pay no commission," I said, "in a case like this. If the chair was here, you would have had a sovereign for what you'd done."

The man looked ready to burst.

"Well, it ain't my fault," he blustered.

Fitch uncovered and turned and looked at him.

The sexton clapped a hand to his mouth. Then he ran into his cottage and shut the door.

We drove on, to stop at the forge...

"Well, we lost the chair, Big James."

The blacksmith nodded.

"Ay, sir," he said. "You shouldn't have been so outspoken. That sexton goes to Akers, and Akers gets a dealer from Dovetail, to wipe your eye. But it seems he missed an old master – an' was he wild? A firs'-class row, they had, because o' the money they'd dropped, each suspectin' the other of schemin' to do him down. That's the way o' the wicked, you know. An' then the sexton turns rusty, an' Akers blacks his eye."

"Tell me," said Daphne, "where did the picture go?"

"Nobody knows," said the smith. "A stranger walks in an' buys it for eighteenpence. An' the dealer swears it's worth fifteen hundred pounds. You should have had that, Miss Daphne. It would have looked well at White Ladies, if half what he says is true."

"It will look well there," I said, "when it's been done up. It's gone to London this morning, to be restored. You must come and see it, Big James, as soon as it's back."

The farrier stared upon me. Then he threw back his head and laughed till the tears hopped down his cheeks.

"By gad, you've done 'em," he crowed. "You picked un out an' you won un – for eighteenpence. An' you give them the chair to play with, to keep them quiet. Oh, but this does my heart good! You've bit the biter, Miss Daphne. An' there's a fine picture gone to its proper place."

I pointed to Fitch.

"There's the stranger," I said, "that did the deal."

Big James smacked his thigh and stamped with delight.

"I might 'a' known," he cried, "that you'd be up to their weight."

"Listen, Big James," said Daphne. "We wanted the chair for you, but it's too late now. We've one very like it at White Ladies. If you'd like a copy of that, we'll have one made."

"Nay, nay, Miss Daphne. Jus' for me to sit in? 'Tis wanton waste."

"It isn't at all. A fine thing gives you pleasure, as it does us. And, but for you, we shouldn't have had the picture. Any way, you're coming on Sunday, and we'll go into it then."

"As you will, Miss Daphne. But to think of you foolin' them rogues! What do they care for beauty? All they think of is lucre, gotten by hook or by crook. But now it'll hang at White Ladies. Ah, but that warms my heart."

So clean an outlook warmed ours. That we had enriched ourselves meant nothing to him: spared the dust of the market, a work of art had gone to a decent home.

Three weeks had gone by.

Jonah was holding the steps, I was bearing the picture, Berry was finding the places at which the two hooks must hang, and Daphne and Jill were waiting for the Claude to go up.

"What's half sixty-three?" said Berry, measuring-rule on the panelling, pencil in hand.

"Thirty-one and a half," said Daphne.

Her husband made a mark with a pencil upon the oak.

"And now what's half thirty-nine?"

"Eighteen – nineteen and a half."

Here Berry dropped his pencil, which Jill retrieved.

Once again he applied himself to the wall.

As he made to mark the distance, the rule collapsed.

"Oh, give me strength," said Berry. "Can't someone produce a wholesome measuring-rod? Can't someone furnish a yard-stick instead of this brazen serpent?"

"Other way round," said Jonah. "Then it can't shut up, because of the wall."

"Yes, and then the figures are wrong. Never mind. What's eighteen and a half from thirty-six?"

"Nineteen and a half," corrected Daphne.

Before we could stop him –

"Nineteen and a half," said Berry, making a mark.

"No, that's wrong," we cried.

"What's wrong?" said Berry, pushing himself from the wall.

"The mark you've made. It isn't nineteen and a half."

"Don't talk to me," said Berry. "I've got the blasted rule." He dabbed at the graven numbers. "There's nineteen, and there's – "

"But the figure's wrong," cried his wife.

"The figure?" screamed Berry. "But I asked you. I put myself in your hands. I subjected my intellect to yours. How the devil d'you expect me to do mental arithmetic at an angle of forty-five?"

Jill began to shake with laughter.

"My sweet," said Daphne, "you've got it wrong."

"*I've* got it wrong? Oh, I can't bear it," said Berry. "I ask you – you misinform me – and then I've got it wrong. Goats and monkeys! I'll do the swab-stuff myself. Eighteen and a half from forty-five. That's – "

"No, no, no," screamed everyone.

"What's the matter?" said Berry.

"The figure you want," said I, "is sixteen and a half. If you put the rule as you had it – the wrong way up…"

Berry looked round.

"Is everybody agreed that that figure is right?"

"Yes," said everyone.

All things considered, it was not surprising that he was now unable to find his original mark.

As he peered to and fro, growling –

"It must be there somewhere," said Daphne.

"But what a brain," said Berry, straightening his back. "What insight! What powers of deduction! Or did a little bird tell you?" He laughed hideously. "Give me the rule. Oh, I've got it. What was the original distance?"

"I think," said I, "I think you said sixty-three."

Once more Berry applied himself to the wall.

Then he looked over his shoulder.

"You observe my posture," he said. "The trunk contorted. The spine well out of truth. The strain upon the entrails is frightful."

"Well, do be quick," said his wife.

"What's half sixty-three?"

"Thirty-one and a half, darling."

"Thirty-one and a half," said Berry, taking his pencil out: but, before he could mark the spot, the rule, now the right way up, once more collapsed.

Before this new misfortune we all broke down, while Berry thundered from his pulpit, denouncing all such as subscribed to the making, sale or use of collapsible rules and comparing our sense of decency unfavourably with that of the wart-hog.

As the flurry died down –

"Half a minute," said Jonah. "I've got it now. Don't worry about the centre. Hang one hook a foot from the window and the other a foot from the Cuyp. If sixty-three is the distance you'll find that's exactly right."

"D'you really mean that?" said Berry.

"I do. I've just worked it out."

"Give me the hooks, someone."

"In your pocket," said I.

"So they are."

The hooks went up.

With a protruding tongue, Berry checked their position. As he withdrew the rule, he knocked one down,

Berry straightened his back and looked round.

We fought not to laugh, while Jill retrieved the hook and handed it back…

"And now the picture." said Berry.

Holding the glass to my chest, I stood to the wall: then I raised my arms, and Berry leaned down for the chains which we had already attached.

One chain he hung upon its hook, and I let that side of the picture take the strain. As he made to hang the other, the hook fell down.

Berry placed his hands together in the attitude of prayer.

"Be gracious, St Swine," he said. "If you will correct your offspring, I hereby vow to vomit next Slow Bellies' Eve."

Too weak with laughter to protest, my sister picked up the hook and handed it hack.

"And if anyone thinks," snarled Berry, "that I'm going to measure that distance over again – "

"Be quick," said I. "Plate-glass weighs quite a lot."

"And what about me?" said Berry. "For twenty minutes my organs have been displaced. Give me that blasted chain."

This time he attached the chain before hanging the hook on the wall; and a moment later the Claude was fairly up.

"Is the chain straight?" said Berry.

"A shade more to the right," said Daphne.

The move was made.

Then Berry came down, and Jonah removed the steps.

The Claude was not straight. It was sloping gently but surely from left to right.

There was a painful silence. Then –

"I – I think it looks fine," said Berry.

"Don't be absurd," said his wife. "We can't leave it like that."

"Why, what's the matter?" said Berry.

"It isn't straight," said Jill.

"That's probably the wall," said Berry. "Besides, I like it like that."

"Well, I don't," said Daphne. "That right-hand chain's too long."

"In fact, it isn't," said I. "I counted the links. And if we move it one link, it'll be too much."

"Leave well alone," said Berry.

"It isn't well," shrieked his wife. "It isn't straight with the panels. It's crooked – all down on one side. Just because you don't want to – "

"Nothing," said Berry, piously, "could be further from my thoughts."

"Oh, you liar," said Jill.

"You wicked child," said Berry. "You wicked, irreverent – Besides, I enjoyed the exercise. If you want to change it with the Cuyp, you've only to say the word. I – I'll hold the steps next time."

"It's the hooks," said Jonah. Berry stifled a scream. "The one on the right's too long. Or the one on the left's too short. Which ever you like."

While my cousin replaced the steps, I sought for another hook. Then I mounted the steps and hung this upon the rail.

It was immediately clear that Jonah was right.

The right hook was longer than the left: but the new one was not.

While Berry supported the picture, I made the change.

In so doing, I dropped a hook.

"Clumsy fool," said Berry. "Here am I, to my wounding upholding a fearful weight – "

"It's the discard," said I. "Come on."

A moment later, Jonah was removing the steps...

The Claude was straight now, and I must say it looked superb. As we had hoped, the strong side light was plumbing the depths of the picture, not only presenting the landscape as we had not seen it before, but discovering the delicate detail and, best of all, the cunning with which the painter had caught and then used the sunlight he loved so well.

"*My favourite picture*," breathed Daphne. "Poor old fellow. And I'm not a bit surprised. You've only to look at that scene, and you feel at peace."

This was most true.

Berry turned to his wife found her fingers and put them up to his lips.

"To you the glory, my sweet. Even I can see it now. But you had the eyes to see it, when it was out of sight."

4

In Which We Play For the Village,
and I Consider a Conversation Piece

Nearly seven years had gone by; Spring was ushering Summer; and I was making the most of the Whitsuntide recess.

Jill was home for good; I was at the Bar; Berry had grown a moustache; and we had become established motorists. Otherwise, little had changed.

We had just finished lunch and were taking our ease in the library, quick with the scent of sweet-peas.

"Must you go on Monday?" said Jill.

"Certainly not," said Berry. "I'm very comfortable here, and it would be very bad for me."

"I'm asking Boy."

"Of course he must," said Berry. "He's got a case to lose in the Clerkenwell County Court."

"Must you, Boy?"

I sighed.

"I'm afraid so, my sweet."

"Weekends?"

"Yes," said I, "till July. Then I shall be marshalling Granite for two or three weeks."

"That means you'll be at Brooch."

"For a week, yes. If we finish early at Forage, I may get a day or two here – complete with Judge."

"But you'll be off duty?"

"Oh, yes. He'll amuse himself. As long as I get him to Brooch on Sunday night…"

"I suspect that saying," said Berry. "Guests like Sir William Granite don't amuse themselves. They have to be catered for. If you retire, the burden will fall upon us. He'll probably want to walk all over the blasted place – and I shall have to stagger about with him."

Although I did not say so, I felt that Berry's forecast was good. The Judge preferred walking to being driven about.

Daphne looked up from *The Sketch*.

"Who shall I ask to meet him?"

"Anyone, darling. Sir Anthony, Derry and Jane."

"He'd probably like Lady Touchstone. She's more his age."

"That's a brilliant idea," said I.

"I know," said Jill. "Let's have tea at Privilege Splash."

"Fine," said Berry. "The Judge and I can walk there – it's only eleven miles. He can carry the spirit-lamp."

"Oh, blow the Judge," said Jill. "I mean, today."

"I've much to do," said Berry. "And if I stay here, I shall do it. So that'll suit me. Besides, we shall pay for this weather, so why not call the tune?"

"Can we come back by Dovetail?" said Daphne. "That's all I ask."

"Of course," said I. "Why Dovetail?"

"I know," said Jill. "Cream cheese."

"That's right," said my sister. "Janet's cream cheese is still the best in the world."

Harboured by Minever Enclosure, Privilege Splash was retired. Whenever we had been there, we had had the spot to ourselves, and the forest road that ran into and out of the water had never shown signs of traffic of any kind. (This may have been because the ford was unusually deep.) Of course the verderers knew it – the little foot-bridge was sound: but, so far as we saw, the world had passed it by. Perhaps because of this, the very spirit of the greenwood seemed to inhabit the place. The little sward remembered *As You Like It*: a truly magnificent oak might well have sheltered outlaws: a patient tapestry of foliage arrassed a council-room.

We had left the high road and were approaching Minever, when I saw a blind man coming, perhaps a hundred yards off. He was feeling his way with a stick, and, since the way was narrow, I slowed down, to pass him gently, in case of accidents. I was watching the fellow closely, and, when he was thirty yards off, I saw his face change. And when I say 'change', I mean it – he looked a different man. Now few people would have seen it, for thirty yards is some way: but my sight was then very keen, and I saw the change take place. The man had grimaced – thrust out his lip and drawn his mouth down on one side. More than that, perhaps: for, as I have said, he looked quite different. And so he continued to look, until the car had gone by.

This interested me, and, as we gathered speed, I watched the man in the mirror beside my seat. Sure enough, when we were some eighty yards off, he stopped and turned and stood watching… He was not blind.

This fact engaged me so much that I forgot where we were.

"Stop, Boy, stop," cried Jill. "You've passed the gate."

Minever Enclosure was shut by two or more gates.

"Sorry. I wasn't thinking. There's a lane a little way on. I'll turn the car there."

So I did.

As we came back to the gate, I saw that the 'blind' man was gone.

When we had entered the Enclosure, I told the others what I had seen.

"D'you mean he's a fraud?" said Daphne.

I nodded.

"He is neither blind, nor revolting. That face was put on."

"I find that strange," said Berry. "Blindness excites compassion. But such is human nature that people will give more freely to a man with a pleasant face."

"But what a strain," said Daphne, "to make a face all day long."

"I know. I don't understand it. He put on the face for us. And I'll tell you another thing – he was decently shaved."

The thing was too hard for us, and we put it away.

Two minutes later, I brought the car to rest by the side of the clearest water you ever saw, flowing steadily under the footbridge, rendering the grateful sunshine and offering for inspection every polished pebble that rested upon its bed.

My sister left the car and looked pleasedly round.

"Always the same," she said. "Time stands still here, I think. I always feel, when I come here, I'm stealing a march."

"I know what you mean," said Berry. "I used to have the same feeling about Loch Spiel o' the Whisht."

"There's no such place," bubbled Jill.

"You ask the Golosh," said Berry. "It marches with his estate. When I was Mary, Queen of Scots, I used to steal a march there all by myself. Rizzio used to bring his banjo, and – "

"That's more than enough," said Daphne.

"That's right," said Berry. "Break the beautiful thread. Think what some antiquary would give for these sidelights – these precious gobbets, filched from the maw of Time. There's a lovely conceit. I don't know how I do it."

"Come and lie down," said Daphne. "You'll feel better then."

"That sounds familiar," said Berry. "I think you must have been one of my tiring-maids."

As they made for the sward, Jill and I took our seats on the foot-bridge, from which it was always our habit to watch the life of the stream. If we sat very still…

Our patience had its reward. After a quarter of an hour, a water-rat coaxed its offspring into the flood.

When Berry denied our report, we desired him to come to the bridge and see for himself.

He did better than sit – he lay down. So, he was less conspicuous. It was as he leaned away from the planks that his gold cigarette-case slid out of his left breast pocket, to sink in three feet of water, immediately under the bridge.

"Of course that's done it," said Jill. "You've frightened them off."

Berry let out a maniac laugh.

"I suppose gold scares them," he said. "How very thoughtless of me." With a shaking finger he indicated his case. "How beautiful it looks, doesn't it? And yet, you know, I've a feeling we might as well get it out."

"It's up to you," said I.

"Don't be obscene," said Berry. "I came here at your invitation. Against my better judgment, I – "

"Oh, you liar," said Jill. "We told you to – "

"At considerable personal inconvenience, to do you pleasure, I lay down upon my belly – "

"I will not," said Daphne, "allow you to use that filthy word."

"I see," said her husband. "Well, b-bellies are b-bagatelles to the b-blanks which I shall clothe, if that case is not restored within two minutes of time. Damn it, you gave it me. D'you want it to be done in?"

"You dropped it," said Jill. "Why should poor Boy – "

"I," said Berry, "am the head of an illustrious house. It is the privilege of the younger members to assist and comfort their lord. That's matter of tradition."

"I'll help to dry you," said I.

In a pregnant silence, my brother-in-law gained the bank, removed his coat and laid it upon the turf. Then he rolled up his sleeves.

"Have we got a walking-stick?"

I shook my head.

"What about the tire-pump?"

"If you ask me," said I, "there's – "

"I don't ask you," snapped Berry. "I wouldn't demean myself by seeking counsel of you. Your duty is plain. Thanks to your treachery, a valuable trinket of mine has been cast into the draught. The least you can do is to restore it."

"There's nothing doing," said I, and went for the pump…

The water was three feet deep and the distance from the bridge to the water was two feet six. By lying flat on the planks, Berry could reach the case with the end of the pump; but, when he endeavoured to push it towards the bank, it merely turned and settled, time and again.

"What you want is a rake," said Daphne.

Her husband was breathing through his nose.

"The next person," he said, "to name any of the innumerable requisites, such as diving-bells, which would avail me, but are not available, will do so at his peril."

With that, he rose to his feet, strode to the bank, threw the pump into the bracken and tore off his shirt.

By the time I had found the pump, Daphne and Jill had retired and Berry was in his shorts.

As I opened my mouth –

"I'm much obliged," said Berry. "I know that look, It ushers that gorgeous protasis, 'If I were you.' But I don't want any 'words to the wise'. I am well aware that, being neither acrobat nor contortionist, I can only recover my case by immersing the whole of my person, with the possible exception of a zone, five inches in depth about my trunk. With luck, that may remain dry. Possibly some portion of the buttocks may escape – a solemn thought. I shall enter and leave the flood by way of the foot-bridge. You will assist me in – and assist me out. And now – *en avant*."

With that, he led the way, with the air of a cardinal.

All went very well. Berry had recovered his case and was shaking the water from his head, when I saw him peer at the under side of the planks.

"That's funny," he said, standing up. "There's a letter-box under the bridge." He gave me the case. "Right at the end. Lie down and see for yourself."

I did as he said.

Screwed to the centre plank was an ordinary letter-box, such as is sometimes seen within a front-door. Its lid was shut and secured by a staple and hasp.

"Anything inside?" said Berry. "My hands are wet."

I opened the lid and drew out a little package, heavy enough for its size. An oil-skin tobacco-pouch was wrapping a stout linen envelope, folded once.

"Wait till I'm out," said Berry. "Now give me a hand."

One minute later, seated upon the sward, we examined our spoil.

The envelope bore no writing. It was sealed in the usual way. There seemed to be a paper inside: there were certainly a number of coins.

Berry regarded me.

"What price the blind wallah?" he said. "The blind man who could see?"

I struck the turf with my palm.

"By God, you're right," said I. "That's why he was watching the car. When I *didn't* turn into Minever, he went on his way."

"An uneasy mind," said Berry. "I think we should show this to Lake."

Colonel Lake was the Chief Constable. His pleasant house stood a mile and a half from Dovetail, close to the Bloodstock road.

"I expect you're right," said I.

I wrapped the packet again and stowed it away. While Berry put on his clothes, I dried his case.

As we rejoined the girls –

"I'm hungry," said Berry. "Astonishing how immersion can whet the appetite."

My sister looked round from the kettle. "Nearly ready," she said. "Is the case all right?"

"I think it's improved," said Berry. "Where is the food?"

"There's some bread and butter there, if you really can't wait?"

"What, real bread and butter? What a treat! Aren't there any anchovy sandwiches?"

"If you're really hungry," said his wife...

The kettle declined to boil, until I screened the lamp with a rug from the car. Jill and I held this up, while Daphne watched the pot. I could feel no breeze, but lamps are sensitive things. At last the tea was ready.

Offered bread and butter, Berry refused.

"I've had two slices," he said.

"But you said you were hungry," said Daphne.

"I know. It's all this waiting. The – the urge has passed."

"Well, have some cake," said his wife.

"No, thank you. I'm thirsty now. I'll just have some tea."

"Well, I'll have some cake," said Daphne.

"Where is it?" said Jill.

"In the other jar, darling."

"No, it isn't. I've looked. They can't have put it in."

"Oh, I can't bear it," said Daphne. "Besides, Falcon asked if he should slice it."

"Just as well I'm not hungry," said her husband.

I turned and looked at him.

"What were you doing," I said, "while we were screening the lamp?"

"Doing?" said Berry, wide-eyed. "Bread and butter in hand, I strolled down to the water again. I thought, if I stood very still – "

Daphne and Jill were upon him, before he could move.

After a violent struggle, a sheet of grease-proof paper, folded again and again, was found in his jacket-pocket. That it had contained rich cake, there could be no doubt.

Flushed and panting, my sister sat back on her heels.

"You're not fit to live with," she said. "It's like the animals. While we three are making tea in which you're going to share, you bolt our cake – eight slices."

"Only six," said Berry. "Falcon must have miscounted. I thought there should have been eight."

"And I meant," said Jill, "I meant to give a piece to the rat."

"He can have my bread and butter," said Berry. "Where's my tea?"

"I've poured it away," said Jill.

"Oh, the vixen," said Berry. "No, damn it, I'm parched with thirst."

"I'll bet you are," said Daphne. "And so you'll stay."

With that, she emptied the teapot before his eyes.

"Of course that's wanton," said her husband. "You won't be forgiven for that. Think of the starving tramps that would sell their souls for – "

"Yes, you thought of them, didn't you? Which d'you think they'd like best – six slices of Dundee cake or a cup of tea?"

"The cake wasn't wasted," said Berry. "I was failing, and it restored me. My God, I'm thirsty." He looked pleadingly at Jill. "Let me have one mouthful, my sweet. You know, just a sip."

"Not a tea-spoon," said Jill. "Besides, if I said yes, you'd swallow the lot and then say you'd made a mistake."

"I shouldn't dream of such a thing" – piously. "I'm not like that. Haven't you got any water? My tongue's beginning to swell."

"Not a drop," said Daphne.

"There's always the stream," said I.

"Yes, I don't fancy that," said Berry. "We're not near enough to its source."

"There's some spirit left," said Jill, "if you like to boil some more."

Berry shuddered. Then he glanced at his watch.

"I think we should be going," he said.

"Why?" said Daphne. "It's only a quarter to five. As long as we're at Dovetail by six…"

Berry stifled a scream.

"I – I must be home," he declared, "by half-past five. I'm expecting a telephone-call."

"Who from?" said Jill.

"Derry Bagot," said Berry boldly.

"That's all right," said Daphne. "He's coming to tennis on Thursday and he can tell you then."

"That won't do. It's business."

The association of Derry with business made us all laugh.

"It's about the match," said Berry. "Bilberry's playing Gamecock on Saturday afternoon. Derry wants to know if I'm going to turn out."

"Of course you're playing," said I. "And so am I. I'll ring him up and tell him at eight o'clock. And don't get worried – Janet'll give you some milk."

"And what's the beer done? But the point is I want it now. My salivary glands aren't working. My gorge can't rise."

"It serves you right," said Jill. "When I think of that rat and its baby… They would have loved it so."

Berry swallowed – with difficulty.

"I, er, did it without thinking," he said. "Busy with my reflections, absorbed in thought, I consumed what there was. Had there been forty pieces, I might have devoured them all."

"Abstractedly?" said I.

"That's right," said Berry. "That's the word. I don't think I ought to suffer because of that."

"Don't you, indeed?" said his wife. "And what about us? We've lost our cake, and then we're to leave an hour early because you've eaten it all. Is it Gamecock The Butcher plays for?"

"Not on your life," said Berry. "He works for Riding Hood." He turned to me. "Your turn this year, my hearty. I hope he won't smash your nose."

Cricket. One or more of us always played for the village, provided that we were at home. This was an understood thing. The one match we did not enjoy was that against Riding Hood. This was because of The Butcher, who fairly deserved his name. The wickets he took were few, but he got his men. Three years ago, when Riding Hood had played Dovetail, four of the Dovetail batsmen had had to be helped from the ground. Berry and I took it in turns to face him. Last year it was Berry's turn, and he was hit on the throat. The bowling was lawful, but of a fearful kind. And village wickets are imperfect. To say that the ball 'rose sharply' is nothing at all.

"But I shan't be here," said I.

"Yes, you will. You're coming here with Granite."

"That's the Cleric match. Riding Hood's the week before."

"Then you'll have to come back," said Berry.

"I can't," said I. "I shall be attending the Judge. That afternoon we shall entrain for Forage."

Berry looked dazedly round.

"D'you mean to say," he said, "that I've got to face that murderer again? That, after what I suffered last year, I've got to stand up there and be maimed or disfigured for life?" He clasped his head in his hands. "I had to be massaged last time – for weeks on end. Damn it, I've only just recovered."

"I'm very sorry," I said. "I'd be here if I could."

"The thing's a scandal," said Daphne. "Can't something be done?"

"Everyone's waiting," said I, "on everyone else. If Cleric lodges a protest, Cleric lays itself open to a charge of cowardice. It's the same with Gamecock and us. Look at Dovetail: four men 'retired hurt' in one innings: but Dovetail wouldn't protest. The truth, of course, is that it's up to Riding Hood. They shouldn't play the man."

"Is he such a good bowler?"

"He's rotten," said I. "Unfortunately, most of us are very indifferent bats. Any county batsman would put him where he belonged."

"It's really shameful," said Jill. "I mean, it isn't as if the ball was soft."

"You're telling me," said Berry, feeling his throat. "What I went through last year. The wonder is I'm alive. And now I've got to go through it all over again. This time, I suppose, he'll knock my teeth down my throat. The pillory isn't in it. After all, dead cats may smell, but they've got some give. And now what about this rat? Let's see if some bread and butter will help it up."

Under Jill's direction, he laid a slice upon the lip of the hole from which the rats had emerged. Before we left for Dovetail, we had the very great pleasure of watching the mother taste and then commend it to her child. While they were making their meal, the father returned, and, by his advice or instruction, what remained of the slice was drawn carefully into the hole and out of our view.

"There you are," said Berry. "You couldn't have done that with cake."

Forty-eight hours had gone by, and Derry Bagot and Daphne were playing Jane Bagot and me.

"Love fifteen," said Derry, and served out of court.

His second service was treated as it deserved.

"Sorry, my dear," said Derry. "I seem to be out of form. If only Jane were better – a bad opponent invariably puts me off."

The game went to deuce four times, but we won it at last.

Three all. We were very evenly matched.

Surrounded by limes and chestnuts, the court was a pleasant court, and its turf was good. Since we were ten years old, we had, all of us, larded its earth. It knew no tournaments. Always we played for pleasure – and nothing else. Not even for exercise. So, I think, games should be played. On one side, a miniature terrace served lookers-on; from a height of four feet, one could see the play very well.

I was about to serve, when Berry appeared.

"Lake – and friend," he said. "They feel they'd like to see you. I'll take your place."

"And here's trouble," said Derry. "Who have you killed?"

"Very secret," said Berry. "We'll tell you as soon as we may."

"Espionage," said Derry. "And you be careful – one of my aunts is French."

I took my coat and made my way to the house...

The Assistant Commissioner was speaking.

"So, you see, it's a very big thing. Your blind man is the wallah we've wanted for years. He is 'above suspicion', but now we're under his guard." He pointed to the packet beside him. "That's going back tonight. If it's been looked for, we're sunk. But I hope the box will be cleared on Sunday next. Whoever clears it will never be out of our sight. In that way, we should get home – by which I mean that we should get your blind man.

"That packet contains twenty sovereigns – for information received. It also contains two pages of information desired – highly important information, in the sight of the German Naval Staff. But that information, it says, is not to be put in that box. 'Method Q' is to be followed. That's why we must trail the recipient by day and night. By using 'Method Q' he will lead us to your blind man. And then we shall be home, for his finger-prints are all over his questionnaire."

"Any time limit, sir?"

"Happily, yes. He says he must have what he wants by July the nineteenth. Must. I believe there's something coming – anyway, that's what he says. I shouldn't think we'll need you. I hope we shall take him red-handed. But if we do, I take it you'd know him again."

I raised my eyebrows.

"I might," said I. "I daren't put it higher than that. With his grimace, I'd know him anywhere. But he was thirty yards off, when he made his face. And that's some way, sir."

The Assistant Commissioner nodded.

"Go on."

"I've a vague idea of what he looked like – before he made his face. He had a curious look. His face was faintly suggestive of that of a skull. Square and grim. That's the impression I had – at thirty yards. I'm sorry I can't do better, but there we are."

"Not at all your fault, Mr Pleydell. You've done very well. And you're up against a big shot. He was ready for you, but you weren't ready for him. But at least you've noticed the man – which is more than anyone else has ever done.

"Now I hope very much that X – that's the petty traitor – will lead us to Y. But, just in case he doesn't, please bear Y's face in mind and keep your eyes wide open wherever you go. You never know – you might see him crossing Pall Mall. Bear him in mind, Mr Pleydell, wherever you go."

"And if I should see him, sir?"

"On no account lose him. As soon as you can, call a policeman and say that he's to detain him and ring my office up. Wait a minute – I'll give you a card."

He took out a pencil and wrote on a slip of paste-board –

The bearer has my confidence. Do as he says.

"That will show you two things, Mr Pleydell. First, that I trust you implicitly: and, secondly, how very badly I want this man."

I saw our guests off and made my way back to the court. But I was not thinking of tennis. My thoughts were of Minever Lane and the man whose face had been altered when he was thirty yards off. Square and grim – that was right. Faintly suggestive of a skull. And something else...

Seven weeks had gone by, and the Judge and I were at Forage, when a letter from Berry arrived.

July, 1914.

Dear Brother,

I am happy to inform you that the Riding Hood match is over, and, that except for a cracked rib, I am whole. I am still more happy to inform you that Mr Frederick Ballast, surnamed The Butcher, is, however, halt and like to stay halt, if not for years, at least for the remainder of the season. I tell you these glad tidings that you may hasten to the nearest place of refreshment and there order and consume a gallon of malt liquor to the honour and glory of St. Bertram of White Ladies, whose belated canonization is to be celebrated by the installation, equally belated, of a small soak-pit behind the Post Office.

This was the way of it.

Mr Ballast was bowling with the gleeful malignancy sometimes attributed to a fiend of Hell, who has been charged with and specially released for the discomfiture of the godly. That the Vicar was his first victim, I need hardly say. Hit him over the heart. Forty minutes later Young Tom was standing up well and beating the ball. He'd made twenty-five, when The Butcher sent down a fair – Let me put it like this. Had his delivery borne arms, these would have been distinguished by the bend sinister. Such was its pace that I couldn't see where it pitched; but it rose like a rocket and took Young Tom under the chin. Well, they carried him off, and I strode down to the wicket, seeing blood-red. I was a crusader: my bat had become a morning star. I hit him for four twice running, and he didn't like that. First ball, next over, I hit him for four again. To judge from the sinister manner in which he protruded his tongue – ostensibly to moisten the palms of his monstrous hands – he liked this still

117

*less. In a word, it was painfully clear that it was in his mind
to bring to a horrid conclusion my services as a bat. I believe
the euphemism is 'dismiss': I prefer the downright 'dispatch'.
Be that as it may, he sent down another b-b-b-ball, which got
me full in the ribs. Of the agony, I will say nothing. Enough
that I lost my balance and damned near fell into my wicket.
But let that pass. The point is that I was annoyed. Could Mr
Ballast have searched my heart, he'd have left the field, asked
for police protection and hidden himself in a wood. Still, I
think he was disconcerted – perhaps, by the look in my eye,
for, immediately after that, he played clean into my hands. He
sent one down dead straight, which kept very low: and I let
him have it straight back with every ounce that I'd got. He
tried to get out of the way, but he hadn't time... We ran right
away after that, and beat them handsomely.*

*Less good news from Lake. As you already know, X, the
petty traitor, was being most carefully watched. Four days
ago they watched him walk into an omnibus or hackney
coach – but not by the door. He is now in hospital, with a
fractured skull. Owing to this indisposition, he will be unable
to keep his engagement with Y. And as no one has any idea
of what 'Method Q' may be, the Special Branch is not exactly
sanguine of laying Y by the heels. In fact, unless he should
accost you and then do his famous nose-trick before your
eyes – and that I feel to be unlikely – there seems to be little
hope of his arrest. But watch and pray, luv. You never know.*

*All is ready for your coming on Thursday next. The floors
have been smeared over, the ginger-beer ordered, the water
in the flower-vases changed. We assume that you will sleep
in the same room as his lordship, and, as we have no truckle-
bed, a pallet will be spread to leeward of his four-poster. And
your place will be laid next to his at meals, so that you
can taste his food without inconvenience. Indeed, as is my
wont, I have thought of everything. But there you are. To live*

*for others has always been my motto, and a stiff upper lip,
my crest.*

Kind regards to Gran-Gran.

*Your beloved cousin and brother-in-law,
Berry.*

PS. The car will be at Bloodstock, to meet the 3.15.
*PPS. Our women are well, and Jonah has arrived. He has
come from Germany – and prophesies no good, but evil.*

The news about X depressed me. And when I told the Judge,
he shook his head. Fortune's smile had faded. My chances of
seeing – let alone recognizing Y, were painfully thin. For what it
was worth, I must, of course, keep my eyes open: but now, as
luck would have it, my days were spent in court and I could not
go out and about, as I usually did.

I think that my Judge found favour wherever he went. Be that as
it may, he found immediate favour with Daphne and Jill.

As the car stole up to White Ladies, the two appeared.

Sir William Granite – Mrs Pleydell, Miss Mansel."

"Please excuse my husband, Sir William. He's sitting on the
Riding Hood Bench."

The Judge smiled.

"My learned brother is excused."

As they passed into the house, I put the Judge's servant in
Falcon's charge.

Five minutes later –

"I expect you'll like my brother to show you your rooms.
Please do as you like while you're here. I mean, tea will be
served on the lawn in half an hour: but if you would like some
upstairs – well, the servants have orders to do as your servant
asks."

"My dear," said the Judge. "I am here to enjoy myself. I shall
therefore appear on the lawn at a quarter to five."

In fact he was there before then, for when I came down in flannels, Jill and he were examining the yew peacocks and discussing topiary work.

Jonah joined us at tea.

As I introduced him –

"I remember your father," said the Judge. "He dined with me at White's and I dined with him 'on guard'."

"Which reminds me," said Daphne, "I've asked some people to dinner tomorrow night. Colonel Lake and his wife – he's our Chief Constable: Lady Touchstone from Bell Hammer: Sir Anthony Bagot of Merry Down and his son and daughter-in-law. Except for that explosion, we shall be very quiet."

"I like being quiet," said the Judge. "But I shall be very happy to meet your friends. And I trust you to do as you would, if I was not here. I have the reputation of being an easy guest."

"We will, if you'll do as you please."

"I shall, indeed, Mrs Pleydell. Did I hear there was cricket on Saturday?"

"That's right. The match of the season. Bilberry v. Cleric. All three of the men are playing, if you won't think that rude."

"Will you think the fourth rude," said the Judge, "if he attends the match?"

"Oh, I hoped he'd say that," said Jill.

Then Jonah and I played tennis, and the girls carried off Sir William, to show him over the house.

Before the day was out, the Judge had referred to what was in everyone's mind. When Daphne and Jill had left the dining-room he passed the port and then sat back in his chair.

With his eyes on Jonah –

"I think," he said, "you have just left Germany."

"That's right, sir. A week ago."

"Does that country mean to make war?"

"That's my belief, sir," said Jonah. "I never saw the tide of arrogance running so high: and it's still coming in."

"No signs of anxiety?"

"None, sir, so far as I saw. The Army is intensely excited."

The Judge pursed his lips.

"France, they despise," said Berry. "But they've hated us for years, because they know that we are better than they. Not more powerful – just better. We're better bred: we deliver better goods: we behave. And now they feel they've a chance of curing that inferiority complex."

"By, er, eliminating their superiors?"

"Yes, sir. The Kaiser dreams of strutting at Windsor: the Army of swaggering down St James's Street: the politician of annexation: the merchant of markets in which his goods are the best: and the man in the street of treating the British like dirt."

"Are they all insane?" said the Judge.

"Not all," said Jonah. "But those that are not believe war to be inevitable and hope, with confidence, for the best."

"With confidence?"

"Yes, sir. Many think it will be a walk-over. That their armies can be beaten, no one believes."

The Judge raised his eyebrows.

"If war is at hand," be said, "a very handsome era is about to come to an end. Much that we take for granted will go by the board. Security – by which I mean freedom from care – will disappear. The old order will change." He sighed. "The fabric of our civilization is not homespun today. It is easier to rend and very difficult to patch. When it is patched with new stuff, the old will give way."

Berry looked up and round.

"Will this survive, sir?"

"With you behind it – yes. But only devotion will preserve such a period piece."

"Let's hope I'm wrong, sir," said Jonah.

"By all means. But just in case you're right, let us enjoy to the full the days that are left. Soon they may be 'the old days'." He turned to Berry. "I'm sure you did justice today. Have you got a good clerk?"

Berry looked down his nose.

"We haven't been taken to the Divisional Court lately, sir."

The Judge laughed.

"Then you have a good clerk," he said. "But I hope you don't let him run you."

"Oh, no. He knows his place. But he has a difficult time. We have one obstreperous Justice, whose private solicitor he is. There are occasions upon which duty and business, so to speak, seethe together. The process is painful to watch, but most engaging."

"I remember a case," said the Judge...

A quarter of an hour went by, before we put out the candles and left the room.

His lordship lived up to his Epicurean creed.

The following day, Jill and he were abroad before I was up. From their report at breakfast, they seemed to have walked five miles. After breakfast he proved the gardens – and disappeared. I found him at last in the harness-room, discussing with Peters the virtue of various bits. Seeing the gig turned out, he asked my permission to mount and to take the reins. Then he picked my sister up and drove her into the village and over to Ightham's farm. After lunch, while we played tennis, he did the duty of umpire, until we stopped for tea; then he strolled off, to call on the Vicar and visit the little church.

Dinner that night was festive.

On Berry's right, Lady Touchstone, in black and silver, sparkled with wit: she, Derry Bagot and Berry were better than any play: on Berry's left, Mrs Lake and Jonah were laughing helplessly. Jane Bagot, in white and cherry, was pulling the Colonel's leg. My sister, looking peerless in gold, was sitting back, smiling, between the Judge and Sir Anthony, laughing together over some elegant jest. And Jill, beside me, something resembling a seraph in powder blue, was making me free of her pleasure in the comfortable scene.

"Those are the Bagot sapphires that Jane's got on. Isn't that necklace lovely? Of course, she's a perfect skin. I love the Judge, when he puts his eyeglass up. And Lady Touchstone's earrings – look at them, Boy darling. They're so white, they seem to be blue. But Daphne has it – as always. She looks like some beautiful painting; and the emeralds go with that dress. But anything would look lovely upon her arms. I'm sure the bracelets have never looked so fine. What queen were they made for, Boy? I always forget."

Before I could answer, the Judge was lifting his glass. He was looking at Lady Touchstone.

"A glass of wine with you, madam."

Lady Touchstone threw up her head.

"That's the second time. Shame on you, Judge. I may be disorderly, but I refuse to be drunk. And when I'm before you at Brooch, it'll be 'I'm surprised to see a woman of your advanced years…' "

"That's all right," said Berry. "You'll come before me. And I can tell you now it'll be half a crown or seven days. Of course, if you cling to the railings, it'll be three and six."

"Boy shall defend you," said the Colonel. "If you don't go into the box – "

"You'll all be in it," said Lady Touchstone. "I'll see to that. What a *cause célèbre* it will be! How d'you sub-poena a Judge? And now is everyone satisfied that I am not a nice woman? For ladies of my age, to be styled 'a nice woman' is the end."

"I'm with you," said Berry. " 'Because thou art *thirtyish*, shall there be no more cakes and ale?' "

Lady Touchstone looked at Daphne.

"My dear," she said, "I don't wonder you married him."

At last the cloth was drawn, and ten minutes later my sister caught Lady Touchstone's eye. But not until coffee had been served and the servants had gone did colonel Lake mention Y – the blind man who could see.

"This accident to X," he said slowly, "is a catastrophe. In view of the way things are going, Y would have been a great prize. If there's to be a war, we can pull in the petty traitors in twenty-four hours. We know quite ninety per cent. But this is a different case. X, now in hospital, is a German Naval officer. He's been a barber at Portsmouth for nearly nine months. That twenty pounds was for him to spend upon drinks. And Y, to whom he was reporting, is a much bigger man. Worse. He's a man of position – we have no doubt about that. And during a war he could be most dangerous."

There was a little silence.

Then –

"Is he, too, German?" said the Judge.

"I think he must be," said Lake. "The German he writes is flawless. But he may have been naturalized." He shrugged his shoulders. "We've let so many in – let so many establish themselves, that now it's like looking for a needle in a bottle of hay."

I put in my oar.

"Y asked to receive the information by Sunday next. When 'Method Q' is not used, will he try the letter-box?"

The Chief Constable shook his head.

"I can't believe that he will. He'll know that something is wrong. We shall watch the box at the foot-bridge, just in case: but spies don't make mistakes: and, when a spy is late, his fellows know what it means. Oh, no. I'm afraid we've lost him – unless he walks into your arms."

The Judge was speaking again.

"Is there any district, Colonel, which you suspect? I mean, if my marshal can help you, I'll give him leave."

"No thank you, Judge. If there was, we'd have asked for him. But we have no idea. Y may reside in this county, or he may not. Cars have made movement so easy, and distance has lost its sting."

"What is Y like?" said Jonah.

I groaned.

"I was waiting for that," said I. "I won't say he was too far off: but I only have an impression of what his true face was like."

"Shut your eyes," said my cousin, "and picture Minever Lane." I did as he said. "Now you've just seen the man – some forty yards off: and because of the way in which he is using his stick, you realize that he's blind. So you lift your foot and watch him. Now – at thirty yards – you see him alter his face. Alter his face – *from what*?"

"Square and – Wait a minute." I struck my fist into my palm. "By God, I've got it! I've been trying so hard to remember, and now it's come back. *The fellow's got no eyebrows.* I couldn't see that then, but I noticed that, as he was approaching the car. Now then. Square and grim...no eyebrows...faintly suggestive of a skull. I really believe, if I saw him, I'd know the swine."

"Of course you will," said Berry. "I'd almost know him myself."

"He will, if he sees him," said the Judge.

"I agree," said Lake. "If he sees him. But what a hope!"

"Are you sure," said the Judge, "that you wouldn't like him released?"

The Chief Constable hesitated.

Then –

"May I let you know on Sunday?" he said. "By then I shall have seen the Assistant Commissioner again. I'm going to Town tomorrow and returning on Sunday night. May I leave a note at the Lodging?"

"By all means," said the Judge. "He must swear the Grand Jury on Monday. After that, if you want him, he's yours. I'll wire for a nephew of mine, to take his place."

To swear a Grand Jury, as a Grand Jury should be sworn, was a trick which could not be mastered overnight. It was the Judge's Marshal's duty to learn and administer the oaths. The oath which the Foreman took was one hundred and twenty-six words long: that of his fellows was shorter; but, since a Grand Jury consisted of twenty-three men, the Marshal administered this no less than twenty-two times. Then, again, the Bench was always some distance from the Grand Jury's Box, so the Marshal had to speak out, in a clear, loud voice. Finally, no Judge who set store by his dignity, would take to himself a Marshal that could not do this duty and do it well.

"Very good, sir," said Colonel Lake. "A note shall be at the Lodging on Sunday night."

Five minutes later, we rose and made for the gallery. As we were climbing the stairs, the lilt of a famous valse came floating down to our ears.

"Dancing, Sir William," said Berry. "As soon as you're bored, there's a fire in the library."

"I shan't be bored," said the Judge. "Dancing does not become age; but records have to be changed and, if you'll teach me to do it, I shan't feel out of things."

We had, all of us, learned to dance in the L-shaped gallery – I remember Berry in Etons dancing with Daphne, aged eight – and, perhaps for this reason, that fine, familiar chamber has always been for me the home of such exercise. It has three oriels – one at the corner of the L, and there, when we were dancing, the gramophone stood. I sometimes think that it looked its best at night, with the crimson curtains drawn and the chandeliers ablaze and the gilded frames of the pictures glowing against the oak. And more than the frames. The rare old pigments kindled to the touch of the hanging lights, absorbing the gold and rendering jewels, instead.

Although I say it, a picture was added that night: Jill and I hung on our heels, to savour the scene. Sir Anthony, staunch Etonian, had put on *The Boating Song*, and, though we were but five couples, the room seemed full of the rhythm of gracious movement, of colour whirling and gliding down all its length – blue and cherry and gold and emerald green, of the exquisite flash of gems and the glancing white of stiff shirts, of the elegant turn and twinkle of shining feet, and of Daphne's clear soprano, singing the time-honoured words.

The Judge's voice breathed in my ear.

"Complete the picture, I beg you. I see the Queen of Hearts, but I miss the Fairy Princess."

I was glad to do as he said.

It was after midnight, when we left for the library.

Lady Touchstone inspected her wrist.

"I'm pretending my watch is misleading. All the same, another ten minutes, and I must go. I'm sure I don't have to say I've enjoyed myself. The fact must stand out."

Sir Anthony smiled.

"You speak for us all, Harriet. But, by the way, what a beautiful dancer you are."

"That's because I'm fat," said Lady Touchstone. "I was never bad, but now that I've put on weight, I'm extremely good. The fatter I grow, the better I seem to perform. In another five years, I shall be giving exhibitions. After that, I suppose it'll be the circus. You'll have to come with me, Tony. D'you still carry bulls about?"

In the prime of life, Sir Anthony had been fabulously strong.

"Not quite. But if you go, I will. I can still lift a chair by its leg, and that's quite good enough."

"Good," said Lady Touchstone. "And the Judge shall be our showman. And after the show, we'll all have supper together in my caravan. Crab and stout. Oh, 'Motley's the only wear'."

His lordship looked round.

"When I think," he said, "that all next week I must go robed in scarlet and ride in a coach, the prospect of sleeping off crab and stout in a tent is most alluring."

Lady Touchstone leaned forward.

"I'm lunching at Brooch on Thursday. May I come and sit on the Bench for half an hour?"

"God forbid," said the Judge. "I'm sure I should catch your eye. Besides, you're not a nice woman."

It was nearly one o'clock when our guests were sped.

We have always been proud of the village cricket ground. for the timber that rises about it – elm and lime and chestnut – is beautiful stuff, and the little, old church and its yard, to the north of the handsome meadow, make up as English a picture as any that Constable saw. But, indeed, the very spirit of England was living and moving about the sward that day – that pride of fellowship, precious to high and low, that knows no condescension or disrespect, that no other country on earth can so much as understand. Old Lord Udal of Rosewood had come to cheer Cleric on and had brought a groom and a gardener to play their part on the green. And Mrs de Lisle was there – I heard her charging her butler before the game began. 'Now do be careful, Worsted, until you get set. Remember what happened at Dovetail. Play yourself in.' Colonel Buckshot had given the Curate a seat in his car; and Admiral Foley, driving his four-wheeled dog-cart, had brought the baker's assistant and one of the saddler's sons. And, of course, the Bagots were there: and so were the Ighthams and Lady Elizabeth Veil. So much for the opening of play. But after lunch, two-thirds of the village were present and many came over from Cleric to watch the match.

Two tents had been pitched beside the changing-room, and garden seats and chairs had been collected and set in the shade of the trees. With the help of the Scouts, Peters and Furness, the grocer, had done this cheerful duty; and now they were busy attending to everyone's comfort and making all things smooth.

"Just beside the big chestnut, my lord. You'll see very well from there. Come up close to the trunk, Jim, and then bring them round very sharp. Yes, my lord, there's stabling reserved at *The Rose*. Good morning, Sir Giles. Will you follow his lordship's carriage? Stop anywhere there, sir. Your groom can take the mare, and we can manhandle the dog-cart wherever you please. Well, Arthur, you're looking fit. Is Dolly coming along to see us cut you down? Good morning, madam. We're putting the cars over there. Just to the right of that elm, if that'll suit you. Jump on the step, Billy, and show the chauffeur where we're putting the cars. An' don't forget to open the door…"

Cleric won the toss and batted first.

Bilberry started well, for four good wickets were down for thirty-two runs: but then the smith and Worsted stopped the rot, and the hundred went up before the latter was bowled. At lunch the score was a hundred and twelve for six, and, when we went in to bat, at five minutes to three, we faced a total of a hundred and fifty-eight.

Berry was inconsolable.

"And to think I dropped Fred Able before he had scored!"

Fred Able was the blacksmith. After his 'life' he had hit up forty-two.

"These things happen," said I.

"You shut your face," said Berry. "That was an oratorical apostrophe. When you hear a lament like that, you should go on your knees. Comment is indecent. 'Fell sorrow's tooth doth never rankle more, Than when it b-bites, but lanceth not the sore.' "

"Darling," said Daphne, "the sun was in your eyes."

"No, it wasn't," said Berry. "It was in the small of my back. Except that 'the leathery duke' was rough with these delicate palms, I have no excuse. O Hanwell, Hanwell, had I but served my side as you shall serve my turn – No, that's wrong."

"I thought you had it," said Jonah.

"So," said Berry, "did I. I was just going to throw it up, as they do at Lords. And then it fell on to my foot."

"I once did worse," said the Judge. "I ran our best batsman out, when he'd just got set. And that was at Lords. I remember praying for an earthquake, as I watched him walk off the ground."

"Was that the year, sir," I said, "when you took nine wickets and hit the stumps eight times?"

"It was. And that's my point. Your brother-in-law will more than repair his mistake. I've seen it happen so often."

Derry Bagot came up, smiling.

With his hand upon Berry's shoulder –

"Allow me," he said, "to offer you this consolation. In the changing-room just now, Ted Halsey spoke for us all. 'He can drop what catches he likes – Mas'r Berry can. He's done his bit this season by laying The Butcher out.' Didn't you hear the applause?"

I fear the scoring was slow, but Cleric's saddler's son kept a beautiful length. At five o'clock, the outlook was none too good, for five of our wickets were down for eighty-nine. And stumps would be drawn at six. Seventy runs to make, and an hour to go.

As Berry came by, to join me –

"Now's your chance," said I. "Beat the ball into the sky."

"You bet," said my brother-in-law.

He was as good as his word.

At once he went for the bowling and hit the saddler's son all over the field. The village roared its delight, and the Judge was waving his hat on the end of his stick. In half an hour we had put on forty-five runs. And then I was caught in the slips. Still, things were looking much better. Twenty-five runs to make, and twenty-eight minutes to go. But Worsted was bowling his best.

Berry was joined by William, our second groom. Together they put on six, before William was bowled.

"Oh, I can't bear it," said Daphne. "It isn't fair. If we're to beat Cleric, we've got to beat the clock."

With an eye on the church-tower –

"Nineteen to get," said I, "and fourteen minutes to go. It has been done."

Ted Halsey came hastening out...

He survived the rest of the over, but made no runs. Then Berry faced the baker's assistant, who knew how to pitch them up.

We waited breathlessly…

Then Berry slammed a ball past mid-off.

"Come on," he roared… "And again" – and bolted back down the pitch.

"Oh, he's done," shrieked Janet.

"*How's that?*" howled Cleric.

But Berry was home by inches, and the umpire shook his head.

The next ball he let alone.

His next two strokes were boundaries, and the village yelled itself hoarse.

Then Berry hit a one very nicely, and 'Over' was called.

"Eight runs to make," breathed Jill, with her eyes on the clock. "Is this the last over, Boy?"

"I'm afraid so," said I. "Hullo, they're taking off Worsted. The Curate's going on."

The Curate's leg-breaks were famous; but Berry was taking no risks.

He ran out and met the first one…

Six runs to make, and just five minutes to go.

The second ball Berry mis-hit, but one run was scored.

Ted Halsey was palpably nervous: but he had learned of Berry and kept his head. He ran out to meet the next ball and left it in the midst of the pitch… Before a fielder could reach it, Berry was back and was facing the Curate again.

I never remember such a silence.

Then the Curate sent down a full toss – and Berry squared his shoulders and hit it out of the ground.

With a squeal of delight, Jill flung her arms round my neck. The clock must have chimed and struck, but nobody present heard it, because of the cheers. Sir Anthony was standing on a chair and roaring like any bull, and the Judge had his hands to his mouth and was shouting 'Well done': Mrs de Lisle was waving her parasol, and Lady Elizabeth had hold of Daphne's hands: Derry Bagot and Peters were fussing over Berry and bringing him in, and Admiral Foley stopped them, to shake his hand. 'There are some victories, my boy, that the vanquished cannot grudge. Come across and see old Udal, before he goes.' I think that he spoke for Cleric, for I never saw a defeat that was taken so well. And the old Earl was very cordial. 'Your match, Pleydell, your match. Off your own bat, you won it – and won it well. Haven't enjoyed myself so much for twenty years. And here's the Judge. Judge, I say it's his match – and you'll bear me out.' And we all made much of Ted Halsey; and Ightham and Mrs Ightham were waiting to say how happy they were; and Fergus led the cheers, when at last Berry made his way to the changing-room.

Four hours had gone by. Dinner was over and done, and we were all at our ease about the library fire. A slow wood fire, just to take the chill off the chamber; for great old rooms can be cool on a summer's night. I left my seat by Daphne, to search the shelves for some book, and, when I turned to come back, with the book in my hand, I stood quite still for a moment, regarding what might be called 'a conversation piece'.

Two stout, oak logs were slowly growing rose-red upon the hearth – stately, comfortable embers, soon to go grey: now and again a baby flame would leap from behind the wood, to flare and fret for a moment, before it died. In a recess to the right, the crimson casement-curtains hung still as death – except for two, that trembled and swayed now and then, to speak to the air beyond. Daphne, deep in her chair, with her feet to the hearth, was lifting her lovely profile, to dwell upon the canvas by Herring that, ever since I can remember, has hung on the panels above the mantelpiece. On the opposite side sat Berry, his comely features outlined against the spines of books: chin down, legs crossed, he was lazily drafting a letter upon a writing-block. From time to time he drew upon his cigar. As I watched, he picked up his brandy glass and, finding it empty, raised his eyes to heaven and put it down. Jonah was sitting to a table upon the arm of a chair. Pipe in mouth, as always, his keen and handsome face was bent to a map of Europe. Now and again, he would thoughtfully measure a distance, using, because he was Jonah, a pair of compasses. And side by side on the sofa, Jill and Sir William Granite were sharing with murmured rapture a volume of reproductions of Holbein the Younger's work. The two themselves made a picture which many a master, I think, would have wished to paint. My little cousin still looked but a beautiful child – that is playing at being an adult by piling her golden hair on the top of her head. Her eager air was compelling: her artlessness, not of this world. Jill is made of a stuff which will not go into words. And the fine, old head beside hers was that of a man whose school is now extinct. Breeding, wisdom and strength were declared by those splendid features, then sixty-seven years old. I had seen them grave so often; but now they were gay – intent upon Jill's pink finger, picking some exquisite detail out of the gorgeous page.

I shall never know why I stopped to value these things. But now I remember them gladly, because they belong to the last night I spent at White Ladies before the outbreak of war.

Berry let his block fall and got to his feet.

"I know no fate more foul than to be a conscientious trustee. I'm perfectly sure that Sir William will bear me out."

"That I will," said the Judge warmly. "I've suffered enough myself. But you should be above trusteeship on such a day."

"I am, sir," said Berry. "But I cannot escape my conscience. I ought to have written that letter two days ago."

"I'll keep your conscience till Monday. May I go to Church tomorrow – to Matins?"

"Of course," said Daphne. "Unless you would rather walk, Boy or Jonah will drive us up in the car."

"I'll walk, if you please, my dear. Do you have the Vicar to lunch?"

"He's a standing invitation."

"In that case, I'll bring him back. After lunch I must read depositions which I should have read before. You five have corrupted me. You've pointed the path of pleasure and urged me down." Here the Judge took out his eye-glass and wiped it carefully. Then he looked up and round. "I haven't been so happy for many years."

"Isn't that fun?" said Jill. And when she bade him good night, she put up her face to be kissed.

It was upon the following evening, when the Judge and I were at dinner in the Judge's Lodging at Brooch, that a servant brought in a note from Colonel Lake.

The Judge broke the seal and read it and passed it to me.

Dear Judge.

While the Assistant Commissioner is not prepared to inconvenience you to the extent of asking for your Marshal to be released, he would like him to stand by for a summons at any time. If I may see you for five minutes after your Charge to the Grand Jury tomorrow morning, I can be more explicit.

In great haste.

Yours very truly,
Jasper Lake.

"Is the bearer waiting?" said the Judge.

"Yes, Sir William."

"Then bring me a writing-pad."

Two minutes later his answer went off.

Dear Colonel,

Certainly. Be in my room at the Castle at a quarter-past ten.

Yours sincerely,
W Granite.

His lordship was 'churched' the next morning; but I was not there, for I had to be at the Castle, before he arrived.

I had done what I had to do and was on my way to the gateway, to meet the coach, when I ran into Colonel Lake.

As he opened his mouth, I heard the fanfare of trumpets which meant that the coach was there.

"Wait in his room," I cried, and took to my heels.

I was just in time to receive the Judge on his entry and take my place in the little procession formed.

One minute later we were upon the Bench.

The Grand Jury was in its box, some twelve feet above the floor. The Judge bowed to them, as usual, before he took his seat. Then the Clerk of Assize called their names. When he had done, I rose and looked at the Foreman. He looked at me, too nervous to find his voice.

I raised my own.

"I think, sir, you have a request you would like to make."

"Er, yes. We – that is, the Grand Jury would be glad if they could be sworn in the old-fashioned way."

(It was at my instance that this request was made. The old-fashioned way was more simple and took less time.)

I glanced at the Judge.

"Certainly, gentlemen."

I raised my eyes to the box and began to administer the oath.

"You, sir, as Foreman of this Grand Inquest – "

And there I stopped dead.

To the left and the rear of the Foreman was standing my blind man. I had no shadow of doubt. His face was square and grim and was faintly suggesting a skull. He had no eyebrows. If proof were needed, the fellow was staring at me, as though my head were that of Medusa herself.

The Judge was speaking under his breath.

"What is it, Pleydell? What is it?"

"It's Y," I breathed. "He's standing there, looking at me."

"Leave the Bench and see Lake. He'll know what to do. And then come back."

As I turned, I heard him speaking.

"I must apologize for this delay, gentlemen. The Marshal will swear you in a minute or two. Until you are sworn, no one will leave the box."

As I entered the Judge's room, the Chief Constable rose to his feet.

"Y," I cried. "He's sitting on the Grand Jury. He's wearing a black tie, with a pearl pin – the only one, I think. And a red button-hole."

"Name?"

"I don't know. But he can't escape, if you put a man on the door."

"Certain, Boy?"

"Certain. And I saw him recognize me."

Lake ran out of the room and I returned to the Bench.

"All right?" said the Judge.

"All right, sir."

"Then carry on."

I raised my eyes to the box.

"You, sir, as Foreman of this Grand Inquest…"

Four minutes later I swore a German spy.

It was while we were sitting at lunch in the Judge's room that the Chief Constable opened the door and put in his head.

"All over," he said. "He took poison ten minutes ago. He knew the game was up, when we gave them each a paper to read and sign. Finger-prints. Details later, sir, I've got to get in touch with the Yard."

Two days later we had the truth in our hands.

Dear Judge,

Y was — Esq., of Ploughboys, some twenty-two miles from Brooch. His true name was Veishner and he was German by birth. He was naturalized in 1902. His role of a respectable country gentleman, with a leaning to botany, was very well played. He was actually elected to the Travellers' in 1908.

Papers of the utmost value have been found at his house. These show that he has been in constant touch with the German Embassy for the last ten years and that, in the event of war, he was to be in charge of a system of espionage which I can only describe as formidable.

Please convey my warmest congratulations to Pleydell on his recognition of this enemy. The Assistant Commissioner is writing to him, himself.

Yours very truly,
Jasper Lake.

The bouquets belonged to Berry. It was Berry that linked the letter-box with the blind man.

5

In Which I Make Daphne a Present, and Berry Favours the Bold

Ten years had gone by.

The war was over and gone: Cousin Jill was married, and so was I: and many another change had taken place. No longer sure of the future, people laid hold upon the present with all their might: an Epicurean outlook was gaining ground.

My sister, Berry and I were still in Town: Jill was in Italy: Adèle was in Boston: Jonah was 'somewhere abroad'.

My sister closed her engagement-book and picked up her cigarette.

"It's been great fun," she said, "but I shall be very glad to sleep at White Ladies again."

"So," said her husband, "shall I. Pomps and vanities are exacting things. To bed at three, and I've got to see Forsyth this morning – the Raby Trust. Moses' bush isn't in it."

"Moses' bush?" said Daphne. "What ever d'you mean?"

"Now don't thwart me," said her husband. "I'm not too good. Moses' bush burned, but was not consumed. That's why it isn't in it. I'm burned up at both ends."

"How d'you feel really?"

Berry regarded his wristwatch.

"Ask me about five o'clock," he said. "I may or may not know then. Weather forecast, laousy – with an a. Is there any coffee left?"

As she refilled his cup –

"The Raby Trust," said Daphne. "How long will that go on?"

"It'll see me out," said Berry. "The child's at school."

My sister expired.

"You must not consent," she said, "to act any more."

"I won't, my darling, I won't. I've given my word to Forsyth. Why people pick upon me, I cannot conceive."

Others could. An exceptionally scrupulous Trustee, who charges nothing at all, is worth having.

"Lunch?" said Daphne.

Berry shook his head.

"I must lunch at the Club. I promised to see Jo Carey. See you at Christie's later."

"Perhaps," said Daphne.

My sister did not remind him that we had been sworn to attend a private view. In fact, her one idea was that Berry should not be there. We all disliked 'modernist painting'; but Berry's comments upon it were most embarrassing.

To fortify our souls for the visit, we lunched at the Berkeley Grill.

As we entered the gallery –

"We needn't stay long," said Daphne. "Just once round. Oh, my God, there he is – with Lady Morayne. He would choose her." Lady Morayne was at once outspoken and deaf. "Quick, Boy. Before he sees us."

But Berry's eye was not dim.

"Ah, there's my wife and her brother. Lady Morayne and I were waiting for you. We want to share this repast – this luscious collation, conceived and served by the master squirts of Montmartre – telegraphic address, *Slop-pail.*"

Lady Morayne let out a high-pitched laugh. Then she took Daphne's arm.

"My dear," she said, "no one will look at the pictures as long as you're here. And what possessed you to visit this outcrop of minds diseased? Kindness of heart, for a monkey."

"And you, Lady Morayne?"

"I've come because I like getting angry. Before I'm through, I shall probably foam at the mouth. Never mind – we'll go round together. What's the name of this insult, Berry?"

"Number Seven," said Berry, opening his catalogue. "Here we are. Seven – *Beyond the Mules*."

"Beyond the what?"

"Mules," said Berry. "You know. Large, obstructive mammals. We used to have them in the war."

"Don't be a fool," said the lady. "What's the title mean?"

The inquiry was justified. The canvas was covered with dirty yellow paint, upon which a few unrecognizable objects were casting impossible shadows of great intensity. Between two square cocoanuts was lying a boomerang: what might have been the neck of a vulture was indicated by a pointing finger, such as one sometimes sees upon notice-boards: in the bottom left-hand corner was a crude representation of something which it would be charity to describe as garbage.

Berry fingered his chin.

"*Beyond the Mules*," he murmured. "Well, I suppose we've outpaced them. We're, so to speak, ahead. The mules will arrive later. That's right. This is what the mules are going to find when they get here."

"Well, I hope they like it better than I do," shrilled Lady Morayne. "So much rotten balderdash – that's what it is."

"You must admit," said Berry, "that the housework – I mean, the brush-work is very fine."

"Brush-work!" spat Lady Morayne. "The impudent felon that did it can't even paint. And what's that mess in the corner?"

"That," said Berry, "I associate with the mules."

"But you said they hadn't got here."

"Nor they have," said Berry. "They are going to have a surprise, aren't they? I mean, talk about a home from home…"

In desperation, Daphne urged Lady Morayne towards a dark green canvas, covered with yellow blobs.

"And what," said that lady, "is the name of this masterpiece?"

"Number Ten," said Berry. "*Sugar.*"

"Did you say *Sugar*?"

"I did. That's what it says here."

"You know," shouted Lady Morayne, "this is one long series of obscene libels. We all know what sugar looks like. What resemblance does anything there bear to that useful commodity?"

"The green," said Berry, "is a lawn – a b-beautiful sward.

Upon this were playing some children, all of whom were sucking b-barley-sugar. Suddenly the school b-bell rings. Each child at once, er, parks its sugar against its return. They were still in school, when the artist – "

"Fudge," said Lady Morayne. "The thing's a filthy outrage, and you know it as well as I. What's that over there?"

We advanced upon a large canvas, entitled *Slender Thought*.

Upon a fantastic sunset were superimposed three bottles, tied together with tape. Beneath this, a kiosk was being approached by a naked, human leg. The remains of a kaleidoscope, a backdoor, a pair of trousers and an enormous eyebrow completed the work of art.

"*Slender Thought*," said Lady Morayne grimly. "And some damned fool is going to purchase that beastly drivel and hang it up on his wall. It's only fit to floor a fowl-house with."

"That would be dangerous," said Berry. "The chickens would be born with hare-beaks. Now if it was called *Roofing Felt*, we should know where we were."

"But that would be honest. You don't expect honesty here. The whole thing is based upon fraud. Half a salmon on a pavement is honest – and usually very well done. But this is a ramp. This filth is produced by failures and foisted on fools. I'd rather have half a salmon on a flag-stone and hang it up m my hail than the whole of this gallery. There's Adela Churt. Adela, isn't this bestial?"

The Dowager Countess of Churt was understood to concur.

"It's the war, my dear. Before the war it wouldn't have been allowed. Well, Daphne, and why are you here? None of this will go with White Ladies."

"We're not purchasers, Lady Churt. We've come to keep abreast of the times."

"There's a winner here," said Berry. "Oh, how d'you do, Lady Chart. Come and look at *Dry Rot*. I can't think how they think of the names."

A moment later we were confronting a canvas, some four feet square. Yellow paint had been daubed upon this in elliptical whirls. The only objects were a tent-peg, entire, and the head and shoulders of a hot-water bottle.

"You see," said my brother-in-law, "it's all disappeared. The artist has painted the absence of what was there. Most artists paint the presence. You see what I mean. If this fellow painted your portrait, he'd wait till you'd gone. Then he'd paint the void which your presence fills. Once you've got it, it's very simple."

"But where's the dry rot?"

"Gone," said Berry. "I'm sorry. If we'd been here two years ago… But now we're too late. The woodwork has disappeared. All that remains is a tent-peg, too hard for the worms to digest."

"And why the hot-water bottle?"

"That's very subtle," said Berry. "One of the best worms, whose name was Sobstuff, was a martyr to sciatica. Reluctant to lose his services, the other worms – "

"When I," said Lady Morayne, "was of tender years, I used to play 'Shops'. I used to take my doll's tea service and fill the platters with berries and pebbles and pips. I remember it perfectly. And my mother used to come by and ask the price of the goods. That was a game – for a child of tender years. But this is no game. Adults are offering adults rubbish tricked out as art. Frames such as these have been set about old masters. Famous works have been hung in this gallery. And now these antics, which would offend a maniac – these contemptible scrawls which no pavement-artist would dare to perpetrate are displayed with honour and actually offered for sale. And not in vain. Because they are here, people are going to buy them. If they were offered horse-dung, they would refuse. But I'd rather have a shovel of horse-dung than ten of these."

"Lady Morayne," said a voice, "is among the prophets."

Lady Morayne looked round and inclined her head.

"I should have been less downright, had I known that Your Excellency was there."

"But I agree with you, Madame. But who are we, when the powers that be have determined that this is to be the vogue? Believe me, it is easier for a camel to enter the eye of a needle than for a rich fool to withstand the vogue. All these, er, productions will be sold. Prices that Velasquez never dreamed of will be paid for these meaningless daubs. Museums will compete for the honour of hanging them on their walls."

"Oh, I can't bear it," said Berry. "After all, sir – "

The Ambassador set a hand upon his shoulder.

"Before," he said, "you are as old as I am now, you will see this putrid trash hanging under the same roof as Rembrandt, Watteau, Reynolds and the rest."

Under cover of the discussion, Daphne and I made a belated escape.

Christie's was not over-crowded. Though the furniture was fine, there was nothing sensational. Good prices were being paid.

"Lot two hundred and three. The picture-clock."

The bidding began at five pounds, and I bought it for twenty-one.

I gave my name and address to the auctioneer's clerk.

" If I may, I'll take it with me."

"Certainly, sir."

He nodded to one of the men, and the latter picked up my purchase and made his way to the stairs.

As I rejoined my sister –

"To be cleaned," I said. "I don't believe it's been touched for fifty years. If we drive to Rodsham's they can take the clock out, and – "

"Tomorrow," said Daphne. "Let's take it home and have a look at it first."

"As you please, my darling."

Ten minutes later, we were regarding our spoil.

The canvas was very dirty, but the painting had been well done. It was an English scene – the skirt of a little hamlet, whose decent inn was commanding a pleasant green: cows stood knee-deep in a horse-pond, with rising woods beyond: comfortable clouds rode in a pale-blue heaven, and, peering between the trees was the tower of the village church. And in the tower was a dial – a little silver dial the size of a two-shilling piece.

Behind the canvas was the clock-case; and, when you lifted the frame, the face of the clock left the picture to stay with the works, for a hole had been cut in the painting, to fit the dial.

The picture was not dated; nor was it signed. The clock was dated 1754. This had three gongs – two for the chimes, and one for the stroke of the hour. There was no key to wind it, but, when I let fall the hammers, the notes were sweet.

"What fun," said Daphne. "You know, I love conceits – the conceits of yesterday. They are so elegant. Of course, they got awful later. Remember that clock that played hymns – at six and nine?"

"I do, indeed. Ormolu. A fearful thing. But it sold for ninety pounds."

"I know. The vogue, again. I'd rather have ninety pence. Never mind. I love my present." She took my face in her hands. "You're very good to your sister. Not all men are."

"*Tout passe,*" I quoted: "*l'amitié reste.*"

Daphne kissed my nose.

"I'd rather you'd said that, Boy, than anything else."

When Berry returned, we exhibited our acquisition.

After a thorough inspection –

"Lovely," he said. "Dear old Bughaven. They'll fairly swarm in that casing. We'd better hang it in the garage."

"Don't be absurd," said Daphne. "If there aren't any now – "

"How d'you know there aren't any now? They only come out by night. There they are in those cracks, listening to all we're saying – "

"Rot," said Daphne. "According to that, every old cupboard or picture – "

"No, no. It's the chimes," said Berry. "Bugs are mad about music. Look at the barrel-organ. Always crammed with bugs. Hence its name."

"I don't believe a word of it," said Daphne. "And why – hence its name?"

"Barrel-organ's a corruption," said Berry. "It was originally the bushel-organ. And bushel is itself a corruption of bug-shell. My sweet, it's well known. All the great composers had to be regularly deloused. Why, when I was Beethoven's *fiancée* – "

"Later, darling," said Daphne. "The Willoughbys specially asked us not to be late."

"What, Madge's birthday? Tonight? Oh, I can't bear it," said Berry. "I felt like death today until after lunch."

"Only three more days," said I.

"Thank God for that," said Berry. "What do we do it for?"

"I couldn't tell you," I said. "I suppose because it's the vogue."

"Hush," said Berry. He stooped, to set an ear to the picture-clock. " 'Down in the *crevice* something *jeered.*' "

After four hours' sleep the next morning, I found a letter from Christie's lying beside my plate.

July, 1924.

Sir,

*When yesterday's sale was over, we were approached by a
Mr Coker Falk, at present of 210 Mortimer Street, regarding
the picture-clock, for which we enclose our account. This
gentleman had intended to bid for this lot, but only reached
our rooms after it had been sold. He desired us to give him
your name and address. This, according to our practice, we
declined to do; but he was so insistent that we ventured to
undertake to give you his name and address, so that you
could communicate with him, should you feel so disposed.*

We are, Sir,

Your obedient servants…

I did not feel so disposed – and enclosed a note with my
cheque to that effect. Daphne liked her present, and no
consideration should make me take it away. Indeed, despite
Berry's misgivings, she had already decided where it should
hang – outside her room at White Ladies, so that its chimes
could be shared with the rest of the floor.

Later, I drove to Rodsham's and had the clock taken out.
There they said at once that the timepiece was French. "And a
very nice piece of work, sir. When once it's cleaned, you'll find
it'll go very well." I arranged to let them know when the picture
was hung: then they would send down a man to put back the
clock.

Then I drove to the picture-liner's, and left the canvas there.
This was to be sent to White Ladies in ten days' time.

From there I walked to the Club, to be joined by Berry about
a quarter-past twelve.

"Give me a drink," he said. "A triple brandy, or something.
I've just left a friend of yours."

"Has he proved so exhausting?" said I.

"Exhausting?" said Berry. "He's corrosive. He eats you away." Here a waiter appeared. "Two dry martinis, Latham, and make them strong."

"A friend of mine?" said I.

"That's right," said Berry. "A Mr Coker Falk. He's after Bughaven."

"Good God," said I. "But how – "

"I've no idea," said Berry. "And I can't face any questions. I'm not myself. I can make a dying deposition, and that is all. I tell you, the man's vitriolic. Twenty minutes with him, and your brain is scarred."

"Twenty minutes?"

"It may have been more," said Berry. "And I wasn't fit to go out, except in an ambulance."

Here the cocktails arrived.

As I laid the money down –

"Have one of these," I said.

"I'm going to have both," said Berry. "When I think – "

"All right. And another one, Latham. And now let's have it, brother. I want to know."

Berry emptied one glass and lighted a cigarette.

"About half-past eleven," he said, "I left the house. I can't remember where I was going – that's Coker's fault. Oh, I know. I was going to have my hair cut. Damn it, I had an appointment. That's what Coker does – he stuns your brain. Well, I left the house and walked straight into his arms. Of course he thought I was you, and was off like a rogue. He began with a poor imitation of Deborah's song. He, Coker Falk, had circumvented Christie's, who, poor fish, had refused to give him your address. That, be said, was always the way. America was the locomotive, and England was the trucks: and when the trucks withstood the locomotive, they found themselves pushed around. Look at the war. England and France had tried to beat Germany for four years, and the United States had beaten her in four months. That was because America got down to things. He then told me what he would do to Christie's, if he was the Managing Director. He spoke of Bargain Basements and Ladies' Rooms. Finally he seized the lapel of this excellent coat and said he was going to have the picture-clock. He said he'd never wanted anything so much in all his life, and when Coker Falk felt that way, the angels watched their step. There he paused for breath: so I said, that while I fully appreciated his outlook, unless both his god-parents were of German extraction, the acquisition of British nationality was a matter of some difficulty. I added that trout-streams were, however, available at a price and that if he made a noise like a lipstick outside the back door of Lambeth Palace, His Grace would serve him after closing time and before the mast. Before he had recovered from this counter-attack, I urged him to release my coat, as it had been left me by a hot-drop forger who had died of bubonic plague. I followed this request with an invitation – which he immediately accepted – to lunch with me today at the old Bailey at one o'clock. He certainly let go my lapel, but when I sought to be gone, he fell into step beside me and started again. He said I could have Lambeth Palace and the trout-streams. All he wanted of me was the picture-clock. He said it was 'just poitry' – the cutest operational gadget he'd ever seen. He was going to take it to Chunkit – that's his home town – and hang it right up in his parlour and then ask the folks to step in. He said the noise they'd make would be heard in Dayton and that, when it said its piece, they'd just pass out. I said that was fine. Then I pointed out that I hadn't been near Christie's for a fortnight and had never purchased or possessed such a thing as a picture-clock. This statement appeared to afford him infinite mirth, for he made a noise like a hooter, slammed me upon the back, pitched a penny into the gutter and then spat upon it with remarkable accuracy. That, he said, was for my bluff. When he did that at Chunkit, folks put the storm-shutters up. And then he was really off. He'd got to have that clock. He'd write me a cheque on the Farmer's Glory Bank that'd make what I'd paid Christie's look like a tag in a five-cent bargain-sale. Reminiscence, prophecy and metaphor foamed from his lips. He wouldn't let me speak and he wouldn't let me go, and, when I stopped a taxi, he followed me in. I don't wonder he gets what he wants. If the clock had been mine, he'd have had it – and that's the truth. You've got to stop him somehow, or you'll go raving mad.

"When he heard me say, 'Drive to Christie's,' he quietened down. You see, he thought he was home. He was fairly hugging himself, as he followed me up the steps. I asked to see —. When he came, I asked him if he had been selling yesterday afternoon. He said yes. 'Then will you tell this gentleman whether or no it was I that purchased a picture-clock.' 'It wasn't you,' says —. 'In fact, I don't think you were there.' 'And you didn't bid for me?' 'Certainly not.' I turned to Coker. 'Is that good enough?' I said. He looked from — to me and savaged his thumb. 'You're B Pleydell,' he said, 'of thirty-eight Cholmondeley Street.' I nodded. 'And you didn't buy that clock?' 'I've been telling you so,' I said, 'for half an hour.' 'Then there's dirty work somewhere,' he said. 'I'll have to begin again.' With that, he started on —, and I slipped down the stairs and drove to the Stores. I tell you, I was taking no chances. When I was sure I'd lost him, I left by another door and took a taxi here. And now what?"

"Don't ask me," said I. "If you can't beat him, I can't."

"If he comes back," said Berry, "you'll have to hand Bughaven over. And if you take my advice, you'll do it at once."

I'm damned if I will," said I. "Besides, it's broken up. The clock and the picture are parted – they're being severally cleaned."

"That won't stop Coker," said Berry. "If you gave it to the British Museum, he'd have it out."

"Well, we go out of Town on Friday."

"I know. And the moment he sees White Ladies, he'll want that, too."

We had been at White Ladies a week, and I was sitting at Riding Hood, under some limes, waiting to pick up Berry, who was upon the Bench. After another five minutes, I left the car and made my way quietly into the little court.

Berry was in the Chair, and a Chinaman stood in the dock.

"You say you're a seaman?" said Berry.

The prisoner inclined his head.

"How do you come to be here?"

"I wished for the country, sir, before I signed on again."

"Do you mean to return to China?"

"Yes, sir. I beg that you will beat me and let me go."

Berry frowned.

"Because you're a stranger," he said, "the charge has been reduced to one of common assault. Had you been English, you would have been sent for trial on a much more serious charge. Do you understand?"

"Yes, sir."

"To draw a knife on a man is a very serious thing."

"I lose my temper, because he has insulted the bold."

"An insult is no excuse for trying to take his life. But you are a stranger and a seaman. If you were a landsman and English, we should send you to prison for six months."

"I am very sorry, sir."

"As it is, we shall only send you to prison for six weeks, with hard labour."

The Chinaman clung to the dock.

"Beat me, my lord, beat me – and let me go."

"I have no power to have you beaten."

"But prison – no."

"I'm sorry," said Berry. "But you have done something which we have not the right to pass. We're being very lenient. When you come out, the police will help you to get a ship."

The man bowed his head. As the jailer touched his arm, he let out a terrible cry.

"The bold, the bold!"

Berry looked round.

"What does he mean?" he demanded. "Who are the bold?"

An Inspector of Police stood up.

"I think it's his puppy, sir. We've got it outside."

Berry looked at the prisoner.

"Is The Bold your dog?"

The Chinaman bowed his head.

"I am his servant," he said. "The blood is royal."

There was a little silence, while Berry fingered his chin. Then –

"I begin to see daylight," he said. "Bring the dog in."

One minute later, the most perfect Pekingese puppy I ever saw stood upon the solicitors' table, looking imperiously round. He was very small, because he was very young; but a full-grown mastiff had not his dignity. Strange as were his surroundings, he knew no fear. His little head was up, and his tiny tail was lying along his spine. His hair was not in – he was furry. He looked like something a woman might have worn at her throat. Richer, I think, than sable: but rather more grey.

"Let him go to him," said Berry.

The prisoner left the dock and stepped to the puppy's side. Then he spoke to him in Chinese, as though indeed he were his equerry.

When he had done, the puppy surveyed him proudly and put out a tiny paw. The other bowed his head and it touched his brow with its tongue. But the tail never moved.

"Listen," said Berry. "Your trouble is that you don't want to leave The Bold?"

The Chinaman looked at him and inclined his head.

"While you are in prison," said Berry, "he shall be lodged in my house. He shall be fed and cared for in every way. When you come out, he will be ready and waiting to sail to China with you. Tell him what I have said in your own tongue."

The prisoner addressed the puppy – rather as his adviser addresses a King.

When he had done, he stood back.

"Thank you, my lord," he said quietly. "Now I will go."

As the door closed behind him, Berry nodded to me and got to his feet. As he left the Bench, I moved to the table and picked the puppy up.

"Has he eaten?" I asked the Inspector.

"Not a bite, sir. He won't take nothing from us. He's a proud little dog – stares you down, you know. An' clean as clean. An' he can't be more than two months. He's had a little water."

"He's no ordinary dog," said I. "If a Chinaman says he's royal, he probably is."

"What, a dog o' royal blood, sir?"

"That's right. It's a terribly ancient breed."

"Soun's like a fairy-tale, sir."

"So it does," said I. "But I think it's probably fact."

As we settled ourselves in the car –

"What else could I do?" said Berry. "He damned near did wilful murder for love of this scrap. Saw red, of course. But you can't pass things like that."

"I think," said I, "he's extremely fortunate."

"I don't know about that. You see, British Justice is very rightly renowned. And when we have an alien before us, I always bear that in mind. If he's a swine, he gets more than an Englishman – why should he come over here to do his dirt? But if he's a decent bloke, he receives consideration, so that when he goes back to his country, he'll always speak well of us. I admit it's not in the Manual, but I think it's common sense. And what do we feed him on? Goat's flesh, seethed in sour milk, or rotten fish? They eat such filth in China that what the scraps can be like, I tremble to think."

"Bread and milk," said I. "And a little raw meat. He wants building up. And mind what you say of his country. He's most intelligent."

Berry regarded the puppy, snug in the crook of his arm.

"Daphne," he said, "will never let him out of her sight. You must be a good dog, The Bold, and we'll be good dogs to you. A very fine lady is going to be your friend. One of your rank, you know. But you mustn't look down on us, for we have our points. And mind you're civil to the servants." He turned to me. "You might have a word with Nobby. I know he'll be full of goodwill, but he's rather impetuous. I mean, this'll be a new one on him."

"I'll see to that," said I. "He'll be all right, as soon as he knows the facts."

"Well, do be ready," said Berry. "When you've been away for ten minutes, he has a bewitching habit of leaping into the car and of climbing all over my face in order to get at yours. If he does that today, and uses The Bold as a foothold…"

He need have had no concern.

As the Rolls stole up the drive, I saw at a glance that my Sealyham was deeply engaged.

He was standing square on the gravel, with his tail well over his back and his eyes on the door of a green all-weather coupé, berthed by the side of the lawn. His demeanour was eloquent.

Framed in the coupé's window were the head and shoulders of a man I had never seen. He was wearing a circular hat and his face was red. But I knew who it was before Berry spoke his name.

"And this," said the latter, "is where I leave the tram. Nobby's got him where he belongs. You can make all things clear and then take your leave. He'll have to go – or spend the night in the drive."

I stopped, and he left the Rolls. Then I drove slowly on, until I was abreast of the captive, till then unaware that he was no longer alone.

"Get this darned dog away," he yelped. "I wanner get out."

Nobby looked at me, and my lips framed the words 'Good dog.' Thus reassured, he lowered his chin to his toes and let out a bark.

"Mr Falk," I said, "you're only wasting your time."

"Get that dog away, and I guess I'll change your outlook. Before I'm through, sonny, you're going to be born again. I told your senior he couldn't faze Coker Falk. I won't say he hasn't edged me, because he has. And I don't think much of his Club. All cops and corner bums, as far as I saw. But you can't side-track a land-slide. An' when Coker Falk says 'Mine', wise guys throw in their hands. What d'you want for the honey, Mister? Don't be afraid."

"Look here," said I. "I don't know how long you're prepared to stay in that car, but my dog is prepared to watch it until it leaves. Make it forty-eight hours if you like – it won't faze him."

"See here. You get him away."

I shook my head.

"He's serving my turn," I said. "This interview is not of my seeking and I have no time to spare. Please get this once for all – the picture-clock is not here and is not for sale."

"See here, Junior, when Coker Falk wants what's his, it's quicker to have a war than to stand him down. If your cops knew their job, they wouldn' o' held me at Chiswick an' let you take that gadget out of my jaws. An' when a guy does that, as soon as he sees his error, he puts it back. That's Chunkit's way, Buddy, but maybe Chunkit's ahead. So Coker Falk's buying you out. You move the hound, an' I'll – "

"By pursuing the matter," said I, "you're throwing away a chance which will never occur again."

"How's that?"

"Tomorrow evening an exhibition will close, and its famous works of art will be dispersed. They *are* for sale – at a price. The price may be more than you are prepared to pay – "

"See here, Junior, if Coker Falk – "

" – but if they don't shake Chunkit up, then nothing will. More. They're the latest thing. I was there with two ladies of title, a week ago: and they had seen nothing like them – they said so, in so many words. And one has a room full of van Dycks; so she ought to know."

"Name, please," said Mr Falk, notebook in hand.

"Adela, Countess of Churt."

The name went down.

"There's a glorious study there, *Beyond the Mules*. Or if that's sold, there's another, called *Slender Thought*. They're more than I can afford, but – "

"What's the address?"

I gave the gallery's name and got out of the Rolls.

"*Slender Thought* and *Beyond the Mules*," repeated Mr Falk. He put his note-book away. "Now let me out of this car."

I shook my head.

"That's my last word, Mr Falk. I've given you the low-down on those pictures. I've told you what Lady Churt thinks. If Chunkit knows better than she does, then let them go. But don't blame me if, before we're very much older, you see *Beyond the Mules* on some well-known gallery's walls."

With that, I made much of Nobby and entered the house, while Mr Falk, in a foaming diatribe, compared British hospitality unfavourably with that of the United States.

Five minutes later, I heard the coupé leave...

As I appeared upon the terrace, my sister sat back on her heels.

"I suppose it's real," she said. "I mean, when we wake tomorrow it won't be gone."

The Bold was standing still at the head of the terrace steps, surveying his present dominion with the dignity of a lion. He resembled a little image that stands on a mantelpiece.

I bent my head to Nobby, under my arm.

"There he is," I whispered. "You see, he's very small, and, although he covers it up, I think he must feel very strange. So be gentle with him, old fellow."

Nobby put up his muzzle and licked my face.

The Bold descended the steps, as best he could. Happily, they were shallow; but I am inclined to think that they were the first he had used. But they had to be traversed, if he was to reach the grass – and The Bold knew how to behave.

I let him prove the lawn. Then I put Nobby down…

The meeting was well timed, for The Bold had just found that the lawn was uncomfortably big. After all, he was very tiny, and the sward must have seemed immense. Be that as it may, for the first time his tail went down, and he stood, a forlorn little figure, awed by his giant surroundings and plainly not at all sure of the way he had come. And then he turned to see Nobby, two paces away.

In a flash his tail was up and he faced the Sealyham squarely, as though he knew no fear. Nobby moved his tail and lay down – and The Bold came stumbling towards him and lay down, too.

So they played upon the lawn together, Nobby suffering him, and The Bold no longer a prince, but an urchin boy.

But when, later on, we went in to dress for dinner, Nobby stood still and The Bold stepped in before him, chin in air.

Indeed, as long as he was with us, he always took pride of place – and Nobby accepted this and always gave him the wall. He would sway his tail for the servants, but never for us. But with us he would be familiar; with us he would play and bicker; from us he would take his orders – often enough with a high and mighty air; and Daphne was his goddess – for her he would turn on his back and wave his paws in the air. And when she picked him up, he would sob with content. After all, he was very tiny and very young.

As we took our seats at table –

"And now," said my sister, "about this awful man. What have you done with him?"

"He's gone for the moment," said I. "But I'm not sure he won't come back."

"Of course he'll come back," said Berry. "He's Coker Falk. What's yours is his, and he wants what he wants when he wants it – and that's right now. Mind you get that, Sugar, and get it good. When Coker Falk says 'See here', wise guys go into the wash-room and lock the door."

"Oh, do be quiet," said Daphne.

"That's nothing at all," said Berry. "That's Tallis' Responses, compared with Coker Falk. After five minutes with him, your nerves are flayed."

"Go on, Boy," said my sister. "How did you drive him away?"

"I put him on to those very beautiful pictures we saw ten days ago. I suggested that, if he really wanted to blind Chunkit – for that, I assume, is the idea – he couldn't do better than show it *Beyond The Mules*. I took Lady Churt's name in vain, and that made him think."

"If he comes back," said Berry, "you'll have to give him the clock. We can't go on like this. It's bad for my heart."

"Nonsense," said Daphne. "Just because – "

"My sweet," said Berry. "You've had no communion with Coker. Neither has Boy really, because today he was treed. But once let him get his hooks in, and after a little while you'll give him what ever he asks. The tension he induces is so frightful, that you simply have to relieve it at any cost. How he's escaped mutilation, I can't conceive: if he's *persona grata* at Chunkit, I tremble to think what life in that town can be like."

"If I have to sock him," said I, "he won't have the picture-clock. But if Nobby could tree him, I don't think he'd wait for that. After all, he may not return. I've thrown him quite a good fly. And I fear he considers us sticky. He didn't care for the Central Criminal Court, and he felt very strongly that he should have been asked to stay."

"What here?" said Berry. "Oh, go on."

"He'd brought his suitcase. He said so, before he went. I sat in the hall and listened. They're a funny lot at Chunkit. It seems that if I went there, to force somebody's hand, I should be loaded with gifts and fêted for several months."

157

"Or robbed and murdered," said Berry. "Don't you go. Never mind. Let's hope and pray that *Beyond the Mules* is sold. That'll be enough for Coker. Lunch at Bell Hammer tomorrow? Or am I wrong?"

"No, that's right," said Daphne. "But I forgot to tell you – Sir Andrew won't be there. He can't leave Town until Tuesday. So, as he wants to see you, he'll lunch here on his way down."

Sir Andrew Plague, KC, was a notable man. He was also a survival. Few brains could compare with his: his temper was that of a bull: his personality was devastating. Rough as he was with them, his servants worshipped him. Since his marriage with Lady Touchstone, some ten months back, he had become less fiery; but, once he was roused, Sir Andrew knew no law. We liked him well and held him in great respect – and I like to think he liked us, for there were, in fact, few houses to which he would go. My brother-in-law and he were co-Trustees.

"Good," said Berry. "Er, good. Has the household been warned?"

"It will be. And he's sure to bring Spigot with him."

Let me put it like this. When Sir Andrew went visiting, his valet was quite invaluable – not so much to Sir Andrew as to his host.

"I think, perhaps," added Daphne, "that just while he's here, The Bold should be out of sight."

"I entirely agree," said Berry. "Two such majestic personalities would almost certainly clash. I mean, when Sir Andrew's mellow, he looks at you as if you were dirt, and The Bold's imperious stare would send the blood to his head. By the way, where's The Bold to sleep?"

"Well, I thought in Boy's room."

"Not on your life," said I.

"But, darling, he won't feel lonely if Nobby's there."

"But – "

"What could be better?" said Berry, unctuously. "And if he wants to go out about half-past three – well, then he can go, can't he?"

"This is monstrous," said I. "You took him on. I heard you promise that Chink – "

"I was very careful," said Berry, "to use the passive voice. 'The dog,' I said, 'will be cared for.' Besides, at three a.m. life's at its lowest ebb. If I were aroused about then, it might be the end. And what if it's raining? Am I eating Arthur's Seat? It's really extraordinarily good."

"Arthur's Seat?" screamed Daphne.

"I mean, Dover Sole," said Berry. "When I was Judge Jeffreys, I used to buy my gooseberries at Turnham Green. Some years later, when I was on the Bloody Assize, the apprentice that gave me short measure gave evidence for the defence. And there you are. As I said to him before sentence, be sure your sin will find you out. It upset me terribly."

There were now many cars abroad, but the roads which we used the next morning were little known, and for much of the way we had no company. With one consent, we drove slowly, for the country was looking its best, and, since it had rained in the night, the air was as sweet as the prospects on every side. The timber was especially lovely. There was a bulwark of woodland, thick and close as tapestry laid upon the arm of a chair: yet, when we stole beside it and could see its warp and its woof, a glancing, diaphanous mansion, lodging zephyr and sunbeam and fit for the pretty progress of Shakespeare's maids. And here, at a corner, was standing a wayside oak – the very embodiment of England, slow, resolute, majestic, unearthly strong: one mighty branch hung over the way itself, offering shade and shelter and printing upon the road its splendid effigy. For those that have ears to hear, such trees give tongue. Then there were hedgerow elms – jacketed men-at-arms, that took up their escort duty four hundred years ago.

Four magnificent chestnuts were squiring a Norman tower, and a quarter of a mile farther on two copper beeches, new burnished, filled the eye. So the pageant went on, with lime and ash and walnut, still taking their ancient order, while a watch of firs upon a hilltop still did its sober duty by many a mile.

So we came to Bell Hammer, just as the stable-clock was telling the time. A quarter to one.

As we left the car, Valerie Lyveden came running across the lawn.

"My very dears, how are you? Anthony's changing – he only got back from his village ten minutes ago. And how is everything?"

"If you're thinking of Town," said Berry, "it's now one large, steep place – with the Gadarene swine rushing down it, by day and night. We've pulled out at last, but, once you're going, it's terribly hard to stop. But we've come to hear news – not give it."

"First tell me – how's White Ladies?"

"Looking up," said Daphne. "I've got the laundry going, I'm thankful to say. The money it's going to save us. Half our stuff has been ruined by sending it out."

"Laundry!" cried Valerie Lyveden. "I can't even staff the house."

"Yes, but the future's assured. When Anthony really gets going, you'll have a waiting list."

Two things had happened to Lyveden within the year: he had inherited a very great fortune and had married a very rich girl. Young and able and active, he could not fold his hands; but even while he was wondering what he could find to do, the little village of Pouncet, lying at the gates of Bell Hammer, had come to be sold. And many acres with it. Lyveden had bought them forthwith, and now was to use his fortune to make of Pouncet an Auburn of 1924.

Here the new landlord appeared...

"But this is absurd," said Berry. "He can't go about like that. He must wear a large double-Albert and tails and a square felt hat. He must carry a stick with a knob, which he holds to his chin, suck his teeth before speaking and – "

"Be quiet," said Daphne. "Anthony, where are the plans?"

"On the billiard-table – all ready. When you've digested them, I'll take you down to the borough and see what you think."

"What about the pub?" said Berry.

"I've had a find there," said Lyveden. "They're pulling one down at Bristol, which is over two hundred years old. I've got the bar and the shelves, two beautiful old bow-windows, full of original panes, the floor and a lovely fireplace and four good doors."

"You don't mean to say you let the cellars go?"

"But I've got a peach of a sign-board: *The Godly Shipman* – that's a new one on me. Another pub's going at Portsmouth, and I've got the settles from that."

"And the village hall?" said Daphne.

"I'm copying one from Oxford – of course, on a tiny scale: that'll make one side of a quad. Almshouses on the others, with a porter's lodge and a gate. But that's all to come. Water and light and drainage come before everything else. Of the present habitations, five out of six are outwardly very nice: but most are far too small: so, as the leases fall in, I shall just knock two into one."

"You can do what you like?" said I.

"Pretty well, I think. Sir Andrew's behind me there. I can make certain rules. No char-à-bancs, for instance. No tea-rooms. I will not have a resort."

"It's fascinating," said Daphne.

"Well, I want it to be Pouncet's show. They're a very decent lot, and it is such a pretty spot that I hate the idea of their drifting into the towns."

"Almshouses," said Berry. "Along three sides of a square. Will you want as many as that?"

"*Touché*," cried Valerie. "That's a concession to architecture."

"Then devote one side to your staff. Do as they do in France, and let some live out."

"What a tidal brainwave," said Valerie, clapping her hands. "Next door to the hall, and all. And when they grow old in our service, they've only to cross the floor."

Here Lady Plague arrived.

"I insist upon knowing," she said. "Have you told them about the baths?"

"Not yet," said Anthony.

"Discourse," said Berry. "Discourse."

"Well, it's silly to put in bathrooms, so I'm having a bathhouse built. That's going under the hall. Hot water every, evening from six to nine: hot water every morning for washing clothes. I don't know whether it'll work."

"What could be better?" said Berry. " '*The flesh* at night, *the vest* and *drawers* by *day*.' "

"Really!" said Daphne.

"Gluckstein," said Berry. "I mean, Goldsmith. Out of *The Converted Village*. I remember it perfectly. 'And *those* who came to *wash* remained to *bathe*.' "

"Berry," said Lady Plague, "I give you best. *The Converted Village* alone is worth a weekend. And you're only going to have lunch."

"Come and name our new cocktail," said Valerie, "and you shall stay for a month."

As we followed her and my sister into the house –

"You know," said Lady Plague, "it's like sawbones."

"Sawbones?" said I.

"Yes. That silly game that everyone was playing before the war. There were family quarrels about it. When someone had done two-thirds of Rembrandt's *Night Watch* – "

"You mean, jigsaws," said I.

"Do I? Never mind. They used to give them to the sick – a most extraordinary procedure. If I was ill, the last thing I should want to do would be to reconstruct Rembrandt's *Night Watch*. But as we're all well and strong we've fallen for this new game. Andrew's quite silly about it. The billiard-room is our wash-pot. The table's been covered with cork, and the cork with plans. And we have a board for 'Ideas'. What are you thinking, Boy?"

I glanced over my shoulder. Berry and Anthony Lyveden were not to be seen.

"Strictly between you and me, is Pouncet going to like it?"

"Of course not," said Lady Plague. "Pouncet is going to loathe it with all its might. It'll loathe the pub and the hall and, except to pinch the soap, it won't go near the baths. The drainage it regards as an insult – that we know. And, to mark its disapproval, half the village will leave – and cut off its rotten nose to spite its rotten face. But Anthony's ready for that. Their homes will be swept and garnished, and then will be possessed by disabled ex-service men. That's what's at the back of his mind. He's got a young architect who's lost a leg in the war, and he's ear-marked a sergeant-major to run the pub."

I sighed.

"It's a great thing," said I, "to be a monarch. If we owned Bilberry…"

"What then?"

"You must ask Berry," I said. "The sorry tale is his."

The cocktail was very good. Berry named it *Dry Auburn* – which I thought was better still.

Appealed to at lunch, he related our tale of woe.

"This," he said, "is a Saturday afternoon. By rights, we should be playing cricket – and putting Gamecock or Dovetail where they belong. That we are not is due to our Mr Doogle, an unattractive swine, for whom humanity falls into two classes only – blood-suckers and wage-slaves. Mr Doogle appeared in the village some eighteen months ago. That he came in haste and by stealth cannot, I think, be denied, and Doogle" – he spelt it – "seems to me a queer name. The less sympathetic suggest that his surreptitious arrival was due to a desire to avoid bloodshed and that, had he remained in the North, more than one of his veins would most certainly have been opened in the crudest possible way. To this view, I incline, for he has been heard to boast that, while his conscience prevented him from serving his King in the field, such was his personal energy in fomenting strikes that, during the critical years, he cost his country more than a million working hours. Now our Mr Doogle is cunning – I'll give him that. Of White Ladies he speaks no ill. Instead, he continually proclaims how fortunate – nay, blest the village is in such a neighbour. With a loud voice, he applauds our condescension in worshipping in the same Church, in patronizing the same shops, in joining in the same games as 'the common man'. He begs the village to consider how much it costs us so to demean ourselves. Finally, when I came out of Church after reading the lessons, he led the cheers. There were, of course, no cheers to lead. Well, I give the brute best. Our Mr Doogle has done his job – the job he is paid to do, for he has money to spend, but he does no work. Every gesture we make is now suspect. The old fellows love us still: but the younger – see through us. Class hatred has come to stay."

A painful silence succeeded Berry's words.

Then –

"I'm not surprised," said Valerie. "White Ladies was bound to stand high on the Communists' danger-list."

"And what of their agent?" Lady Plague's eyes were afire. "Better for him that a millstone were hanged about his neck. My God, what fools people are!"

"What," said Anthony Lyveden, "is Doogle like?"

"Undersized," said Berry. "A rat of a man. Thin, reddish hair, and protruding eyes. Age about forty. Can you place him?"

"I think I can. I believe his true name is Elgood – that would be Doogle reversed."

"Well done, indeed," cried Daphne – and spoke for us all.

"Go on," said Berry. "Go on."

"Well an agitator called Elgood left Durham early last year. On the eve of an inquest on a woman who took her life. He'd been blackmailing her. Some search was made for him, but no charge could be made and so he wasn't pursued. The coroner was – very outspoken. I happen to know these things, because the woman was the wife of a sergeant-major I know. He was once my first servant, and I hope he's coming to Pouncet to run the pub. As a matter of fact, he's coming to Bell Hammer next week. Warren, his name is – one of the best of men. And I've little doubt that he'd like a word with Elgood – or, as he once described him, 'that little red rat'."

"He can have it," said Berry, "for certain on Saturday night. From what Fitch, our chauffeur says, that's guest night at *The Rose*. Doogle's guest night, I mean. He dilutes his doctrines with whiskey. After two or three rounds, they turn into obvious truths."

Anthony fingered his chin.

"You mustn't be on in this act, and neither must I. I'll have a word with Warren, and you have a word with Fitch. And Warren shall report to Fitch at nine on Saturday night. I think it must be the man."

"It must be," said everyone.

"If it is," said Lyveden, "when he's discharged from hospital, I feel that he will cross Bilberry off his map."

"Let's hope he tries Pouncet," said Berry. "By that time Warren will certainly be installed: and when Doogle limps into *The Godly Shipman*, in search of a double Scotch – well, he'll feel the world's against him, won't he? And now to return to our *moutons* (very low French). I understand Pouncet is peevish – doesn't want to be washed and brushed. If you want to disperse her dudgeon, set up an elegant conduit in the midst of your quad. This must have two pipes – one connected to the main water, and one to the pub. And then on high days and holidays, such as the anniversary of the discovery of smallpox, the fountain can run with beer."

Neither Berry nor Daphne nor I will ever forget the highly fantastic trick which Fortune played before us upon the next day but two.

For Sir Andrew Plague's visit, arrangements had been carefully made. The Bold had been confined to the house-keeper's room – a sentence for which he had summoned his most indignant stare. Nobby had been bathed and cautioned. A simple lunch had been ordered – Sir Andrew liked plain food. His appetite being healthy, a cold steak-and-kidney pie – a delicacy to which he was partial – was in reserve. And the household was standing by at a quarter-past twelve.

Since I was upon the lawn, but the others were in the house, I alone of us three saw the outrage take place.

At five and twenty to one Sir Andrew's car had turned in at our entrance-gates, when a van turned in behind it and then, by the use of its hooter, demanded way. Sir Andrew's chauffeur naturally took no notice, for, apart from anything else, the drive was very ancient and, therefore, none too wide. Upon this, with his hooter screaming, the driver of the van deliberately forced his way by, compelling Sir Andrew's chauffeur to take his car on to the turf and over the roots of a tree.

As Berry and Daphne appeared, the van was pulled up all standing before the door, and Coker Falk flung out and ran to its back. As he and his accomplice were lifting out a large picture, the car came to rest, alongside, but slightly in rear.

Sir Andrew was half out of his window, stick in hand.

"You murdering blackguards," he roared. "You bloody-minded felons. Lemme out of this car, Spigot. I'll show them what murder means. I'll teach them to cram their betters on private roads."

It was a fearful business.

Sir Andrew was enormously fat and a giant of a man. His face was normally red, but now it was blue. He had leaned so far out of the window, that now, when he sought to do so, he could not retire: indeed, had the door been opened, he must, I think, have gone with it, and Spigot wisely refrained from doing as he was bid.

Coker Falk disregarded his yells, addressing Berry and Daphne, as though the stage was his.

"Well, folks, I guess you'll allow Coker Falk can do his stuff. Don't you notice this boyo: he's only sore 'cause I pushed him. When Coker Falk is moving, wise guys get under the seat. See here, Charming, you couldn't afford these cunning compositions – Junior told me so: an' so I've brought them along, to hang in the old ancestral in place of the picture-clock." He ripped its wrapping away, to expose *Beyond the Mules*. "You've got to stand back for this one." Here he stepped back – within range. "But once – "

Sir Andrew's stick fell upon his shoulder – and shivered with the force of the blow. With a howl of pain, Coker swung round, to meet a blast of invective that took his breath away.

"And that's nothing," yelled Sir Andrew. "Wait till I'm out. That's not even an earnest of what you're going to get. I'll tear your head from your body. I'll – "

"See here, gargoyle," shrilled Coker, "you can't get funny like this with Coker Falk. I'm an American citizen, an' – "

Sir Andrew laughed – a laugh of such hideous menace as made the blood run cold.

"So was Crippen," he blared: "but he died over here. My God, lemme out of this car. You all of you heard him say 'gargoyle'. I'll kill him for that. And that filthy offal there shall serve as his winding-sheet."

"See here, ogre, if you think you can bluff Coker Falk – "

"Bluff?" screeched Sir Andrew. "*Bluff?* Goats and monkeys, I'll show him. I'll…"

Coker had not stopped talking: Sir Andrew's disapproval was superimposed upon his.

" – get tougher, bogey, I guess I'll have to show you the ugly way. If you'd been chased when you were a little rosebud…"

" – an alien scourge. And then you can have his vile body and cast it into the draught."

Here, with a madman's effort, the ravening knight fought his shoulders out of the window and into the car. And then the door was open, and he was down in the drive.

As he launched himself at Coker, the latter started back and, catching his heel in its wrapping, fell into *Beyond the Mules*. The canvas, of course, gave way, and Coker went through the frame, which his trembling accomplice continued to hold upright.

This brought Sir Andrew up short, and Spigot seized the occasion and caught his arm.

"Steady, Sir Andrew. The man's not worth your attention."

His master turned upon Spigot and shook him off.

"Stand back," he roared. "I'm going to abate a nuisance – a filthy, verminous nuisance, that wears the shape of a man."

My sister was by his side.

"Sir Andrew," she said, "my husband has sent for the servants and…"

But Berry and I were not waiting. Between us, we picked up Coker and flung him into the van. Then I seized *Beyond the Mules* and pitched that in upon him, and Berry slammed the doors.

Then he addressed the accomplice.

"Get into the cab and drive off. And tell Mr Coker Falk that, if he appears again, I shall have him thrown into a cellar and send for the police. He's molested me and insulted one of my guests. And he will return at his peril – and so will you."

As the fellow started his engine, Coker was thrashing the panel behind the driver's seat.

"Here, you," he howled, "you're taking your orders from me. You leave this truck where it is and let me out. That fat thug's lammed my shoulder and spoiled a museum piece. I'll say I'm sore. An' when Coker Falk gets sore, wise guys…"

Amid the storming of gears, the rest of the adage was lost.

Berry turned to the gardeners who had come up at a run.

"See that van out, and close the entrance-gates."

Daphne met us, as we re-entered the house.

"Cocktails on the terrace," she said. "I'm going to drink two. Sir Andrew will have his upstairs. Spigot says he'll be quite all right in a quarter of an hour."

"I shan't," said Berry. "I shan't be all right for years. To emerge with the object of greeting a highly punctilious guest; instead, to be confronted with a quarrel – not to say, brawl, which is not so much indecent as obscene, in which to interfere is as much as one's life is worth, is not conducive to that sweet and regular rhythm which the valves of the heart should preserve. Which reminds me, great heart, how did you lure the rogue lion away from his kill? I mean, we were occupied."

"I invoked Lady Touchstone," said Daphne. "I mean, Lady Plague. I said I was sure that she would be greatly upset if he soiled his hands with such trash. He looked at me very hard. Then he said, 'Her mantle becomes you', and let me lead him away."

"Gorgeous," said Berry. "Can anyone tell me how the love-scene began?"

I related what I had seen before he arrived.

"That's Coker all over," said Berry. "One of these days that energetic blow-fly will come to a violent end. He'll be dismembered, or something. Between you and me, I thought he was doomed today. He may talk big about Chunkit, but I'm inclined to believe he's been fired from his native land. America has her faults, but no people on earth could stick behaviour like this. I mean, it's beyond the mules. I'm only so sorry he didn't do his 'penny trick': Sir Andrew would have loved that, wouldn't he? Oh, and where was that godsend, Nobby? If only he'd done his duty – "

"I can answer that question," said Daphne. "Nobby is lying outside the housekeeper's room."

Six days had gone by, and Fitch was gravely reporting what had occurred in the public bar of *The Rose*.

"It all went off very well, sir, accordin' to plan. I comes in, as usual, at half-pas' nine: and I sits down with Mr Fergus, to drink my beer. Doogle's up at the bar, lettin' go, as usual, about the idle rich, with eight or ten lappin' it up an' drinkin' his Scotch. Just about ten minutes later, Warren comes in. He stands quite still inside an' throws a look round. An' then he sees Doogle – an' points, like a dog with a gun. But Doogle never sees him, but goes straight on with his talk. Then Warren straightens up an' lets his voice go.

" 'Well, Elgood,' he says…

"I tell you, sir, it was like a scene in a play.

"Doogle starts like he'd been shocked an' knocks over his glass: then he swings round an' sees Warren, an' the blood goes out of his face: an' then he begins to tremble…

"Warren goes on –

" 'Thought you was safe, did you? Thought you'd lie up here with a change of name? You'll never be safe, Elgood. I'll always rout you out wherever you go.' Then he takes out a newspaper-cutting an' looks at us all. 'This is Mr Elgood, of Durham – he's turned his name round. An' if you'll excuse me, gents, I'm goin' to read you a short report of an inquest – the inquest upon my wife. Mr Elgood's name is mentioned…' An' then he reads the report from beginnin' to end."

Fitch hesitated there, and a hand went up to his mouth.

"That poor girl's letter…an' the things the Coroner said… An' Doogle shakin' all over an' hidin' his face in his hands…

"Then he puts the paper away, goes up to Doogle, takes him by the scruff of his neck an' puts him outside. An' then he starts in…

"When he's done, he leaves him down in the gutter and comes in an' has a pint. Never says a word about Doogle, but talks about the Army an' this an' that. An' then he says 'Good night all', an' walks out of the house.

"I stopped on, as arranged, sir, an' met him back in the stables before he left. He's a proper man, sir, Warren... An' Doogle's gone. Packed up and left this morning at six o'clock. Jem Hollis saw him takin' the station road. He didn't know him at first, his face was that out of shape."

"That's very good hearing," said Berry. "And now that their master's exposed, let's hope that Elgood's disciples will reconsider the doctrines which he has dispensed."

Fitch smiled.

"Shaken 'em up all right, sir. Their faces last night... They didn't know where to look."

As we strolled back to the house –

"We can't complain," said Berry. "On the whole, we've had a good week. The wicked have been discomfited. Coker has been discouraged: the spirit and manner of the operation were soul-shaking, but the fact remains. Then, Doogle has been reduced – thanks to Anthony's intuition, with sweet efficiency. Finally, a blasphemous imposition has been destroyed: Coker made a good job of that: *Beyond the Mules, after Falk* becomes *Beyond Repair.*"

6

In Which Berry is Attacked by Lumbago, and Jill is Escorted to France

"A-a-ah," screamed Berry.

Daphne, Jill and I jumped nearly out of our skins, and Nobby and The Bold were barking each other down.

When order had been restored –

"Must you do that?" said my sister, with a hand to her heart.

"I must," said Berry. "My agony must be expressed. If your lumbar region was enriched by the sudden introduction of a red-hot skewer, you would almost certainly remark upon the fact."

"You must see a doctor," said Jill.

"I don't want a doctor," said Berry. "I want an exorcist. I'm possessed by a devil of great malignancy. Unless it's cast out, it'll stay indefinitely. Why the swine should enter my body, I can't conceive. I suppose it's because it's the best he could find about here. Remember those lovely lines of Wordsworth? *The wasp will choose the choicest fruit, The skunk will pick the best-cut suit.* And now could someone help me to orange marmalade? It was in a glorious failure to reach that delicacy that the spasm was induced."

As she charged his plate –

"But what about Thursday?" said Jill.

"If I have to be carried," said Berry, "I'm going to start. Besides, the change of air may make my tenant think. And his passport mayn't be in order."

Cousin Jill had been at White Ladies for nearly three weeks and now was to join her babies, who were at Pau. I was to drive her down, and Berry had declared his intention of coming with us.

"My darling, you can't," said Daphne. "Unless your back is better, you can't start off on a run of six hundred miles."

"We can drop him at Rouen," said I, "if the pain's too bad. *The Hôtel de la Poste* is all right. And I can pick him up there, when I come back."

"That's right," said Berry. "And I shall subsist on squeezed duck – *specialité de la maison*. All the same, I'm not mad about Rouen. If I have to be dropped, I think it should be at Chartres. After all, the *pâtés de Chartres* approach ambrosia."

"As a matter of fact," said I, "you'd be most comfortable at Tours."

"So I should," said Berry. "And the table *The* — keeps is above reproach. They've a pastry-chef there that ought to be canonized. Tours has it – unless, of course, I can go on." He drew my attention to his cup. "I hate to trouble you, brother, but the promotion of that vessel is unhappily beyond my power."

As I passed his cup to Daphne –

"You used to swear," said Jill, "by the table at Angoulême."

"She's right," said Berry. "She's right. Their *omelettes aux truffes* belong to another world. Well, let's make it Angoulême."

I fingered my chin.

"From Angoulême to Pau is not very far, and the aunt of our cousin-in-law has a quite exceptional chef."

"So she has, God bless her," said Berry. "He's a way of doing sweet-breads that makes you swoon. If I get to Angoulême, I'd better go on."

Her elbow upon the table, her chin cupped in a palm –

"How you can do it," said Daphne, "I do not know. Even while you're gorging, you're carefully weighing the chances of where your back will allow you to make a beast of yourself."

"Beloved," said Berry, "I protest. In the ordinary way my victuals mean nothing to me. But when one member fails, one turns for comfort to another. The small of my back gives in. What more natural than that I should look for consolation to, er, its opposite number. When you have a headache, I order the best champagne."

"I don't care," said his wife. "It's indecent. When Chartres is mentioned, most people think of the cathedral. You don't. You think of *foie gras*."

"Not *foie gras*," said Berry. "Partridge. Besides, I do think of the cathedral. I remember it perfectly. Hell of a flight of steps and a wicked wind. Will somebody pick up my napkin? I want to blow my nose."

"Today," said Daphne, "is Monday. Unless you are very much better, to leave for Pau on Thursday will be the act of a fool. And what about lunch tomorrow? You can't go on like this when strangers are here."

With infinite care, her husband rose to his feet. Then he looked majestically round.

"I trust," he said, "that my guests will lament their host's distress." With that, he turned – just too sharply, and let out a roar of pain. "And now I'm stuck, good and proper. Afraid to move. Don't sit there, staring, like so many Barbary apes. Get a litter or bier or something, to carry me on. But you'll have to be very careful. No 'by numbers', thank you. I've got to be moved in one piece."

"Don't be absurd," said Daphne.

"I'm not being absurd," screamed her husband. "I tell you, I'm in a strait jacket. If a tiger burst into the room, I couldn't withdraw."

"I bet you'd try," said Jill.

"You impious child," said Berry. "You wicked, irreverent siren. Here am I, your overlord, for some inscrutable reason struck down in my prime, and, so far from succouring me, you actually deride a spectacle before which the very stones would cry out. That's why I don't go on the terrace. Supposing the flags were to rise up and call me blessed."

Here the door was opened, and Falcon came in.

"Captain Rage is here, sir. If you can give him ten minutes, he will be much obliged."

"Of course," said Berry. "Show him into the library."

"Very good, sir."

As Falcon withdrew –

"Whatever's the matter?" said Daphne. "It's only just ten."

"Heaven knows – with Toby. I only hope he hasn't run somebody down."

Toby Rage was a very good friend of ours. So was Mrs Medallion, Toby's aunt. Toby was staying with her, some twenty miles off. The two were – dissimilar. Each had a heart of gold: but, while in Toby's case this was evident, Mrs Medallion's goodwill was not immediately apparent. Her outlook was strict, and she had not moved with the times: but Toby was up to date. His excellent aunt was proposing to make him her heir: in return, she demanded a behaviour which Toby did his best to observe.

Berry shuffled towards the door, in the wake of Daphne and Jill. I followed behind, to render such aid as I could.

As we gained the library –

"My dears," said Toby, "I'm in it up to the chin – and, though you'll hardly believe it, for once it is *not my fault*. I've been at Rokesby ten days, and I've never put a foot wrong. Family prayers at eight – I've always been on parade. Blood and tears for one, but I've never been late. I've never smoked in my bedroom; I've squired the Vicar's daughters; I've taken the sack round in Church. You never saw such a show. There was I, at the end of the pew, when a beery wallah looms up with a velvet pouch. I tried to shove something in it, but he wouldn't have that. 'Don't be a fool,' says Aunt Ira. 'He wants you to take it round.' 'But I'm not a lay-reader,' says I. 'The presumption is,' says she, 'you're an honest man. Accept it at once.' You know, I'm not made for such things... And now, when I've flown all these fences, an onlooker crosses the course an' brings me down."

"Expound, Sir Belch," said Berry. "How can a stranger have put you wrong with the aunt?"

"Not his fault, either," said Toby. "The old bogey means no wrong. But they've both of them got the stick by the dirty end. And I'm damned if I blame them – it's fairly plastered with dung. But if they don't drop it, I'm sunk. I give you my word, I'm half-way down the drain."

As Berry let himself carefully into an easy chair –

"Toby dear," said Daphne, "please give us the facts. You know that, if we can help – "

"You can't do that," said Toby. "Nobody can. But at least you will believe me: and that's what I want. I have my faults as you know; but the widow an' orphan are safe from blokes like me. And I don't go about denuding elderly bogeys at dead of night. And that's the offence I'm charged with – and what they believe I've done."

I took Captain Rage by the shoulder and gave him a cigarette.

"And now come down," I said. "We'll have the high lights later. Tell us exactly what's happened from first to last."

"I expect you're right," said Toby. "Well, here we go.

"Aunt Ira's solicitor is one Congreve of Bedford Row. He's on the aged side, but a nice old duck. She won't go to see him, so he has to come to her. He came down yesterday, said his piece in the evening and stayed the night. Have you ever been over Rokesby?"

We shook our heads.

"We know the ground floor," said Daphne. "I have been upstairs, but I can't remember the rooms."

"Well, right at the end of the house, there's a very old wing. Fifteenth century, I think, but it's old as old. And there's the hell of a chamber – it's called the Arras Room. I'll say it gives you the willies on Midsummer Day. Stone walls, hung with black arras from bottom to top: a huge four-poster, hung with black curtains again: and a yawning fireplace that looks like the mouth of Hell. Talk about deaths and burials... I wouldn't have slept in that boudoir for a thousand golden pounds. I mean, it *must* be haunted. It issues a standing invitation to every ghost within range. If you ask me, the swine feel at home there. But that's by the way.

"Now once, years ago, I stated this obvious fact. I said I thought it likely that apparitions frequented the Arras Room..." Toby covered his eyes and sighed. "I can still remember the scene that innocent chatter provoked. You might have thought I'd suggested that she should attend a celebration of the Black Mass. You see, Aunt Ira doesn't believe in ghosts. More. For anyone who does, she has a violent contempt. That her own flesh and blood – to say nothing of her heir presumptive – should so much as toy with such a notion constituted a deadly insult to the ancient house of Rage.

"Well, I learned my lesson all right and from that day to this I've kept my beliefs to myself. From that day to this..."

Toby leaned forward.

"This morning I came down as usual at five to eight. But not to family prayers. These had been cancelled. Instead, the butler desires me to go to the drawing-room. There are Aunt Ira and Congreve, looking like blocks of black ice. When I asked what the trouble was, they spoke of shame and horror, of vulgar outrage and gross effrontery. 'Monstrous' and 'abominable' were among their epithets. In a word, it seemed very clear that I had given offence.

"Well, of course I'm used to Aunt Ira. She's old and she's built that way. Thorns to burn, but she's been a good rose to me. But Congreve had no right to speak to me as he did. So I took him on. I said that he was a lawyer, and I was not; but that I'd always understood that it was a principle of law that, before a bloke was convicted, he should be informed of the charge. That shook him, I think, for he looked at me very hard. And then he stated his case.

"At half-past ten last night he retired – to the Arras Room. About half-past one this morning he woke, to find his feet cold. This was not surprising, because they were not covered up. The bed-clothes – sheet and blankets – had been untucked and turned back from the foot of the bed. Well, he thought that was very queer, but supposed that in his sleep he'd loosened and kicked them off. So he wraps up his toes again and goes back to sleep. At two o'clock he wakes up, to find the clothes going away – being drawn off his body and over the foot of the bed. He seizes the sheet and holds it with all his might: but the blankets go on – he feels them sliding away. And his sheet's being pulled. He calls out, but nobody answers: and nobody hears him, of course, 'cause he's too far off. There's no electric light, so he gets a knee on the sheet and feels for a match. As he finds the box, the sheet goes away, and, when he can light his candle, there are the clothes on the floor at the foot of the bed. As he looks round the room, the candle goes out; and when he lights it again, there's nobody there.

"That is Congreve's tale; and I've not the slightest doubt that it's perfectly true. That blasted room is haunted and always was; and some damned ghost or other was doing his stuff last night. But the point is *they think it was me*. Neither Aunt Ira nor Congreve can accept the supernatural: you might as well ask them to believe in a well-read giraffe. They are, therefore, forced to the conclusion that the outrage was committed by me. The servants, of course, are washed out – they're all too old. But Captain Toby Rage… If history may be believed, some fifty years ago the practical joke was the vogue, and its most faithful exponent was the dashing young Guardsman. And Aunt Ira the Good and Congreve still live in seventy-five.

"Net result – Congreve is 'inexpressibly pained and never would have believed'; Aunt Ira is 'horrified and filled with the utmost disgust' – and so incensed that she can hardly sit still; Toby is sunk. You see, it's a matter of deduction. If it wasn't a ghost, it was Toby: and as ghosts don't exist, then it must have been me. And I went to bed at eleven, and never woke up till Sarah brought me my tea. Incidentally, you wouldn't get me into the Arras Room after dark for any money."

There was a little silence.

Then –

"Has Congreve gone?" said Berry.

"You bet," said Toby. "He had an appointment in Town at twelve o'clock. Besides, he's a Will to alter. What do I do?"

"You go back and take your leave – very respectfully, of course. You feel that you cannot stay any longer in a house in which your solemn word is disbelieved. Even your aunt's house. If ever she should have occasion to vary the unhappy conclusion to which she has come, nothing will give you greater pleasure than to return."

"She won't," said Toby. "Why should she? You know, I don't blame the old girl. She doesn't *want* to think that I have insulted her guest, but her outlook leaves her no alternative. If someone could shake her conviction that ghosts do not exist – "

"I hope they will," said Berry, "almost at once." We all regarded him. "Tomorrow two eminent men are coming to lunch with us. One is a distinguished art-critic: the other is Wrotham, the well-known architect. Wrotham we know – slightly; and a very nice fellow he is. But we don't know Basing at all, except by repute. For all that, here and now, I'm going to ring him up. You see, he's not only a critic. He is also the president of some society or other that believes in and investigates the activities of what are called ghosts."

Toby went down on his knees.

I shall always consider that Berry did very well.

He spoke to Thomas Basing and shortly told him the facts. Then he asked him to visit Congreve without delay. "Much will depend," he told him, "on how you handle this man, for Congreve alone can procure you admission to Rokesby Hall. If you shake Congreve, he will shake Mrs Medallion – enough to make her receive you and hear what you say. Then, after lunching with us, you can drive over to Rokesby and see the Arras Room. Perhaps she will let you sleep there, if that should be your desire."

Basing was greatly excited and promised to act at once. And so he must have done, for that afternoon he rang up, to say that he had seen Congreve, who was returning to Rokesby the following day. "Mrs Medallion will receive me at four o'clock. Whether I can convince her, I do not know. But Congreve is clearly shaken and dreads that a grave injustice may have been done."

Toby Rage had withdrawn to his Club; and there we had undertaken to ring him up. But not until after dinner. In any event it was better that he should keep out of the way.

Berry glanced at his watch and, using the greatest caution, rose to his feet.

"The stage," he declared, "is set. If Mrs Medallion determines to stop her ears, there's an end of the matter – and Toby, too. Of course she's a very hard case, and more than once, in the past, our Toby has put a foot wrong. But Basing sounded all right and he's got some way. That Congreve's returning to Rokesby is excellent news. And now I'm going to shamble about the lawn. It can't make my back any worse, and I must have some air."

"I'll come in five minutes," said Daphne. "I must see Bridget about the laundry-maid."

(As her mother before her, Bridget Ightham had risen to be our housekeeper: and, as her mother before her, she had come to command our affection and our respect.)

Jill and I made our way to the tennis-court...

"Poor Toby," said my small cousin. "I do think Mrs Medallion should take his word."

"So she should," said I. "Except to save another, Toby would never lie. The lady is in a cleft stick. If she takes Toby's word, she must allow that there are such things as ghosts. And that she cannot do. Ghosts are to her as miracles are to us. We don't believe in miracles. And – "

"I do," said Jill simply.

"I know, my sweet. But then you have a faith that most of us don't possess."

"I can't see why," said Jill. "Why we all shouldn't have it, I mean. I've never seen a miracle done, but when you look at the world – and the dawn and the dusk and the seasons…a frosty night without a breath of wind or a cloud in the sky… I know people take them for granted, but those are miracles, Boy. Of course they were done a great many years ago, and I suppose we've got used to them. But when you think of putting the sun in the heaven or even of growing an oak from a tiny acorn, the size of my finger-tip – well, it isn't such a great matter to make a lame man walk."

"That's very true," said I. "And I'll give you this – if more people had your faith, I think we should see more miracles done today."

"It's science," said Jill. "And Mrs Medallion's like science. She can't believe a thing, unless she can understand it. And that's pre-presumptionous. Our brains aren't big enough. And the silly thing is that she'll watch a conjurer and say how clever he is; but she's not the slightest idea how he does his tricks. And it's just the same with science. When a conjurer does his stuff – a good one, I mean, they say it's marvellous. They can't think how he does it, and things like that. But when the dawn comes up, it's up to them to explain the miracle."

It is written, 'Out of the mouth of babes and sucklings…'

Before we had finished two games, a screech of pain, that rose from the lawn to rend the evening air, suggested that Berry had had another attack: but when the screech was succeeded by roars for help, we left the court and ran as fast as we could.

Berry was down on all fours, in the midst of the lawn: and The Bold and Nobby were barking and leaping about him in heathenish ecstasy. As we arrived, The Bold contrived to scramble upon his back – a king-of-the-castle effect, to which Nobby at once subscribed by launching furious assaults. Such massage was too rough and too ready for Berry's complaint; yet such was the state of his muscles that to disperse his assailants was quite beyond his power. And so he fell back upon his lungs…

As Daphne, Bridget and Falcon came running out of the house, Jill snatched The Bold from his 'castle', and I seized Nobby and put him under my arm. But Berry continued to bellow, crawling about the lawn like an anthropoid ape, till Daphne and Falcon, between them, had got him on to his feet.

"What ever happened?" said Daphne.

"I must have an injection," said Berry. "You know, when the heart's very weak, they – "

"Don't be a fool," said his wife.

"I'm not being a fool," screamed Berry. "I've had a great shock. My pulse is irregular. I can't find the swine, but it can't be anything else. A brandy and soda, Falcon: I'm not as good as I was."

"At once, sir," said Falcon, turning towards the house.

"And a hot-water bottle, Bridget. Not here. In the library."

"I wish, sir," said Bridget, "you'd let me iron your back."

Berry stifled a scream.

"I'm sorry," he said. "It's just the shocking picture the words present. You know. The mere idea of adding hot iron to my flesh – a flesh already tortured beyond belief, is almost more than the mind of man can bear. You see, if you were to scorch me, I should go out of my mind. My cries would be heard in Brooch. Compline would be interrupted, and – "

"Oh, I shouldn't do that, sir. The iron wouldn't be that hot. And it always does father good."

"So be it," said Berry. "I can't go on like this. What hour will be convenient?"

"When you're in bed, sir," said Bridget. "The very last thing."

"You're very good. Shall we say half-past ten?"

"Whenever you please, sir. You've only to send for me."

"Make it half-past ten, if you please."

As Bridget withdrew –

"And now what happened?" said Jill.

"I dropped the matches," said Berry. "No more than that. A simple and innocent *faux pas* which even the Earl of Chesterfield could not condemn. But, such is the malignancy of my tenant, I could not retrieve the box without going down upon my knees. I, therefore, adopted a posture, convenient, but unbecoming and, indeed, reminiscent of the great Nebuchadnezzar, who, if History may be believed, cropped and devoured herbage, even as the beasts that perish, to the great scandal of mankind. Very well. Having, by numbers, assumed this inelegant pose, I was in the very act of seizing the box, when The Bold appeared from nowhere and stole it away. Of course I crawled after the swine – to his great delight, entreating, conjuring and threatening without avail. Looking more like a gargoyle than ever, he bore the box off in his mouth, always just out of range, with his tail mast-high. I tell you, I could have done murder: my condition, however, was precluding common assault. Congestion of the brain was at hand, when Nobby arrived… With that abnormal instinct upon which you all insist with a frequency which is quite sickening, that paragon saw in a flash that The Bold and I were engaged in a gorgeous game. Whimpering with understanding, he flung himself with rapture into the ring, and before I could get my breath, the two were giving points to the priests of Baal. I was the sacrifice. To rise was beyond my power: and, so long as I remained couchant, I was the goods. Protest was unavailing: indeed, the more rabid my abuse, the faster and more furious became the fun. Bear-baiting wasn't in it. When I sought to grab either sportsman, the gesture served to swell the frolicsome tide. You see, I was pulling my weight. When I missed Nobby's tail, the two of them squealed with mirth – and then returned pell-mell to avenge the abortive assault. My efforts at self-preservation were read as invitations to quicken the pace: my screams were so many halloos: frenzy inspired frenzy, and if you hadn't come when you did, I should have been disembowelled before my eyes."

As Falcon arrived with a salver, Jill addressed the Sealyham, now lying along the sward.

"Poor Berry," she said, pointing. "He's got a bad back."

Nobby is nothing if not sympathetic. In a flash he was up and was leaping, to lick the invalid's nose. Instinctively Berry recoiled – very slightly, of course, but enough to bring into play the muscles which were in balk. That there might be no doubt about this, he let out a yell which must have been heard for miles, clawed hold of Daphne and began to declaim the notice which he wished to appear in *The Times*.

On the twenty-second of August, after incredible suffering and in great agony, BERTRAM, only husband of...

Whilst Jill detained Nobby, I poured the brandy and soda and put the glass into his hand.

"That'll help you up," I said.

Berry took a long draught. Then –

"Oblige me," he said, "by removing these adorable dogs. Lock them up in a cupboard or something, till horse-play's once more in my line. Of course – "

"Not that one, you don't," said a voice. "I've just come here to get him. That's my dog."

As we all swung round, except Berry –

"Good God, more Cokers," said the latter. "Lock them up, too."

A fat man, in plus-fours, was standing six feet away. At rest in the drive was a very large limousine. We had not observed his approach nor that of his car, because, of course, of the flurry to which we had just subscribed.

For a moment we stared upon him.

Then –

"You've made a mistake," I said.

"Not likely," said the other.

"Which dog do you mean?" said Daphne.

"The Peke, in course," said the stranger. "My wife recognized him, she did. Drivin' past in the car, we were; an' she says, 'There 'e is.' "

I turned to look at the road, at least ninety paces away.

"Your wife," I said, "must have astonishing sight."

"She 'as," said the other, shortly. "Come 'ere, Lychee."

Thus addressed, The Bold surveyed him with great contempt.

Berry was speaking.

"He doesn't seem to know you," he said. "May I ask when you lost him?"

That a great deal hung upon the answer, I need not say. That the Chinaman, now in jail, had stolen the dog, I found it hard to believe. Still, if it came to a show-down, to say that the dice would be loaded is putting it low.

"Ten days ago," said the stranger. We breathed again. "I'd know him anywhere."

"Then you've made a mistake," said Berry. "We're taking care of that dog, and he's been with us for a month. I think that settles the matter. Good afternoon."

"Don't talk silly," said the other. "My wife don't make mistakes. That there's her dog, an' – "

Jill let fly.

"How can it be her dog? It was here for twenty days before her dog was lost."

"It may 'ave been more than ten days."

185

"That won't do," said Berry. "Your wife has made a mistake, and you'd better withdraw."

"Wot, without the dog? 'Ere, Lychee."

The Bold stared at the speaker, as though he were filth. As the man took a step towards him, Nobby let out a growl.

A woman's voice came from the car.

"Don't stand there arguin', Walter. I want my dog."

Walter turned and lumbered back to the car. After a violent discussion, he turned again. As he came up –

"It's her dog all right," he said. "An' she wants him back. Can't be sure when he went missing. Maybe three weeks."

Berry expired. Then –

"It is very easy," he said, "to say that a dog is yours. Lots of blackguards do it, because it's an easy way of getting something for nothing, at somebody else's expense."

"If you think – "

"The dog cannot deny it, because he cannot speak. But, if the present owner denies what you say, then you must prove what you say before you can take the dog. You can prove nothing. The dog does not know you, nor does he know his name. When asked when you lost him, at first you say ten days and then three weeks. I *can* prove that this dog has been here a month. Of your capacity for mathematics, I know nothing: but your standard must be deplorably low if you are unable to deduce that the dog which your wife has lost was not yet lost when this dog was put in my charge."

"Can' 'elp that," said the other. "That's my wife's dog, an' I'm goin' to take it away."

"Quite sure?" said Berry.

"You bet."

"And you're neither deaf nor insane?"

"I 'eard."

Berry turned to Falcon.

"Ring up the police. Say that I'm being molested. They'll know what to do."

"Very good, sir."

As the butler withdrew –

"Did you say 'molested'?" said Walter.

"I did," said Berry. "Are you familiar with the word?"

"In course," said the other, "there's somethin' comin' to you."

"What fun," said Berry. "D'you think it'll wear blue, too?" He turned to Daphne. "Come, my dear. The gorgonzolas are waiting. It's past their feeding time. Falcon will let us know when the van arrives."

With that, ignoring Walter, the two of them strolled away, the two dogs moving with them, as dogs will do.

Jill and I fell in behind them, and, after some hesitation, Walter came stamping behind.

"Say you," he cried, "if you think you can bluff me, you're off your beat. That's my wife's dog, as was stole a month ago. That fits, that does. Besides, she's recognized 'im. Knew 'im at once. If 'er lady's-maid was 'ere..."

Berry spoke over his shoulder.

"An impudent if clumsy attempt to appropriate somebody's dog. We had a case very much like it the other day. The Bench has decided to stamp the practice out."

"What are they charged with?" I cried.

Walter began to slow up.

"From now on, with false pretences. That means they're committed for trial."

"Is bail allowed?" I shouted.

"Not to begin with," mouthed Berry. "When they appear on remand, they can apply again. But the cells at Bloodstock were only lime-washed last year. And remand prisoners are privileged. They get two blankets for one thing, and water at both their meals. Then, again, they're not called till five and they don't have to clean their cells before half-past six. After their run, that is..."

With the tail of my eye, I saw Walter stop in his tracks. Then he turned round, to make his way back to the car.

"See him off," I said to Nobby, and grabbed The Bold.

That Walter had no lumbago was just as well. Nobby gave tongue as he landed, two inches from Walter's heels. I have seldom seen a back hollowed with such efficiency. But a horse laugh from his chauffeur seemed to send the blood to his head. He shook his fist at the man and then launched a kick at Nobby that would have done credit to any goalkeeper. As well launch a kick at a fire-fly or one of the swallows, darting below the eaves. While his foot was still in mid-air, the Sealyham bit him sharply in the calf of his other leg.

Their eyes now decently averted, Daphne and Jill were fairly shaking with mirth, but Berry's mouth never twitched. For me, the most humorous feature was Walter's chauffeur's delight. Leaning well out of his window, the fellow let himself go, laughing as a clod at a circus, when a clown sits down on a chair that has been withdrawn. That this should enrage his master was natural enough; and, ignoring the stream of instruction released by his wife, Walter turned upon his servant and rent him savagely.

His back being turned towards us, we could not hear what he said; but, so far from mending his manner, the chauffeur laughed the more and then indicated Nobby, who was considerately waiting till his prey should be disengaged.

"I should 'ave that one," he jeered. " 'E's taken a fency to you."

Such provocation was dreadful, and must, I felt, be followed by battery: but Walter had a shot in his locker he had not used.

What he said, I do not know; but the statement stung his servant, as no reproaches had done.

In a flash the door was open and the chauffeur was down in the drive. As his master recoiled before him, Mrs Walter emerged, screaming – a lady of many inches and worthy, in other respects, of Walter's love. And as the three joined issue, a police car came to rest, ten paces away.

Superintendent Fellows appeared, with the local sergeant behind.

There was no mistaking his words – Fellows had mastered the art of producing his voice.

"What's all this?"

The disputants started and turned. Then they stated their cases, each doing his best to shout the other down.

The Superintendent let fly.

"This isn't the Mile End Road. You can't behave like this in private grounds. You'd better come to the station and settle it there. Get back in your car and follow the police car out."

As a constable turned the police car, his superiors shepherded the trio into the limousine. Not without many protests, which gave way to recrimination, when the former were found to be vain.

"Now you done it," bawled the chauffeur.

Master and mistress were at pains to refute the charge.

As the sergeant took his seat by the chauffeur, Fellows crossed the lawn and put a hand to his hat.

"Good evening, madam. Good evening, sir. I happened to be at the station when you rang up. As long as they go, I take it that's all you want."

"That's all, Superintendent. Sorry to bring you round."

"I'm very glad I was there, sir. I expect the lady's the trouble. The money goes to their heads. And the husband's life isn't worth living, unless he backs her up."

Which goes to show that Fellows knew his world.

As the cortège disappeared –

"If anyone can tell me," said Berry, "why we should be selected to be the butts of wallahs like Walter and Coker Falk – I mean, we seem to attract them. This place is becoming a resort of predatory skunks. Of course, such conduct was unheard-of before the war: but now, because somebody fancies what we possess, they dare to enter our grounds and demand that we shall humour their filthy desires." Mechanically he lowered his voice. "As a matter of hard fact, this dog business might have been damned awkward. If they'd said the dog had been lost a month ago…

"He was much smaller then," said Daphne. "And nobody could have known him ninety yards off."

"I know, I know," said Berry. "But if they'd pursued the matter, we should have had a nice case. 'We're looking after the dog for a friend of ours. Yes, the friend is away… Oh, I think he'll be back soon, but I know he's very busy just now… Well, care of The Governor, His Majesty's Prison, Brooch, will always find him. Yes, it's a funny address, isn't it? No, I'm afraid I don't know his name…' Talk about prejudice. We couldn't have come into court."

"I suppose," said my sister slowly, " I suppose it is all right. I mean…"

"I suppose so," said Berry.

"Anyway," said Jill, "he's much better off with us. Even if he is their dog, they don't even know when they lost him. And I'm sure they'd give him chocolates and things like that."

"I'll make you two bets," said I. "The first is that the Chinaman claims him, when he has done his time. The second is that, when he sees how he is living, he asks us to keep The Bold. If he does that, it will prove that the dog is his."

"And there's wisdom," said Berry. "Well, we shall see. But I'm not going to take either bet, for the odds are too long."

At eleven the following morning Mrs Medallion called.

"I might have known," she declared, "that my nephew would come to you."

"I hope," said Daphne, "I hope you're glad that he did."

"Of course I am, my dear. You're desirable company." The lady surveyed us. "And so you've entered the ring?"

"Not on your life," said Berry. "As Basing was coming to lunch here, I naturally put him in touch with Congreve, before he came. I'm sure you'll agree it's my duty to humour my guests?"

Mrs Medallion looked at him very hard.

"Your interpretation," she said, "of the laws of hospitality is wide indeed."

My brother-in-law swallowed.

"We, er, do our best," he said.

Mrs Medallion frowned.

"Do you subscribe to this preposterous trash?"

"We're forced to," said Daphne quickly. "I mean, Mr Congreve and Toby are, both of them, men of their word."

"My dear," said Mrs Medallion, "I have always sought to be just. But I must decline to let sentiment warp my sense. Only a mind diseased could credit an apparition with common assault."

Jill took her seat on the arm of the lady's chair.

"We've all heard ghost stories," she said. "Whether they're true or not, I couldn't say. But we've heard them told and sometimes we've read them in books. And in some of the worst ones, people have been found hurt." Mrs Medallion stiffened. "Mr Congreve was shamefully treated: and he might have caught a very bad cold. Supposing – just supposing that he had been actually harmed. Almost smothered, or something. Then you'd have *known* that Toby wasn't to blame."

Mrs Medallion looked up at my cousin's eager face.

"My darling," she said, "you've made a very good point. If Congreve had been choked, that Toby had done it would never have entered my head. But pranks stop short of grievous bodily harm... Years ago my nephew made an idle, wanton remark. He said it was his belief that the Arras Room was haunted. Well, I was greatly incensed. That my brother's son should subscribe to so grotesque a belief provoked me very deeply, and I must confess I laid on. I well remember the scene, and Toby, of course, remembers it equally well. Then Congreve comes to stay, and, since the other rooms are being done up, I give instructions for him to be given the Arras Room. Here, then, is Toby's chance to prove the truth of his contention. No harm would be done to Congreve, but I should have to accept the lawyer's word."

"That's not like Toby," said my sister.

Mrs Medallion swallowed.

"No," she said. "It isn't. I'll give you that. And it isn't like Toby to lie. And yet am I to believe that some supernatural agency committed a vulgar assault?"

"One moment," said I. "From what you've just said, I gather that, if another room had been available, you would not have had Mr Congreve put in the Arras Room. If I am not impertinent, may I ask why?"

Mrs Medallion frowned.

"A family prejudice," she said. "My grandfather's grandfather died there in 1754."

"That was Rage of Chelsea?" said Berry.

"So he was called. The room was hung in black for his obsequies, and, for some reason or other, the arras was never changed." The lady's chin went up. "I see you know the reason."

"I can guess it," said Berry. "What I did not know was that he died in that room."

I knew the story, too.

When he was growing old, Rage of Chelsea had married a second wife. At the time of his death, his son and heir was away, and before he could get to Rokesby, the dead man was under ground. That the funeral had been hurried seems to have been beyond doubt. After hearing the report of the servants, her stepson accused the widow of causing his father's death. Poison. No proceedings were taken, but the widow had left the country within the month.

"Are you going to suggest that he haunts it?"

"No," said Berry, "I'm not. But I do observe that you honour 'a family prejudice'."

"That," said Mrs Medallion, "is perfectly true. But you don't have to sleep in the cupboard in which your skeleton lies."

"Why not?" said Berry.

"Because decency forbids. Rightly or wrongly, the room was preserved as a mortuary chapel."

"Surely wrongly," said Berry. "Half the bedrooms in England would be preserved, if a bedroom couldn't be used because someone or other had died within its walls."

"The presumption in this case is that Rage of Chelsea died an unnatural death. The hangings record this notion."

"Which you accepted and honoured, until last Sunday night."

"That," said Mrs Medallion, "is perfectly true. Since I returned to Rokesby, no one has occupied that room. Had it been convenient, they would have – be sure of that. But as, until Congreve came, there were other rooms, the Arras Room has not been occupied." She threw a defiant look round. "I suppose you think you've cornered me now."

"By no means," said Berry. "But I think it will interest Basing, if I may tell him these facts. I mean, it's down his street."

"What a singularly sordid expression – 'down his street'. By the way, what is his street?"

"He's a fellow of Magdalen," said Berry. "At least he used to be. But some years ago he deserted the cloister for the gallery. He is a great authority upon oil-painting. They call him in when somebody questions a Rembrandt – and then he finds a Durer under a Maes. I've never met the man, but Wrotham asked if he could bring him. We've got a Claude he's heard of, and – "

"Not George Wrotham – the architect?"

"That's right."

"Bless my soul," said Mrs Medallion. "I used to play with George Wrotham when I was ten years old. They lived two doors from us in Curzon Street. Send him along with Basing – I'd like to see him again." That the stars were fighting for Toby was very clear. "And now go on about Basing."

"His profession of critic apart, he has for some years displayed an interest in what some people call the supernatural. He has visited many houses which have the reputation of having haunted rooms. He has investigated their, er, attributes. As a result, he has formed certain conclusions. What these are, I don't know. But I know that a case like this would interest him no end. If he thinks Toby's guilty, he'll say so – be sure of that."

"And I'm to accept what ever this expert says?"

"Certainly not," said Berry. "But I hope that you'll weigh his conclusions, because he has studied these things – but we have not."

"He seems to have frightened Congreve."

"To be perfectly frank," said Berry, "I think he's made Congreve think."

"An operation which, in your case, would have been superfluous."

"Yes," said Berry boldly. "Because I know Toby Rage. Had Toby played this trick, he would never have come to us and told us the tale."

Mrs Medallion winced.

"Another odious expression. Why the devil can't you talk English? 'Told us the tale.' Never mind. I see your point. The accused consults his solicitor. Though Toby had lied to me, he'd never have lied to you."

"Never," said Jill stoutly.

Mrs Medallion rose.

"I must be going," she said. "You four have made me uneasy – and that's the truth. Have no fear that I shan't recover. Before I'm back at Rokesby, I shall have hardened my heart. And when Basing comes, I'll put him where he belongs."

"What a vital expression," said Berry. " 'Where he belongs.' "

Mrs Medallion glared. Then she sat down again, put a hand to her eyes and began to shake with laughter.

At ten o'clock that night, we heard the sound of a car. One minute later Basing was ushered into the library.

"I'm really ashamed," he said, "to behave like this. A stranger uses White Ladies as though it were an hotel."

"Counteract that impression," said Daphne, "by staying on. And now sit down, Mr Basing, and give us your news."

As I poured him a whiskey and soda –

"All's very well," said our guest. "By Mrs Medallion's desire, Congreve has spoken this evening with Captain Rage. He's going to see him tomorrow, and Captain Rage is returning the same afternoon."

"Well done," said everyone.

"To you the credit," said Basing. "I may have carried the fortress, but you had breached the walls. The lady was not even hostile. I took care to tell her plainly that I could not prove what I said. I could tell her what I believed and must leave it at that. Congreve was very helpful, and Sir George was a tower of strength."

"What do you believe?" said Berry.

"I believe that Rage of Chelsea met his death by poison at the hand of his second wife. Now the poison which such a woman would be able to obtain was probably very fierce, and anyone seeing his features would know that the victim had died a violent death. In those days it was the fashion for the dead man to lie in state in the chamber in which he died. While the body was there, the household and tenants were marshalled and passed through the room. And now mark this. The features of the corpse were exposed...

"My belief is this – that in this particular case the features were *not* exposed, because they would have declared that Rage of Chelsea had died a violent death. I believe that the sheet was drawn up and over the face. That was, no doubt, the 'report' which the servants made – upon which the son and heir accused his step-mother.

"Well, now we come to the fence.

"Assume that the murdered man's spirit, though it had left his body, was still in the Arras Room. What would have been its impulse – its burning desire, when it saw the file of servants passing the corpse? *To withdraw the sheet and reveal how their master had met his death.*

"It is my solemn belief that that poor ghost acquired too late the energy which it so much desired: that now, demented and helpless, it still frequents the scene; and that, on Sunday night, finding a body lying as once its own had lain, it set to work to strip it, because that impulse rules it and always will."

There was a little silence.

Then –

"Speaking for myself," said Daphne, "I think your interpretation is terribly good."

"It's pure surmise," said Basing. "It can be nothing else. But I have always found that where one has reason to think that some old wrong has been done, from there the strongest evidence of the supernatural will be reported."

"Oh, I'm sure you're right," said Jill. "But it's terribly sad."

"According to my observation, these things always are. The ghost is a tragedy."

"You were lucky in Congreve," said Berry.

"Indeed I was. He is the ideal witness in such a case. He didn't believe in ghosts and he is a practical man. And here is a curious thing. The most startling reports I receive are from practical men. Ghosts seem to turn to them – I can't say why."

"And the lady?" said I.

"She goes as far as this – that if Congreve, Sir George and I believe that on Sunday night some supernatural agency was at work, she is not prepared to withstand the conclusions of three such men. (Congreve, of course, is a convert. His one idea is that Captain Rage shall be righted without delay.) She did not deny her reluctance to use the Arras Room. And when I asked why she was reluctant, she was attractively frank. 'You can have your trick,' she said. 'I'll confess to a superstition of which I am deeply ashamed. I *felt* that it shouldn't be used – and that's the truth.'

"That meant I was halfway home. And of course it explained so much. When Rage said the room was haunted, years ago, although he didn't know it, he was flicking her on the raw. He was affirming the belief of which she was so much ashamed. And so she went off the deep end. And she wouldn't believe him on Monday, because she was sticking so hard to her self-respect.

"She insisted on my staying to dinner – that you know. And when I was going, she said a most charming thing. 'I'm a stiff-necked old fool, Mr Basing. But when I let Toby go, it tore my heart. He's all I've got, you see. Thank you very much for giving him back.' "

All our arrangements had been made.

The Rolls was ready and waiting, and we were to leave for France on Thursday at three o'clock. That night we should cross from Newhaven to Dieppe: and the following evening we hoped to arrive at Pau. This would mean a run of more than five hundred miles; but the Rolls and I could do it – provided the roads were good. The traffic was then so slight that I knew I could count it out. But if the roads were 'patchy'… Anyway, it would be an adventure.

But when, on Thursday morning, Berry came down to breakfast at ten o'clock and then asked me to help him to take his seat, I added my weight to my sister's arguments.

"You're not fit to do it," I said. "Damn it, *my* back will be aching before we get to Bordeaux."

"Good," said Berry. "That'll learn you. As a matter of hard fact, the only ease I've known in the last five days is when I've been in the Rolls. That back seat's just right – far better than any chair."

"Perhaps it is," said I, "for forty or fifty miles at twenty-five miles an hour. But we've got to shift tomorrow: and five hundred miles is the very deuce of a run."

"I won't be thwarted," said Berry. "I will have my change of air."

"But, my darling," said Daphne, "it's absurd. This morning you come down at ten."

"That's not my fault," said Berry. "It took me nearly ten minutes to leave the bath. I occupied it all right, but the evacuation was fearful. And then I couldn't dry between my toes."

"I begged you to let me help you."

"I know, I know, my sweet. But you'd only have strained yourself. What I need is a crane."

"And tomorrow you leave – not the bath, but the ship at half-past five."

Berry stifled a scream – and drank heavily before replying.

"That's – that's all right," he said. "I'll forgo my bath tomorrow. Then I shan't have to get up before half-past three. That'll be just cock-crow, won't it? You know, I never did like fowls."

"But it'll kill you," cried Daphne.

"No, it won't," said her husband. "I shall let a steward into my secret, and he can do up my shoes. That'll save me twenty minutes. And at Rouen we'll stop at a barber's, and I can be shaved."

"That's just what we can't do," said I. "We shan't have time. Besides, the shops won't be open. I hope to be clear of Rouen by half-past six."

"Chartres will do," said Berry.

"Look here," said I. "I don't want to spoil your fun. But I want to get Jill to Pau by tomorrow night. Well, I shan't do that if I'm driving an ambulance."

Berry expired.

"Can you get this?" he said. "I am *not* a sick man. I'm not suffering from typhoid or pneumonia or even bubonic plague. I don't think I've ever felt better. But certain muscles in what is called 'the small' of my back are temporarily out of

198

commission, thus putting it beyond my power to move with that careless carriage which ordinarily distinguishes not only my goings out, but my comings in. This condition has its inconveniences. Should a loved one let fall her nose-wipe, I should be unavoidably prevented from restoring that humble but necessary appendage. But it does not prevent me from being transported from one locality to another. My temperature will not rise – "

"Mine will," said I. "If we strike a bad patch, you'll yell that you're being murdered and that if I don't slow down – "

"In such an unlikely case, I shall withdraw. As previously contemplated, I shall leave the automobile at the next convenient town. The French are very solicitous. The moment they hear my screams – "

"I can see," said I, "that we're in for a lively run. Fancy threading a market town with somebody yelling blue murder down every street."

Daphne cupped her face in her hands and looked at me.

"I wouldn't come with you," she said, "for fifty thousand pounds."

"My sweet," said Berry, "listen. I know this blasted complaint. Unless I take some action, it may very well continue for two or three weeks. No treatment is any earthly. Bridget the Good has ironed me – without the slightest result. But a change of air may do it – a startling change. And that I shall get tomorrow, if I set out today. If I can't go on, I promise I'll stop at Chartres. But I hope that I shall get better with every mile."

"It's very drastic," said Daphne, finger to lip.

"So are my seizures," said Berry. "More than once this morning 'the pains of hell gat hold upon me' – and then some. The worst occasion was when I was engaged with my *coiffure*. You may have heard me exclaim."

"I remember it perfectly," said Daphne.

So did everyone within doors.

"Precisely," said Berry. "And so I seek to lay your alarms by an excursion. Be of good cheer, my poppet. Your lord will return restored." He looked at me. "I believe I could do another kidney. Don't bother to taste it first."

At two of the following morning our packet was berthed at Dieppe. Ten minutes later, the AA man came to my cabin, as I had desired.

"Good morning," I said. "I'm going to disembark at half-past five. Major Pleydell is far from well, and we've got a long way to go. There's two hundred francs for the Customs, if I am on the road at a quarter to six."

"Very good, sir. May I have your papers? They'll be putting the Rolls ashore in a quarter of an hour."

The papers passed.

"And petrol?"

"I'll have two cans here, sir. And then if you'll drive to the garage, we'll fill up there."

"That's the style," said I. "See you at half-past five."

The AA man withdrew, and I went to sleep again for two hours and a half…

From the quay, at half-past five, I watched a procession take shape.

First came Jill, walking backwards and doing her best not to laugh. Then came my brother-in-law, supported by cabin stewards, one upon either side. He was dwelling freely in French on the joys of early rising and confessing to 'a foolish desire' to die in the Pyrenees. As he made to step up on the gangway, he let out a roar of pain, and his two supporters clasped him, imploring him to go gently and not to exhaust himself.

Standing beside me, the only Customs officer on duty was deeply moved. Indeed, it was thanks as much to his emotion as to my two hundred francs that the Rolls slid off the quay at eighteen minutes to six.

As we pulled up at the garage –

"There you are," said Berry. "Who says I don't pull my weight? But for me, you'd have been there for half an hour."

This was true. The bonnet had not been opened and our baggage had not been touched.

Ten minutes later, we whipped past the sleeping hotels and on to the Rouen road.

We met no traffic at all, and the road from Dieppe to Rouen had recently been remade. As we entered the city's suburbs, I glanced at the clock in the dash. Five and twenty minutes to seven. At least, we had started well.

The road out of Rouen was shocking, and, though Berry never complained, I had to slow down. Some of the pot-holes were monstrous. So, for perhaps three miles. But the long, steep bill had been mended; and from there to Pont-de-l'Arche we went like the wind. I whipped the Rolls over the cobbles and let her go at the hill – the long hill that parts the forest, as a barber will part a man's hair. The surface was good, and we scudded up to the crest, as a bird on the wing. But we lost ten minutes in Louviers – more than that: for there it was market-day, and the peasants and all that was theirs were ruling the streets. By the time we were clear of the town, it was five and twenty to eight.

Ten minutes later, we stopped to break our fast by the side of the way…

The morning was big with promise: so far as I saw, there was not a cloud in the sky. Soon it was going to be immensely hot. The countryside was lovely: Husbandry seemed to be at the top of her form.

"It's gorgeous," said Jill. "I knew it was going to be." She turned to Berry, devouring a sausage-roll. "How's your back?"

"It might be worse," said Berry. "Very much worse. Just after leaving Rouen, I thought we'd left the road. In fact, I think I lost consciousness. But except for that explosion of agony, which I trust you will observe I suppressed, my suffering has been more or less normal. And now what about our progress? Are we up to time, brother?"

"I'm afraid we're not," said I. "Sixty miles in just under two hours is no damned good. The French are really hopeless. Louviers, I can forgive. Markets are wholesome things, and I hope they survive. But it's nearly six years since the war, and look at that road out of Rouen – a busy port. Think of the damage done to vehicles using that three-mile stretch."

"That," said Berry, "explains its condition. The *garagistes* of Rouen are paying the Surveyor of the Department five hundred francs a week, so long as that stretch of road is not remade."

"That," said I, "is entirely probable. But if the *garagistes* of all the principal towns on our route have had the same idea – well, we shan't get to Pau tonight."

"Who cares?" said Jill. "I told my babies tomorrow – just in case. At least – I told Meakin to tell them. All the same, why shouldn't we do it? As long as we're in by eleven – we mustn't be later than that."

"I'll do my best, my darling."

"Quite so," said Berry. "Er, quite so. But don't abuse the car. I mean, I should be mentally uneasy if I felt you were doing that. After all, she was constructed to be used on roads – not rockeries."

"Shall I be frank?" said I.

"You can have a stab," said Berry. "From what I've seen of you, I should judge that estate to be beyond your reach."

"Whenever I drive the Rolls, I consider the car first and the passengers afterwards."

"I see," said Berry. "What a very beautiful thought. Is Fitch, whose wages I pay, afflicted with the same outlook?"

I raised my eyebrows.

"I think it more than likely."

"Give me strength," said Berry. "Here am I, a simple – "

With one consent, we hustled him into the car.

202

We made good time to Chartres, and reached the ancient city at half-past nine.

I turned to Berry.

"All right?" I said.

"The faculty of speech," said Berry, "is still retained. I nearly lost it as we were entering Dreux. I am forced to the merciful conclusion that the *garagistes* of Dreux can only afford fifty francs. Never mind. There's quite a good barber – "

"Not on your life," said I. "Besides, you've done your bit."

"Oh, I've shaved all right," said Berry. "But I must have a pine shampoo. They're wonderfully refreshing. Besides, what about the *pâtés*? You can't thread Chartres, without purchasing one of its *pâtés*."

I spoke over my shoulder.

"I'm going to have a damned good try."

"Vandal," said Berry. "Your idle words – "

My cousin raised her voice.

"Let's just look at the windows, Boy. I mean, we can't go past them and not just pay our respects."

"If you put it like that, my sweet..."

I drove to the cathedral forthwith – and there the glory of Chartres detained us for half an hour.

More to silence Berry than anything else, I then made for a shop which purveyed the *pâtés de Chartres*. It was as we were regaining *La Place des Epars* that Cousin Jill let out a cry.

"Stop, Boy, stop. There's Patricia." She leaned out of her window. "Patricia. *Patricia*, darling."

Mrs Simon Beaulieu stopped in her stride. So did most within earshot. Then Jill was out in the street, and Patricia's arms were about her, and everyone was smiling – to see Beauty living with Kindness before their eyes.

It was to our great content that Patricia Bohun, spinster, had married Simon Beaulieu less than a month ago: it was to our great concern that, immediately after their marriage, the two had disappeared. We had an uneasy feeling that here was no honeymoon. Though they were made for each other, they had so little money: and, by her marriage, Patricia had lost what she might have had. And now we had stumbled upon them… Of course we devoted an hour to their splendour of faith and love.

It was long past eleven o'clock when we picked our way out of Chartres. And from Chartres to Pau is more than four hundred miles. Still, the road to Tours was perfect – too good to be true. We crossed the Loire at exactly a quarter-past one.

Behind me, Berry was speaking.

"The hour produces the inn. Not to lunch at *The* — would be evidence of insanity."

"No, you don't," said I. "We've plenty of sausage-rolls."

"Oh, I can't bear it," screamed Berry. "Damn it, we're going right by it: we don't even have to turn off. Thirty minutes of civilization – that's all I ask. Besides, I don't fancy any more sausage-rolls. A cup of cold *Madrilène* – *Oh*, and what about beer? I can't face a sausage-roll without a bottle of beer."

"Be quiet," said Jill. "You had two bottles at Chartres."

"My perspiratory ducts have dealt with them. And one ought to soak the system in weather like this. After all, you water the garden: why not the flesh?"

"We'll stop at a café," I said, "and buy some bottles of beer. And ten minutes later, we'll lunch by the side of the way. There's a steak-and-kidney pie that we haven't touched."

"You can have it for me," snarled Berry.

"That's the idea," said I. "We've got to get on. Of course, if you want to stay here…"

"My back's no worse," said Berry, "if that's what you mean."

"Then we'll do it yet," said I – and spoke as a fool. Ten miles south of Tours, they were mending the road.

We had lunched – I think, very well – and Jill and I were discussing the Beaulieus' happy state, when I sailed round a bend at sixty, to see the shocking apparatus two hundred paces ahead. The epithet is deserved. France does most things by halves – but not her roads. When she remakes a road, she does the whole width at once; and the traffic which has to use it can take its chance.

After ploughing my way through metalling, waiting upon steam-rollers and, finally, helping two mules to drag a laden water-cart out of my path, I coaxed the Rolls on to a surface which would have done yeoman service in one of Chaplin's films. The road had been torn in pieces – and that, for mile after mile.

I was very close to despair when we came to the end of this stretch: but, such is human nature, the sight of a four-mile reach, as straight as a ruler, as smooth as a racing-track, revived the hopes I had had. If we had seen the last of our troubles... I might have known. Three miles south of Chatellerault, without the slightest warning, we flounced clean into a section that might have been planned in Hell.

Only the Surveyor of a Department of France could have issued an order at once so futile and so preposterous. The road, which was pitted with pot-holes, had lately been lavishly tarred. The tar had not been covered, and there had been no rain. The road was no longer a road: it was now a long, long waste of pools of tar.

There are times when I dream of that stretch – some nine miles long. (I should, of course, have turned off. But this was a part of the country I did not know, and I was always hoping that every bend was hiding the end of the tar.) Though we moved at ten miles an hour, our wings were dripping before we had covered two. And a lorry came lurching by, to spatter the windows and wind-screen... As it flung on its way –

"Isn't that nice?" said Berry. "Never mind. They say butter's very good. We'd better have tea at Poitiers. If we save our pats, we can smear them over the door-handles. Then, when we want to get in, we shan't get tar on our gloves. All the same, I can't help feeling they've overdone it. If we meet much more traffic, we shan't be able to see. And I do hope we don't have a puncture. If we do, you must be careful to lay the tools on the step. Otherwise, they might get some tar on them. Oh, I suppose the step's swamped. In that case, I should put them in your pocket... I beg your pardon... Oh, how rude. After all, I was only envisaging such a catastrophe. You see, with my back as it is, I can only advise. And nothing would distress me more than to have to view your embarrassment. Here's another road-hog coming. Put your foot down, brother, and give him some tar to taste."

I did so – with no compunction.

With a howl of apprehension, the driver cowered away...

And then we were half a mile off, but the lorry had come to rest by the side of the way.

Such things are not motoring.

As I have said, our ordeal was nine miles long: but when, two miles short of Ruffec, the same thing started again – the road pock-marked with pot-holes brimming with tar – I determined to turn at that town and hope for the best.

And so I did.

That we could not reach Pau that night was now very clear. I decided to make for Bergerac – not much more than a hundred miles away. Less perhaps; but I only knew my direction and I had not brought a map.

The afternoon was now over, and evening was coming in. And I think we were, all of us, glad of the lesser roads. Their surface was very fair, and because they were none too wide and the wayside trees were full, often enough we drove through a tunnel of living green. Then, again, we ran cheek by jowl with the countryside. We smelled the scent of the meadows and breathed the cool of the woods: we heard the speech of the water, as we passed over a bridge: and these things were better than liquor, after the burden and heat of that trying day.

Only, there were no sign-posts...

"Who cares?" cried Jill. "There never were any sign-posts in fairy-tales."

At half-past seven I stopped by a lazy stream… And Jill produced a sponge… I never remember feeling so much refreshed.

Still, when I re-entered the car, I should have been glad to know where Bergerac lay. We had, of course, asked our way; but that was but waste of time. The French peasant cannot direct. Still, something had to be done. We were, all three, very tired, and though he never complained, I knew that Berry's back was feeling the strain.

And then we ran into St Orlan…

I never had heard of the hamlet; but it seems that fishermen knew it, because it neighbours a water that is a fisherman's dream. And since fishermen must be lodged – and some of them lodged very well – St Orlan has a very fine inn. The house is not pretentious. The hostess cooks, and the host himself leads his *garçons*, with an apron about his loins. But cooking and service are of the very best. And the rooms are clean and pleasant, and the bathrooms, of which there are two, are very well found.

That we deserved such good fortune, I cannot pretend: but when, at a quarter to nine, we sat down, bathed and changed, to a really excellent dinner, served in a jolly garden, behind the house – we all felt truly grateful for what we were receiving and were about to receive.

Great goodwill was shown us by everyone, and when, whilst we were at table, I spoke of the Rolls and asked that she might be washed by nine o'clock the next day –

"She is being cleaned now," said the host. "As soon as I saw her state, I knew that Jean would wish to do her at once. He is an old coachman, Monsieur, and very serious. He will take off the tar with oil. And Alfred is helping him – that is my sister's son. Monsieur need have no fear. She is safe in their hands."

It was when we had drunk our coffee, and Jill and I were strolling, but Berry was sitting still, that our hostess appeared to greet us and say that she trusted the dinner had been to our taste.

After a little conversation, she looked across at Berry, who was making her husband laugh.

"Monsieur is tired," she said. "His face is drawn."

"It's his back," said I. "He's had a rough time today, and he's stood it remarkably well. But – "

And there my brother-in-law began to get to his feet, laying fast hold of the table, as well as the back of his chair. As the other made to assist him –

"You see," I said.

But the lady was gone.

For a moment she trounced her husband.

"What an idiot you are, Pierre. Here is Monsieur in evident pain, and you never tell me. Have I eyes to see from the kitchen the state of my guests? But Monsieur is patient. Wait until you are attacked. They will hear your cries in Bordeaux."

With that, she ran into the house – to reappear one minute later, bearing a little phial.

This was of brown-coloured glass and its cover, which was of skin, was fastened with silk.

As she peeled off the skin –

"Monsieur will drink this," she said. "And tomorrow he will be well."

"You're very kind," said Berry. "I only hope you're right." He took the phial from her. "Do I drink it all?"

"Yes, Monsieur. That is the dose. It is not unpleasant. A little bitter, perhaps."

"Madame," said Berry, "I'd drink a bucket of brine to be rid of this back." He lifted the phial and bowed. "Your very good health." He drank and handed it back. "Herbs, of course. The secret, no doubt, is yours."

"It was my great-grandmother's, Monsieur. And there is more there than herbs."

"Magic," said Jill.

"Madame is right. No physician would ever believe, because he will never believe what he cannot explain. And so his patients must suffer, until they can suffer no more. The herbs, of course, are good: but all depends upon how and when they are gathered – and other things."

"I believe," said Jill.

"Madame does not have to assure me. I have seen Madame's face. And her faith will stand her in stead for so long as she lives, for Nature loves those that are faithful and give her credit for all the wonders she works."

At eight o'clock the next morning, Berry came into my room.

I propped myself on an arm.

"Whatever's the matter?" I said.

Berry's reply was to take off his dressing-gown.

Then he stood up very straight and extended his arms before him, holding his palms downward, as they do at physical drill. Then he leaned slowly forward, keeping his knees unbent. After two or three efforts he managed to touch his toes.

Thirty seconds later, I knocked at Jill's door.

My lady was sitting up, eating bread and honey and drinking *café-au-lait*.

"The traditional diet," I said. "God save Your Majesty."

"You are sweet, aren't you?" said Jill, and put up her face to be kissed.

"Berry's cured," I said. "I've just seen him touch his toes."

"Hurray," said Jill. "And don't say it's an accident."

It's magic," said I. " It must be."

"Oh, I didn't mean that," said Jill. "The magic's done it, of course. But how did we come to St Orlan? We aimed at Pau, but spokes were put in our wheel. Patricia and Simon at Chartres, and then the tar. But for that, you'd never have turned at Ruffec... You know, it's awfully simple, if you can only believe."

I put out my hand for hers.

"My God, I shall miss you," I said.

The fingers tightened on mine.

"*Tout passe*," said Jill quietly. "*L'amitié reste.*"

Four days had gone by, and Daphne was perched on the arm of her husband's chair.

"Well, you know where to go," she said, "if ever you get it again."

"You're telling me," said Berry. "And in any event, you must see it. You've simply got to be in on a place like that. And they'll fall down and worship you."

"Don't be absurd. But I'd like to meet Madame Brulet and thank her for what she's done. By the way, there's a letter from Toby."

Her husband ripped it open and read it aloud.

Dear Berry.

I rather think you know that you've done the trick. God bless you all. I mean, it was touch and go. Poor old Toby was in it, over his knees. And Aunt Ira's actually contrite. I've never seen her like this. I'm the prodigal son with knobs on – thanks to you. If ever you're in a jam, you can have my guts. My love to Daphne and Jill. They're still the best I've seen.

Toby.

"No one can say," said I, "that Toby is inarticulate. What's rather more to the point, he means what he says."

"So does Mrs Medallion," said Berry. "And so does Madame Brulet. What a precious thing honesty is. But I'd love those two to meet. Madame Brulet and Mrs Medallion. Which would you back?"

"Much would depend," I said, "on Mrs Medallion's health."

And there I believe I was right.

Anyway, seeing's believing: and I have told what I saw.

7

In Which Berry Meets Mr Wireworm,
and I Keep the Truth to Myself

"When will he come out?" said Daphne.

"On Wednesday next," said Berry. "The Governor is arranging for him to be put on the bus. That means that he should be here by half-past ten."

"I wonder if The Bold will know him."

"I doubt it," said I. "Six weeks is a lot, when you're only two months old."

My sister regarded her husband over the rim of her glass.

"Poor man," she said. "I think you were very severe."

"In fact, I wasn't," said Berry. "I tempered justice with mercy. And that was before I knew that he had a dog."

"But that explained everything."

"It explained why he lost control. But you can't go about attempting to murder people because they comment adversely upon the looks of your dog. I think he's the King of Beasts, but he does suggest the monster, if you get him against the light. And his nose resembles a spur-rest – you can't get away from that."

"Do be careful," said Daphne, regarding The Bold. "Supposing he tells his master what you've just said."

"In that case," said Berry, "I shall be vivisected before your eyes. But I count upon his good taste. After all, he's broken my bread."

Here The Bold advanced upon him and, rising upon his hind legs, scrabbled upon his trousers with all his might.

"The Bull of Bashan," said Berry, "demands some grouse. He's gaping upon me with his mouth. But have a heart, old fellow. These pretty pants were never made to whet your little claws. There you are. There's a succulent morsel. Don't eat it all at once."

A touch upon my ankle suggested that Nobby had digested this irregularity.

"Damn it," I said, "you're demoralizing my dog."

"It isn't me," said Berry. "It's this damned Royalty."

"He's a law to himself," said Daphne. "But I must confess that he has a most charming way."

"His eyes are bulbous," said Berry. "Every time I see them, I want to ring the bell."

"You are revolting," said Daphne. "And most unkind. Poor little boy. And he's been a perfect guest. I shall miss him terribly. No, not my stockings, darling. Oh, damn. He's done it again."

She regarded an excellent leg, the excellent stocking of which had been ripped by the baby claws.

"The perfect guest," said her husband.

Ignoring the saying, my sister dealt with The Bold.

"Now that's very naughty," she said. "You're a naughty dog. Look at poor Daphne's stocking."

The Bold lowered his tail and passed beneath the table, to lie at her feet. Nobby followed, to offer what comfort he could.

"Nobby'll miss him," I said. "I'm really quite worried about it. He simply adores that scrap."

"But you think he'll ask us to keep him?"

"I think he may. I mean, he's better off here than making a voyage to China before the mast."

"I can't bear to think of it," said Daphne. "Why shouldn't we offer to buy him?"

"In view of his master's outlook, I don't think we can do that."

"I agree," said Berry. "Blood royal is not bought and sold. The suggestion that we should keep him must come from the Chinaman. And even then I don't think we can offer him money. Any way, I'm not going to. I don't want an abdominal wound."

"We can't take him for nothing," said Daphne. "I mean, he must be worth about fifty pounds."

"Can't help that," said Berry. "You wait till you see his demeanour towards that dog. Damn it, he does obeisance."

"Look at it this way," I said. "If the Chinaman asks us to keep him, it will be because he desires to do his best for The Bold. That he is giving him to us won't enter his head. He will be furnishing The Bold with a household befitting his state."

"Offensive, but true," said Berry. "In that fanatic's eyes, we're less than the dung beneath his charge's heels. Never mind. He's probably made a vow to convey The Bold to some filthy temple he knows. There he'll sprawl on a priceless mat, and the faithful will feed him until he's too fat to walk. And the priests will groom him daily and sell the fleas. By the way, did you see Alice Weston?"

"I did," said Daphne, "in vain. She and George are determined to stay at the farm."

Caracol Farm was one of the three we had. The house, which was old and ugly, had been burned to the ground in June; and a very much nicer dwelling was to be built in its stead. Indeed, the plans had been passed and the site had been cleared. But building is a slow business. It seemed likely that, do what we would, the new house would not be ready for several months. And George and Alice Weston declined to leave the farm. Their children had been taken by a convenient aunt, but husband and wife were 'camping out' in a barn. That was all very well in the summer, for George and Alice were young: but the autumn was coming in, and the winter was looming behind.

"I did my best," said Daphne; "but George refuses to leave, and she feels that her place is with him. And they have no comfort at all. George has run up some partitions, and everything's spotlessly clean. But they'll die of cold in the winter."

"Of course they will," said Berry. "What fools they are. The trouble is I can see George's point of view. He's proud and fond of his stock, and he won't live five miles off. If only there was a cottage... I'll go over on Monday and see him again. If the weather breaks before then, that may open his eyes."

"We're lunching at Buckram on Monday."

"So we are," said Berry. "Never mind. Tuesday will do. I do hope they give us melon. The melons of Buckram used to be very good. And the table old Ludlow kept belonged to the books. I remember being sick there when I was five years old."

"You filthy beast," said his wife.

"Don't be absurd," said Berry. "That was a compliment."

Our visit to Buckram Place was over and done.

It had been a very pleasant experience. Our host, George Ludlow, was rising eighty-six, but, if he lived in the past, he never disclosed the fact. Things were certainly done at Buckram as they had always been done. The lawns were mown every morning: the papers were ironed: horses stood in the stables: certain woods were reserved, to provide the household with fuel – and, as they were felled, were replanted, to furnish households to come. But cocktails were served before lunch: the servants had the use of a car: and our host was dressed as we were – soft collar and country clothes. And Jonathan Baldric and Natalie Edgecumb were there, old Ludlow's great-nephew and -niece, each in love with the other for all but them to see. From first to last, the past was scarcely referred to: but when the men were alone, old Ludlow spoke these words.

"White Ladies, Bell Hammer, Buckram – much of the fortune of England depends upon houses like these. They are homes not only for us, but for many beside. My note-paper always lies in the servants' hall: I like them to feel that their address is Buckram – not 'care of me'. But, quite apart from that, such houses point the virtue of having a stake in the country. And that fine idea is absorbed, for five out of six of the people who leave my service, do so to found homes of their own. I always try to help them, for the man that has a stake in the country is a man who, when things go wrong, has something to lose."

And now our visit was over and we were on the way back.

We were running through lovely country, quite unspoiled, when we came to a little bridge. On the farther side, the road turned sharp to the left, to run beside the water and so at right angles to the bridge. And there the road was blocked, for a car was half on to the bridge and the caravan it was drawing was lying athwart the road.

What mistakes its driver had made, I do not know: but now he could not go forward, for his nearside wing would have fouled the parapet: and, if he went back, the caravan would enter the river without any doubt.

A nice-looking man, in his shirt-sleeves, came languidly up to my side.

"Yes," he said. "I did it. I created the obstruction, all by myself." He looked at Daphne and bowed. "I am extremely sorry that you should be inconvenienced; but, if you want to get on, I should take some other way."

As I left the Rolls –

"Perhaps we can help," I said.

"I doubt it," said the other ruefully. "What we need is a mobile crane." He put his hands to his head. "You wouldn't believe what I've been through with this van. If I could find a buyer, I'd sell the blasted thing. Damn it, I'd give it away… They're quite all right, as long as you leave them alone. It's when you take the road that they spoil your life. In the last three

215

days I've covered thirty-four miles. My wife gave in last night and I sent her home by train. She couldn't face any more. The rows I've had – with other road-users, I mean. Of course, I'm in the wrong for trying to drag the swine about the place. But people are unsympathetic. You're very nice about it: but a char-à-banc yesterday evening was very rude. And I should have been back in London on Saturday night. And at my office this morning. And here I am. Are you sure you don't want to buy it? It cost me two hundred and fifty six weeks ago: and you can have it – and welcome-for seventy-five."

"As it stands?" said Berry, opening his door.

I turned to look at him.

"As it stands," said the other. "It's a couple of beds and a bath and a very good cooking-stove: and a sink and a water tank: and lockers to burn. Go and have a look at the brute."

Berry consulted with Daphne. Then he opened the door for my sister, and she got out.

"May we really see it?" she said. "We happen to have two tenants who are short of a house. And while their home's being built…"

"This would be ideal," said the other. "The cooker heats the water, and on a chilly evening she's beautifully warm. As long as she's standing still, I've no complaints: but I can't pretend she's mobile. And a van that isn't mobile is of no use to me."

We crossed the bridge, and my sister entered the van.

When she came out –

"It's absurdly cheap," she said, "at seventy-five. But, to tell you the truth, we don't want to pay any more."

"Madam," said the stranger, "I'm out to cut my loss. If you offered me fifty, I'd take it."

"Seventy-five," said Berry. "You'll take a cheque?"

"Of course," said the other. "Francis Berwick's the name." He took out a cigarette-case. "Here's my card. Come and sit down in the van. And you shall write the cheque and I'll write a receipt."

Five minutes later the curious deal was done.

Then we chocked the wheels of the van and disconnected the car. Thus freed, the car could be backed…

It was an awkward business, because, as I have said, the van was across the road; but at last I coaxed her round and over the bridge. I berthed her some twenty paces behind the Rolls.

Then I left the driver's seat and mopped my face.

"You see," said Berwick. "You're very much better than I am, but – "

"I don't know about that. She's the very devil to handle on roads like this. And if you do make a mistake…"

"Exactly," said Berwick.

He laughed and entered the van, to get his suit-cases out.

While he was transferring his gear, I disconnected the car.

Five minutes later, the latter was ready to leave.

"Well, thank you very much," said her owner. "You've done me a very good turn."

"It's suited us," said Daphne…

Berwick squared his shoulders.

"*The Pilgrim's Progress*," he said. "I feel as Christian did, when his back was freed from the weight of his sack of sins."

One minute later, his car was out of sight.

"And now then," said Berry.

"A decent fellow," said I, "but a full-marks fool. Alone in the car and he brings this thing across country… His only chance was to stick to the main highway. We'll have to have Fitch and the Vane to get it back. And I shall have to help him."

Daphne regarded her husband.

"You'll have to stay here," she said, "and look after the van. Boy and I'll drive – "

"I beg your pardon," said Berry.

"Well, we can't leave it unattended."

"I can," said Berry. "In view of the last half-hour, I can even leave it unwept." He licked a broken knuckle. "If anyone had told me this morning that, before the day was out, I should be

217

coupling and uncoupling my own pantechnicon in a Wiltshire Lane – "

"But what about the contents?" screamed Daphne. "Those mattresses alone – "

"We must lock it up," said her husband. "Lock it up and forget it. And tomorrow Fitch and George Weston can hale it to Caracol."

"That's all right," said I.

And so it would have been, if Francis Berwick had remembered to leave the key.

All three of us ransacked that van in search of that key. First, I did so: then Daphne: confronted with our reports, appalled by their fearful import, Berry refused to accept them and did so again.

With yells of disappointment, he wrenched the lockers open and scrabbled inside: he heaved the mattresses up, to grope beneath and beyond them, muttering fearful things: he scoured the bathroom and pantry, all the time shouting predictions regarding such as saw fit to embarrass the godly, till Daphne and I, weak with laughter, withdrew to the Rolls. And there he presently joined us, with dirt all over his hands and fairly streaming with sweat.

"You didn't tell me," he said, "about the larder. It's beautifully conceived. But you ought to be able to open it when you're outside the van. I mean, I think it's been forgotten. Of course this heat is unusual. But I do think they might have let the sausages out. And now we needn't bother about the key. The first man who opens that door will run for the police. Talk about trunk murder."

"My darling," said Daphne, "you know we can't leave it like this. If someone dishonest comes by – "

"We've been here for over an hour and seen nobody yet."

"I know. But the road is public. Supposing, as soon as we've gone, some gypsies come round that bend."

"Oh, hell," said Berry.

"Exactly. When we returned tomorrow, the van would be stripped. I'm really dreadfully sorry, but Boy will be as quick as he can."

"Yes, I know that bit," said her husband, consulting his watch. "The hour is now half-past five. You won't be back at White Ladies by half-past six. Say, a quarter to seven. Boy leaves again with the Vane at seven o'clock. With luck, he ought to be here by half-past eight. And then the fun begins. And I'm to sit here for three hours and then spend five more hours – "

"Listen," said I. "I shall go back to White Ladies by way of Caracol. There I'll give the Westons the low-down and say that I'll pick up George in a quarter of an hour. I then take Daphne on, find Fitch and return to Caracol. There we pick up George and then return to this spot. I should be here soon after eight. George will spend the night here, and early tomorrow morning Fitch will arrive with the Vane. And he and George together can bring the van home."

"I see," said Berry. "Could you say that again, beginning at 'low-down'? Never mind." He laughed idiotically. "Sounds like a nursery rhyme, doesn't it. 'Boy, Boy, seek Fitch: Fitch, Fitch, drive Vane: Vane, Vane, bring George: George, George, occupy van, or I shan't get home tonight.' And now let's play *Bananas and Jellies, The Bells of Slow Bellies*."

"Will you be quiet?" said Daphne.

"I can't," said Berry. "I'm deranged. I must be. To do you pleasure, I've just spent seventy-five semi-precious pounds to my wounding. In return for that important sum of money, I have acquired not only a verminous pantechnicon, but the apparently inalienable right to watch the same, fasting, for the next four hours."

"My darling, what else can we do?"

"Don't tempt me," said her husband. "I might tell you. Oh, and before you take your departure in this very elegant car, I should like all the cigarettes you've got." We emptied the contents of our cases into his hands. "Thank you. And you might take my case and refill it." I accepted his empty case. "Thank you, again. And if you should see any millstones about my size… Fifteen and a half – don't forget. Oh, no. You have to put them over the head, don't you? Well, say twenty. But I won't pay more than five pounds."

As the Rolls slipped over the bridge, Berry was tiptoeing about his purchase with the traditional ecstasy of a nymph who has encountered an altar, raised to the glory of Pan.

At exactly a quarter-past eight, I re-entered the curling lane that ran beside the water and led to the little bridge.

All had gone very well.

George Weston, greatly excited, was sitting in the back of the Rolls – with his blankets and bag and two lanterns, to light the van fore and aft: Fitch was seated beside me, marking the way I took; and I was looking forward to sharing with Berry the beer which lolled in a bucket by George's feet.

Then the Rolls stole over the bridge, and I saw a car at rest in front of the caravan and a man, with his hands behind him, pacing the road.

As I brought the Rolls to a standstill, my brother-in-law rose up from the step of the van, and the other swung round and came forward, wearing a menacing mien.

He was tall and heavily built, clean-shaven and going grey. His powerful jaw was set, and his mouth was a long, straight line. He was just controlling his temper – but only just.

As Fitch opened my door –

"Mention no names," said Berry. "But kindly tell this gentleman how and when I came to acquire this van."

"You bought it," I said, alighting, "at about a quarter to five this afternoon. At this very spot. Its owner was stuck on the farther side of that bridge: he wanted to get back to Town, and the van was round his neck: he was ripe to give it away, and he sold it to us with his blessing for less than a third of its cost: that suited us very well, for we wanted just such a thing for two of our friends."

Berry turned to the stranger.

"You hear?" he said.

The other stamped upon the road.

"Of course he tells the same lies. You took care to prepare them together, before he left."

Berry expired.

Then he indicated the Rolls.

"According to your information, does that resemble the car that was drawing the caravan?"

"I neither know nor care. Very likely it isn't the same. Your confederate took the one and came back with that"

"But what's the trouble?" said I.

Berry sighed.

"If this gentleman may be believed – "

"What the devil d'you mean, sir?" roared the other.

"Well, you don't believe me," said Berry, "so why should I believe you? And don't interrupt again. I dislike your voice."

"Before you're through, you'll dislike it a damn sight more."

"That were impossible," said Berry. "And now perhaps you'll permit me to put my 'confederate' wise." He returned to me. "If this gentleman may be believed, at about two o'clock today this caravan touched his car."

"Touched?" screamed the other. "*Touched*? It damn well rammed it, sir, as you very well know. Stove it in. Smashed it to matchwood. Three hundred pounds' worth of damage. And I only bought it last week."

"Let us say 'impaired its value'." The other choked. "The occurrence of this *contretemps* or hitch – "

" 'Hitch?' " yelled the other. "How dare you?"

" – coincided with the absence of this gentleman, who had left his car unattended, without some private house. It was not until he emerged, with the object of going his way, that he perceived that, such was the condition of his car, he must either

proceed on foot or procure the services of some other vehicle."
Berry turned to the stranger. "I think that's right."

The latter's reply was to make a rattling noise.

"Exactly. Annoyed by this inconvenience, he approached a
bystander and inquired if, by any chance, he could throw some
light upon the, er, discrepancy between the state of his car, as
he had left it, and its subsequent condition. He was
immediately informed that 'a caravan had done it ' – and,
having done it, had been rapidly withdrawn, to be last seen
proceeding North at a dangerous speed. Upon further inquiry, it
appeared that the caravan had a start of a quarter of an hour,
and, by the time that Mr Wireworm – for that is this
gentleman's name – had procured another car, with which to
take up the pursuit, nearly an hour had elapsed since the
contretemps had occurred.

"In a word, at three o'clock the hunt was up. From then until
six today this gentleman was scouring the countryside, fortified
by a belief, which was obviously well founded, that the process
which is known as that of exhaustion must end in his overtaking
a vehicle whose nature and design were precluding anything
approaching celerity, except upon the straightest of roads. And
so it fell out. At six o'clock this evening, he crossed that
picturesque bridge, to see before him his quarry, at rest by the
side of the way.

"Now whether this is the van that, in fact, impaired the value
of Mr Wireworm's car, I have no idea. There are certainly marks
upon its rear or hind quarters, which I had not before observed,
which may be traces of the contact he so much deplores. But
that, as I tell him, is quite beside the point. Until half-past four
today, neither you nor I nor any one of our house had ever set
eyes upon this van. That being so, it is out of all reason to
associate us with a *contretemps* in which this van was involved
at two o'clock."

"Where did it happen?" said I.

"At some place called Nether Beauchamp. D'you know the name?"

I shook my head.

"At two o'clock," I said, "we were still at table at Buckram."

"I know. I've said so – over and over again. I have declared that, counting the servants, we can bring at least nine or ten people to prove our alibi. But Mr Wireworm won't have it. And I don't know that I should blame him, if he hadn't been so rude."

The other burst out.

"I'll have no more of this."

"You're nearly right," said Berry. "We've got to be getting on."

"No, you don't," snarled the other. "I've got you now, and I'm going to give you in charge."

Berry sighed.

"As I have told you before, that statement is one which only an idiot would make. You might as well say you were going to flay me alive. You can't flay me alive, because, in the first place, the resistance I should certainly offer would place the operation beyond your power: in the second place, I very much doubt if you have the requisite tools: and, in the third place, I'm quite sure you don't know how to flay. I believe it to be a most difficult handicraft... In the same way, you cannot give me in charge, because, in the first place, there is no constable here, and, in the second, if there was, he would assuredly decline to put me under arrest. He would tell you, as I have told you, that this is a case for a summons. Summon me if you will – I've offered you my name and address. But your summons will be dismissed, for I'm not your man."

Mr Wireworm shook his fist.

"I'll see about that, you twister. I know the law. 'Failing to stop after an accident.' "

"Quite right," said Berry. "That is the offence, which, if I may believe you, was committed at Nether Beauchamp early this afternoon."

"By you. And then you bolted. And now I've got you, you're trying to bolt again. What a fool you must think me."

"I do," said Berry. "I think you're a poisonous fool. Except to admit that I'm guilty, I've met you in every way. I've told you how to proceed and I've offered you my name and address. I've shown you how you can prove the truth of my alibi. My cousin has returned to this spot, as I said he would, and, unprompted by me, has borne out all that I said. I told you he'd bring two men with him – and there they are."

"D'you know who I am?" blared the other.

"No, I don't," said Berry wearily. "For all I know you may be a pillar of the Society for the Propagation of Blue-based Baboons, but that doesn't faze me."

"If you did, you'd know I don't stand for treatment like this. You've come to the wrong shop. When I've got my hooks on a blackguard, I never let go."

Berry looked at me.

"You see?" he said. "I've had two hours of this, and I'm getting tired. My tale is strange, but everything bears it out. He finds me alone with the van. If I am, in fact, the delinquent, what have I done with the car? Oh, my confederate took that. Why should he do such a thing? To avoid arrest. In that case, why didn't I accompany him? Because I was looking after the van. He's an answer for everything, no matter how drivelling it is. The truth is he's out for blood, and, so long as he gets it, he doesn't care whose it is."

Fitch approached with a bottle of beer and a glass.

"You must be thirsty, sir."

"Thank you," said Berry. "I am."

Fitch poured the beverage out.

Berry took the glass and offered it to Mr Wireworm.

"I expect there's some more," he said.

The other snatched the glass and flung it over the hedge.

There was a pregnant silence.

Then Berry returned to the chauffeur.

"Another glass," he said.

"Very good, sir."

"George."

"Sir."

"Behold your future home. I should enter and take possession without delay."

"Thank you, sir," and, with that, George took up his gear and entered the van.

Fitch returned with another glass…

Berry drank gratefully. Then he pointed to the stream.

"I expect Captain Pleydell's thirsty. You might wash the glass there and see."

"Very good, sir."

"And then, I think, we'll be going."

Wireworm started forward.

"Not on your life."

Coldly Berry regarded him.

"Are you proposing to detain us, against our will?"

The other swallowed.

"You're coming to the station," he said. "And I'll see you don't get bail."

Berry raised his eyebrows.

"Also among the prophets? I fear I shall prove you false. Damn it, man, I'm sorry your car's been bent. This may or may not be the van that did the mischief. But, whether or no, I've told you that I'm not guilty – and here's my card."

Wireworm snatched the paste-board and tore it up.

"You won't be helped, will you?" said Berry. "Perhaps you'd prefer to take the number of my car. That should enable you to run me to earth."

"It's probably stolen," said Wireworm.

Steadily Berry regarded him.

"You know," he said, "I'm beginning to regret that you weren't beside your car when the contact was made. Bending over…looking into the bonnet."

The other started forward.

"How d'you know she was hit in the bonnet?"

"I don't," said Berry. "That was a bow at a venture. For all I know, she was hit in the camisole. Or hadn't you got your washing out today?"

Mr Wireworm went over the edge, stamping and shouting and vowing most hideous vengeance on 'conduct likely to lead to a breach of the peace'.

When the storm had subsided –

"Allow me to commend," said Berry, "to your consideration a passage in Holy Writ, in which a mote and a beam and a human eye are concerned. In the last two hours you have offered me enough provocation – not for a breach of the peace, but for a whole series of aggravated assaults. So far from committing these, I have made every allowance for your ravening state of mind. But all in vain. I confess that some of my answers have not been soft, but that is because I'm human – if you flog a willing horse, he's apt to lash out. And now I've said my last word." He turned to me. "Have you had your beer?"

I nodded.

"Good. George."

"Sir," said George, from the step of the caravan.

"We're going now. Fitch will be back in the morning at eight o'clock."

"Thank you very much, sir."

"And don't you stand any rot. The van is mine, and you are the tenant in charge."

"I'll see to that, sir. Am I to give any information?"

"You may say what ever you please. I've nothing to hide."

"Thank you, sir."

I turned to the chauffeur.

"I think you'd better drive, Fitch. I'm rather tired."

"Very good, sir."

"In the name of the law," raged Wireworm, "I call upon you to stop."

"Call and be damned," said Berry, and, with that, he got into the Rolls.

The other hesitated. Then he ran for his car.

As he did so, I entered the Rolls.

"Let him follow," I said. "Straight on, Fitch. I'll tell you the way to go."

Berry sank back on the cushions and crossed his legs.

"You see," he said, "of such is Mr Wireworm, I didn't feel like giving Berwick away. Of course, he is the delinquent. That is why he was using the lesser roads. But I didn't want to be the hangman. Besides, of the two, I very much prefer Berwick. Anyone would. And Wireworm is covered by insurance – he said as much. But Berwick has dropped a packet over the van."

"True," said I. "And, in spite of all he says, the damage to Wireworm's car can't be very grave. If it was half as bad as he makes out, the back of the van would be smashed. Still, Berwick bad no right to clear out, while the going was good. I mean, that was a dirty one."

"Yes, it was," said Berry. "You can't get away from that. But Wireworm is such a swine that I could not bring myself to help him to his revenge. The silly thing is he never got as far as asking me for Berwick's name and address. Or for his receipt. And that was just as well, for both were in my cigarette case, and you had that. But what a show. Hadn't we better leave him? I want my dinner in peace."

"We will," I said, "as soon as we get to Cherries. But Fitch doesn't know these roads. First on the right, Fitch, and, after that, the first on the right again. That'll bring us to Cherries, and then you'll know where you are, and we'll run away."

"That's right, sir."

The light was failing now, and our lights were on. So were Mr Wireworm's. I drew the blind behind me, to shut them out.

We were less than a mile from Cherries – a little more than a village and less than a town – when I noticed a tail-light two hundred paces ahead. As I looked, it rounded a bend and was lost to sight. A moment later, however, I saw it again – and something more, *for the caravan that bore it was moving at half our speed. The back of the van was very badly damaged...* The merciless glare of our head-lights showed up the splintered panels, the broken step... The van had been in recent collision, beyond all doubt.

As Fitch exclaimed – .

"Well, I'm damned," said Berry. "Poor old Worm-cast – I mean, Wireworm. And now tie's got to begin all over again. How do we put him wise? If we can help it, I'd rather not be involved."

"Pull out to pass him, Fitch, but go very slow. Keep abreast of the van for a moment, if you can see ahead. The idea is to block the road. Then Mr Wireworm's head-lights will show him the state of the van."

Fitch did the thing very well.

We were still abreast of the van, when a screech of fury rang out from the car behind. Then its electric horn began to open fire.

"He's got it," said I. "Go on, Fitch."

And there was Cherries ahead...

As we swung to the left and on to the main highway –

"Stop a moment," said Berry. "Now that we're out of the wood, I'd like to be in at the death."

We left the Rolls and walked back, to stand unobserved in the shadows against a wall.

Wireworm had passed his prey and had swung across the bows of the car that was trailing the van. Against this obstructive action, some man was bellowing protests of the most violent sort, while Wireworm, now out of his car, was yelling 'Police.' People were standing, staring, and a crowd was beginning to form.

"Go an' learn to drive," bawled the man. "Get out of my way."

"No — fear," howled Wireworm. "I've been chasing you for six hours, you filthy criminal. And now I've got you, I'm not going to let you go. You rammed my car and bolted this afternoon. At Nether Beauchamp."

"You're out of your mind," raved the other. "I've never been near the place."

"Don't lie to me," yelled Wireworm…

"When Greek meets Greek," said Berry. "And now let's go. You see, I know what's coming. I was – present at the rehearsal." We turned to go back to the Rolls. "But what a mercy I didn't let Berwick in."

We reached White Ladies that night at ten o'clock.

As I was leaving the car –

"Excuse me, sir," said Fitch. "But would there be any objection to my getting the van tonight?"

"None," said I, "if you want to. You'll take the Vane, of course. But won't you be very tired?"

"That's all right, sir. By night the roads'll be clear."

"So they will," said I.

"And then again – I mean, after all this fuss, sir, it might be as well to get the van out of the way. The Major's 'ad trouble enough, an' if that driver should manage to bluff Mr Wireworm…"

"He wouldn't bluff me," said I, "with his van in that state. Still, you never know. And if Mr Wireworm harks back…"

"Exactly, sir. If he should – well, then there won't be no van."

"All right. Get some supper first. You won't be back before five."

As I entered the hall –

"But, my darling," said Daphne, "how awful."

"That adjective," said Berry, "in no way meets the case. Indeed, unless one is to overstep the bounds of decency, one cannot fairly describe what one has endured. I couldn't leave the scene, and so I was at the swine's mercy for more than two hours. I couldn't get out of earshot. If I walked down the road, he followed, mouthing maledictions and teaching me terrible things. I handed them on to Berwick, under my breath. But that didn't do much good. And – Oh, I forgot to tell you. Whenever anyone passed, he asked them to fetch the police. And when they asked 'What for?', he started in. Talk about incoherence. Of course they thought he was mad, and I think he is. Never, perhaps, outstanding, his mental apparatus has been deranged. He worshipped his nice, new car. And then he comes out to find that some wallah has done it in. *And* made himself scarce. If you ask me, before that affliction something gave way. The silly thing is he had my sympathy. But whenever I handed it out, he flung it back in my face. Raved about wolves in sheep's clothing, and things like that. And now I must go and wash. You shall have the rest at dinner. Tell Falcon I'll have two cocktails."

"One will do," said his wife. "I've ordered champagne."

Berry took her fingers and put them up to his lips.

"Which gave that order," he said. "Your beautiful head, or your still more beautiful heart?"

The next morning, when I was called, I learned that the van was safe at Caracol Farm.

At ten o'clock on Wednesday the butler entered the room.

"The Chinaman is here, madam."

"Ah," said Berry. "Well, he'd better have some breakfast or something. Have we got any rotten eggs?"

"Be quiet," said Daphne. "Is he all right, Falcon? I mean, well-behaved."

"His manner is perfect, madam. And I thought you would wish him to have something, so Mrs Mason has arranged it. I think he's to have some cold meat."

"Good. Let him come round to the terrace in half an hour."

"Very good, madam."

By five and twenty past ten, the stage was set.

To his indignation, Nobby had been confined: we were, all three, upon the terrace: and The Bold was upon the great lawn, lying upon his side and mouthing his rubber bone.

Hat in hand, with an under-gardener for guide, the Chinaman came into view. Then the former pointed and left, and the latter stood very still. He did not see us. He had eyes for the puppy alone.

So for, perhaps, a minute. Then he looked round about him, surveying the trees and the lawn and, after a little, the house. He saw us then and made as though to come forward. But Berry held up a hand and indicated The Bold.

The Chinaman bowed. Then he turned to the sward and began to move over the turf to where the dog was at play

The Bold neither saw nor heard him, until he was very close. Then he sat up and looked round, to see who was afoot.

The Chinaman fell upon his knees.

Then he addressed the dog with the deepest respect.

The Bold displayed no emotion, but to me it was very clear that he knew him again. After a little, he rose and, as he had done in Court, he put out a little paw. And the Chinaman bent his head, and the puppy leaned forward and touched his brow with his tongue. Then he lay down again, with his eyes on the Chinaman's face.

Then the latter spoke at some length – I think, in Chinese – as though he were offering counsel. Though he spoke for fully two minutes, The Bold heard him out – and that is a thing which, if I had not seen it, I never would have believed.

Then the puppy stood up again, and the Chinaman knelt by his side, pointing to the lawn and the timber and then to the terrace and house. 'All is yours,' he seemed to be saying… And The Bold looked well about him – and then returned to his bone.

For a moment, the Chinaman watched him. Then he turned and moved to the foot of the terrace steps.

There he stood still and bowed.

"It is well, my lord," he said quietly. "If you please, The Bold will stay here."

"D'you mean for good?" said Daphne.

"If you please. It is better so. Now I will go to Southampton, to find a ship."

"Are you sure you mean this?" said Berry.

"I am sure, my lord. Here he is well and happy. His eyes are bright." He bowed again. "I have much to thank you for."

As he turned, I rose, to walk with him round to the drive.

"You're going to Southampton?" I said.

"Yes, sir."

"D'you know how to get there?" I said.

"Yes, by Brooch – the city where I was confined."

"Can we help you in any way? I mean, have you money enough?"

"I have enough," said the man. "This morning, before I left, they gave me my money back."

"Then, er, that's all right," I said feebly.

The Chinaman bowed.

After an awkward silence –

"The Bold," I said, "plays with my terrier, who is a well-bred dog."

"I am glad," said the Chinaman.

"The terrier takes care of him."

"Yes, sir."

As we came to the drive –

"Which reminds me," I said. "Two strangers tried to take him a fortnight ago. They pretended that he was their dog. But they didn't get very far, and my terrier bit the man in the calf of his leg."

"It is well," said the Chinaman quietly. "He would not have been happy with them. They were fat and ill-bred. That is why I took him away."

He turned and left me, standing with a hand to my head.

And so, I believe, I stood, till he passed out of sight.

After considerable reflection, I decided to hold my peace. Receivers or no, The Bold was better with us.

Six months had gone by, and we were drinking sherry in Charles Street, before going home to dine.

Athalia Fairfax's parties were always good. They were not too big – there were twelve of us there this evening – and the guests were carefully chosen, or seemed to be. All knew each other well, but did not meet all the time. The Levels were older than us; the Pemburys were rather younger: Lady Morayne was outspoken; Forsyth was something reserved: but all had a sense of humour and felt the same about things. There was almost a suggestion of the *salon* about the parties that Punch and Athalia gave.

"The world," shouted Lady Morayne, "has gone down the drain."

"I quite agree," said Berry: "but England will get it out. It'll stick before it gets to the cesspool, and England will shove it back."

"Don't be absurd. I'm talking of manners and customs. People used to behave when I was young."

Lord Level laughed.

"History repeats itself, Mary. That's just what your mother said."

"My warrant is stronger than hers. People get drunk at dances. What about that?"

"Out of all order," said Berry.

"Out of all order, my foot. It's indecent – you know it is. Adela Churt gives a dance for that niece of hers. She asks fifty couples and seventy-five turn up. Fifty gate-crashers, thank you. Seven young men get drunk and have to be carried away. And the damage done. The parquet burned to blazes by cigarettes. And holes in two Persian rugs."

"That," said Lady Level, "is indefensible."

"And look at our conversation. We do nothing but talk about money from morning to night. And I was brought up never to mention money. Though you didn't know which way to turn, you didn't expose your sores."

"That," said Forsyth, "I think a venial sin. So many have lost so much that they turn to each other for comfort. They want to share their woes."

"That's right," said Berry. "And four out of five of us here are bursting to do it now. You know we're giving up Cholmondeley Street?"

"You're not," said Lady Level.

"Needs must," said Daphne. "We can't keep two houses up."

"We can't keep up one," said Pembury. "Dot and I are going to withdraw to France."

"Let me be vulgar, too," cried Lady Morayne. "There's Sorcery eating its head off, and I go to bargain-basements to buy my clothes. Yet, if I close the place, there's more than twenty servants out of a job. Decent men and women that look to me. Of course I can sell the pictures…" She turned to Pembury. "Couldn't you live on a barge?"

"Why not?" said Punch. "If you go to France, we shall never see you again."

Berry turned to his wife.

"A barge," he said. "That's what we'd better do. In the winter months, you know. Moored off the Traitors' Gate – I mean, the Savoy. No rates and taxes, Forsyth?"

"None," said the lawyer. "No main services, either."

"That's all right," said Berry, "because you live out. You have a watchman, of course: and he does the beds."

"Thank you very much," said Daphne.

"I'm against a barge," said Athalia. "I'd rather live in France."

"So would I," said Berry. "The Beaulieus are doing that – and doing it well. And living like fighting-cocks. Beer was twopence a bottle, when I was there last year. But of course you must watch your step. If you dine at the *Palais de Splendeur*, a brandy and soda'll cost you one pound ten. Has anyone heard from them lately? The Beaulieus, I mean."

No one had heard.

"There you are," said Punch. "They're off the map"

"Some maps," said Lady Morayne, "are not worth being on. When a man makes a fortune out of *Yes, We have no Bananas*, I'm not sure it isn't time to turn the face to the wall. And look at the Divorce Court."

"Of such is war," said Forsyth. "Heat the pot, and the scum will always rise."

"And here's another saw," said Lord Level. "The watched pot never cools. Don't forget that, Mary. Avert your eyes, my dear. And then one day you'll look round, to find that taste is improving and manners are coming back."

"I resemble Rachel. I will not be comforted. Never mind. As you're all against me – "

"I'm not," said Berry. "The old order is changing, and I decline to believe that the new will be as good. Say we're going through a phase, if you please. Well, I don't like the look of the phase. Why do we talk about money? Because money matters now, as never before. Nothing counts, beside money. Money is 'news'. But it's also the root of all evil, and always was."

Lady Level lifted her voice.

"I have an uneasy feeling that Berry is right. Money is the Lord of Misrule. Some star in America is getting a thousand a week: and Dr — at Oxford is getting four hundred a year. And he's writing a standard work that will outlive time. Once that kind of rot gets going, it's terribly hard to stop."

There was a little silence.

"I should hate," said Lady Morayne, "to write a dictionary."

"I do hope you won't try," said Berry. "As a censor, Lady Morayne is beyond compare. But lexicography is by no means everyone's dunghill. Let the cobbler stick to his blast – last."

"Dr Johnson did both. After defining all day, he sat down and condemned."

235

"What did he condemn?" said Elizabeth Pembury.

"Any departure," said Forsyth, "from what he thought was the proper way to behave. And he was extremely strict."

"In a word," said Punch, "he'd have been pretty busy today."

"I should have loved to hear him," said Berry, "on gate-crashing."

Lord Level laughed.

"You never would have," he said. "The appreciation of the offence would have deprived him of speech."

"How," said Athalia Fairfax, "would you define 'gate-crashing'?"

" 'Vile and verminous conduct,' " said Lady Morayne.

"Too general," said Berry. "So is the skunk's reproach. 'Gate-crashing' is 'the usurping by simulation of the privileges of an invited guest'."

"I will wager," said Lady Morayne, "that my dictionary would sell a damned sight better than yours."

"There you are," said Berry. "Money again. You can't get off the subject. We'd better go back to barges. After all, a barge on the Thames is worth two at the Wash."

"Money again," said Forsyth. "And what has the caravan done?"

"I quite agree," said Daphne. "A caravan gives you a chance. Two of our tenants are living in one in a barn. It's dry and warm and gay. Spend the winter like that, and when the summer comes in, you can take to the road. Why don't you try that, Dick? Whenever I see the Westons, I think how lucky they are. Take ours on from them. They're going into their house at the end of the month."

Pembury shook his head.

"We're through with caravans. The remembrance of them is grievous. You can lock them up, you know, but they can be moved."

"But I thought that that was a virtue."

"It depends who moves them," said Pembury. "The bloke who moved ours usurped the privilege."

"D'you mean it was pinched?" said Athalia.

"Stolen, taken and carried away," said Pembury. He looked at Forsyth. "I believe that to be the wording the law prefers."

Forsyth inclined his head.

"I trust it was used to some purpose before the appropriate Court."

Pembury shook his head.

"The van has never been found. We informed the police, of course, and they were confident. 'He won't get far,' they said. 'You can't hide a caravan.' They warned all districts forthwith. And when a week had gone by, they warned all garages. Then they went to Great Portland Street. I've been there three times myself – by their desire. But the vans I saw were not ours."

"What a rotten shame," said my sister. "Never mind. You shall have ours. We shan't want it after April, and George and Alice have kept it perfectly. If you spend five pounds, it'll be as good as new."

"Oh, we couldn't take it," said Dot.

"My dear, why not? We got it extremely cheap, and we shall get nothing for it – you know what dealers are."

"Where did you lose yours?" said Berry.

"Not far from Shaftesbury. We left it one Saturday morning, to stay with the Fairies at Charing for forty-eight hours. And when we got back, it was gone. In fact, we forgot to lock it, but that is beside the point. Happily, we left nothing in it, except its furniture. Oh, and some sausages." Daphne started violently, but Berry sat like a rock. "We'd meant to throw them away, because they were going bad. If the thief omitted that precaution, whoever opened the larder must have had a pleasant surprise."

"That's right," said Berry. "It damned near knocked me down." He turned to his wife. "Don't you remember, darling?

Wise in your generation, you left it to me to open and prove the frankincense."

"D'you mean," said Daphne faintly, "we bought their caravan?"

"That's right. From that charming fellow, who'd had such a rotten time."

"They always have," murmured Forsyth. "Still, I think the police should have traced it."

Berry shook his head.

"As receivers of stolen goods, we know our job. The van was moved by night. Twelve hours after the sale, it was fifty miles away and standing within a barn."

Forsyth began to laugh.

"If those are the facts, you wouldn't have stood much chance before some of the Courts I know. But what on earth induced you to do such suspicious things?"

"A Mr Wormcast induced us. I mean, Wireworm. A very compelling man."

"Not of Nether Beauchamp?" screamed Dot.

"That's right," said Berry. "D'you know him?"

"Know him?" said Pembury. "We ran into him at – at – "

"Cherries?"

"That's right. We heard that a van was there, and we went to see if it was ours. It wasn't, of course. But some van or other had done in Wireworm's car. During his absence, I mean. And then cleared out. So any caravan was grist to his mill. The state of the one at Cherries suggested extremely strongly that that was the guilty van. But its driver apparently swore to an alibi. So when we rolled up to admit that we had a van, Wireworm fell upon us and swore that we'd done in his car. The thing was absurd, of course. We hadn't been near Nether Beauchamp. Besides, our van had been stolen before his car was done in."

"That wouldn't worry Wireworm," said Berry.

"You're perfectly right," said Dot. "He can't talk sense. We had to have police protection, to get away. But is it really our van? The one you've got, I mean."

"The sausages prove it," said Berry. "Forsyth, what do we do? We receive a van, not knowing it to have been stolen. We have the use of that van for more than six months. What is the judgment of the Court?"

"You do it up," said Forsyth, "and hand it back. But you really must be more careful. Fancy buying a caravan by the side of the way. And now let's hear what happened. Why did you move it by night?"

Berry related the tale.

When he had done, Daphne turned to Elizabeth Pembury.

"I simply can't tell you," she said, "how terribly sorry we are. We did you down good and proper. Until the van is ready, of course you will stay with us. That's the very least we can do. We owe you six months' lodging, look at it how you will."

"That's absurd," said Pembury. "You bought the van in good faith."

"That," said Berry, "is how Mr Wormwood talks. Give us a chance to discharge a monstrous debt."

"I refuse to wait any more," shrieked Lady Morayne. "After hearing this incredible tale, can anyone deny that honesty's gone by the board? Fancy stealing a caravan. Not the contents – the van itself. Fancy daring to steal it away. And then disposing of it – to most respectable people, as I can testify. And so we come back to money. Seventy-five pounds in an afternoon – and that, by selling something that isn't yours. That's the way to get on today. That's five hundred a week. And very nice, too. But that sort of thing wasn't done before the war. I wish I'd been born in 1840. Most of you think I was, but I'm younger than that."

"I confess," said Lord Level, "that sometimes I feel the same. To have died, full of years, in 1910…"

Berry shrugged his shoulders.

"In 1840," he said, "the one and only Duke was satisfied that England was going down."

The argument waxed. But I had no ears to hear. I was wondering what Forsyth would have said, if he had known how we came to acquire The Bold.

8

In Which We Fight For Our Rights, and an Old Acquaintance Does Us a Very Good Turn

"It's bad," said Berry. "I won't eat the blasted thing."

"That's the medlar," said I. "Until it's rotten, it isn't fit to eat."

"But it isn't fit to eat when it is."

"Connoisseurs say so," said I. "They wait till decay has set in."

"They don't wait till it's mobile," said Berry. "I can hardly keep this on my plate. Oh, and why don't you have one?"

"Because," I said, "I am not a connoisseur."

Berry pushed away his plate.

"When I feel like filth," he said, "I can go and pick it out of the gutters – like other dogs. But I don't want it served at my table. You know, I feel quite sick. Have we got any sheep-dip? I mean, mouth-wash?"

My sister strove not to laugh.

"Poor old lady," she said. "The gardeners probably told her that the Rokesby medlars were famous – as they certainly used to be. She's only trying to be nice."

"Funny way of being courteous," said Berry. "Fancy sending a basket of emetics to those you love. It's almost Borgian. I know. Let's send them to Boris. If he has a good gorge, he'll probably pass away."

"That wouldn't help us," said Daphne.

"It'd help me," said Berry violently.

"Well, you oughtn't to say such things. Besides, Vandy's the villain."

"Hush," said Berry piously. "Remember that exquisite precept – 'Speak no ill of the dead.' "

"That didn't stop you," said Daphne, "as soon as you saw his Will."

"No," said her husband. "It didn't. It wouldn't have stopped a Trappist with his mouth full. He might have scourged himself later, but he'd have had his stab."

It was an outrageous business, and that is the truth. A distant cousin of ours had possessed the family portraits, for what they were worth. Their place was, of course, at White Ladies: and how Vandy had come to have them was never clear. They had been removed from White Ladies before our time. Now Vandy had no children, and, with the death of his sister, his line would die. We had, therefore, arranged with him that, when that came about, the pictures should be returned. He had sworn to leave them in Trust and to direct that, on his sister's demise, they should be hung at White Ladies in perpetuity. He had actually sent us a copy of the relevant clause in his Will. In return, we had undertaken to pay his surviving sister five hundred pounds a year for so long as she lived. And then, unknown to us, he had made a new Will, and had left the family portraits to the son of a widow whom he had met at Dieppe. What was almost worse, he had left his sister without a penny piece.

Forsyth, when consulted, had shaken his head. Emma, when told the truth, had bad a break-down. Mr Boris Blurt, when approached, had been what he would have called 'deliciously arch'.

Boris was very modern. He wore his hair very long, he had a high-pitched voice, he believed in *Crème de Menthe* and he was an interior decorator. He considered Chippendale vulgar; St James's Palace, sordid; the National Gallery, subversive. He cared for no quarter of London except Soho. Best of all, be always called Berry 'dear'.

At our first interview –

"And I do so deplore money. I always find it so degrading. After a discussion of money, I always have to lie down. But what would you have, my dears? Of course I couldn't live with them. That Holbein alone..." He shuddered. "I always think Holbein's so unkind. But Algy Watchet says that they're worth the Mint. He's a darling, Algy Watchet – the most enchanting voice. He reads me Goethe sometimes, when I'm very low. And, you see, there's my mission to think of. And Americans are so generous..."

I need hardly say that Berry's report to Daphne of Mr Boris Blurt approached the obscene.

Be that as it may, it looked as though we were sunk.

We could not let Emma down – her distress was really painful. 'I feel dishonoured, Daphne. And I'd always meant you to have them, directly he died.' And Basing had seen the pictures and had roughly valued the twelve at twenty-five thousand pounds. 'The Gainsboroughs aren't very good, but the Reynolds are. The Van Dyck is very nice, and the Holbein is better still. The others are nothing much. But the Holbein will make big money.'

Basing's appreciation had hit us extremely hard. We had never dreamed – nor had Vandy – that the portraits were worth so much. They had, in fact, been insured for seven thousand pounds. And only the week before, we had felt that we could not afford to purchase a new motor-mower until next year.

Ten years had gone by since we had 'received' The Bold and the Pemburys' caravan: and during that difficult time we had come to regard White Ladies as a house that is built upon rock in the midst of a shifting world. We spent little time in London. We visited Jill and her husband – as a rule in the spring at Irikli, their exquisite villa by Como – and felt refreshed. Rarely we stayed in Paris or toured in France. But wherever we went, we were always glad to get back – to an atmosphere which was stable and as it had always been. 'The same yesterday, today and for ever.'

Without our gates, many changes had taken place.

Bell Hammer was closed. The Plagues were in Town for good, and the Lyvedens were travelling abroad. For this lamentable state of affairs, a famous, fatal house-party had been responsible. Reasonable precautions had been taken, but robbery under arms had not been foreseen. Lady Plague and Valerie Lyveden had seen three servants shot dead... And so Bell Hammer was closed. For the model village of Pouncet, an agent was doing his best.

Old Ludlow had died, full of years, and Jonathan and Natalie Baldric reigned in his stead. Punch and Athalia Fairfax were now a power in Mayfair.

Mrs Medallion was dead, and Toby, now lord of Rokesby, had married Cicely Voile – a very attractive girl. But they had let Rokesby furnished for several years. Here, I think they were wise. It was not a home for a bride.

The Beaulieus had become very rich: the Pemburys, now the Larches, were still very poor.

Richard Chandos of Maintenance, Wiltshire, had come to be our very good friend. So had his colleague, George Hanbury – a merry man. And Chandos had married a queen... And then, after four short years, his queen had been killed...with Mr and Mrs Hanbury...flying from France... And now he had married again – a white witch of a girl, whom everyone loved.

Jill was mostly in Italy. Jonah was much abroad, though he had a flat in Town. The war had left him restless: he never seemed so happy as when he was quietly taking his life in his hand. American-born, my wife had her eyes on her country. Her visits there were protracted; but, though I had gone over twice, I could not stand the pace.

That, I suppose, was the trouble with Daphne, with Berry, with me. We 'could not compete'. Perhaps I should say that we did not care to compete. There seemed to be nothing to compete for – nothing one-tenth so precious as that which White Ladies offered for nothing at all.

But even within our gates, we could not feel secure. Uncertainty's lease was running; and Pleasure, Uncertainty's steward, was calling the tune. People were grasping the present, because they had no idea what the future might hold. They lived for the moment – often from hand to mouth. High and low gambled, like madmen. Expenses were continually rising, while income was going down. The best was still to be had – at a fearful price. But craftsmanship was dying. The silversmith could not live: though he beat his vessels out in the sweat of his face, he could not earn a quarter of what the machinist made. People glanced at the headlines and went their way – to spend in less than an evening the price of a pair of shoes that would laugh at Time: and the man that might have made them was staking his dole at 'the dogs'. The old world was giving way to a less substantial structure, whose motive power was so huge that it seemed as though its engines would shake themselves from their seats.

And so we held fast to White Ladies, for there the world stood still. And now our Rock of Ages was to be robbed of its rights…

"You don't really feel sick?" said Daphne.

"Of course I do," said her husband. "I'm not accustomed to refuse. Besides, my stomach is proud."

"A peach," said I, "would be better than any mouth-wash."

"If it could be peeled," said Berry. "Peaches are rather like Holbein. They're so unkind. They always seem to repel me – I can't think why."

His reproduction of Boris was hideously accurate.

"All right. I'll peel it," said Daphne. "But I shall be sick in a minute, if you go on like that. By the way, you never told me. What's Jonah say?"

"He leaves it to us," said Berry. "I knew he would."

"And now what?"

Her husband shrugged his shoulders.

"It can be done," he said, "if darling Boris will play. It won't be a pleasant transaction: but Boris has every right to require his pound of flesh. There's no reason why he shouldn't. But I think he might stop short of the USA. After all, these are English portraits of English men. And twenty-five thousand pounds should set his business up. To say we can afford it is nonsense. It's going to hit us damned hard. And then there's Emma's allowance. But I cannot stomach the fact of those portraits going elsewhere. White Ladies is where they belong. It's not complete without them. They are the illustrations, painted by famous artists, of this old English record of other days."

"Well, how do we do it?" said Daphne. "Assuming that Jill agrees."

"Have to have a meeting," said Berry. "Boris can bring whom he likes, and we'll take Basing along. Our only card is this – that twenty-five thousand pounds is a hell of a bird in the hand. If he sends the pictures to Christie's, he may get more. But he may get considerably less. And he'll have to pay their commission in any event."

"Where will you meet?"

"In his bestial shop, I suppose. There's never anyone there. That, of course, is hardly surprising. It's like a damned awful dream. There are stains all over the walls – I thought it was damp. But, damn it, he's had them put there. He calls them decoration. And he's got a one-sided fireplace."

"I don't believe you," said Daphne, passing the peach.

"It's perfectly true," said I. "There's the grate all right; and on the left there's roughly forty square feet of burnt-brick rockery. I tell you, it's lunatic. The sort of work that belongs to the padded cell. And the district is more than squalid. I mean, a fried-fish shop would actually tone it up."

"It'd finish Boris," said Berry. "I think his personal scent is *Vers l'Aube du Jour*. Cheruit used to sell it. I may be wrong. But the shop's is rather more pungent. After ten minutes there, I wouldn't dare go to the Club."

"Well, if Jill agrees

Here Falcon came in with a cable.

Of course I leave it to you expect me on Thursday next such a wonderful day here Elaine swims just like a fish and a poor woman got stung by a sort of Jelly-fish they had to knock it off her and the life-saver's arms got burnt right through the towels all my love.

Padua.

Basing sat back in his chair and crossed his legs.

"The thing is this, Mr Blurt. If you were a picture-dealer, you'd jump at an offer like this, for dealers know how tricky the markets are. You might get more. You're very much more likely to get much less. Call in Peruke, if you like, and I'll lay he tells you the same. Twenty-five thousand pounds is a very attractive offer. To be honest, I'd take twenty thousand, if I was placed as you are – I would, indeed."

"I don't agree," said Watchet – a long-nailed, bull-necked brute, who was plainly the worse for wear. "Detestable as I find them, there is a section of the public that likes these things. They don't look at the work: the name is enough for them. They can't understand that Gainsborough couldn't paint, because Gainsborough couldn't see."

"How true," said Boris. "Algy darling, you always put things so well." He turned to Berry. "I'm inarticulate, dear. The words I crave for won't come. The feeling's there, you know, but the faculty of speech is denied. Once, long ago, I foamed."

"What, not at the ears?" said Berry.

"No, no, at the mouth. D'you remember when I foamed, Algy? Because the words wouldn't come? Hubert was playing his concerto... I had to go out, you know. I wanted to speak of mountains, riven by storm."

"The gorge was rising," said Berry.

"That's right," cried Boris. "That's right. Emotion had taken charge. They had a terrible time with me. Oscar told me later I cried all night."

"That's bowels," said Berry. "You know. What you yearn with, The seat of all the emotions. When somebody kicks you, the bowels inform the brain. The brain instructs the tear ducts – and there you are. And now what about this offer. How do the bowels react?"

Boris regarded Berry with starting eyes.

At length –

"I – I don't quite know," he stammered, wiping his brow. "At least – I mean, Algy feels very strongly that I oughtn't to give them away."

"Of course you mustn't," said Berry. "It'd mean a major operation for one thing. And who would you give them to?"

"I mean the pictures," screamed Boris. "I mustn't give the pictures away."

"There's no reason on earth why you should. And I hope very much that you won't – unless you give them to us."

"But that's what you're asking me to do."

"I beg your pardon," said Berry.

Boris squirmed.

"You – you make it so difficult, dear. I've told you how it revolts me to talk about dross. I always feel so degraded. And I simply couldn't haggle. But, you see, I must do myself justice. Of course, it doesn't make sense, but Algy says that these daubs are worth at least fifty thousand..."

Basing gave a short laugh.

"I cannot answer," he said, "for Mr Watchet's experience in this particular field: but when I detest a certain class of work, I study neither the artists nor the prices their work will fetch. He finds these pictures detestable: I do not. And so I feel it likely that my opinion is worth rather more than his. And I tell you this, Mr Blurt – the figure of fifty thousand is quite absurd. I'm not going into details, because you have had a copy of my report. But this I will say – that only one of the portraits is an uncertain quantity. And that is the Holbein. The other eleven would make ten thousand pounds. I'm speaking roughly, of course: but thereabouts. The Holbein might make ten or it might make fifteen. It is possible that it would make twenty. But it won't make a penny more."

"But that would be thirty thousand."

"If it were to make twenty – yes. But it might make only ten. I think, if you sold it at Christie's that it would make fifteen."

"More like thirty-five," blared Watchet. "Plenty of mugs about. An' I don' agree that the others are only worth ten. There's a Gon-Gonzales Coques there."

"So the pamphlet says," said Basing. "The pamphlet's wrong. The portrait in question is not by Gonzales Coques, and it's not very good. It's worth about forty pounds, including the frame."

To Boris' obvious consternation, Mr Watchet rose to his feet, swayed to an alcove and threw himself down on a couch.

"Now you've upset him," cried the former, clasping his hands. "Oh, dear, what shall I do? He feels so deeply, dear Algy. You see, he's been given vision. He sees what we cannot see. And when his vision is questioned, he just curls up."

"I see," said Berry gravely. "Will he take refuge in tears?"

"Oh, I do hope he won't. If only he relaxes at once…" Boris rushed to a nightmare cupboard, to pour out a quarter of a tumbler of *Crème de Menthe*. Then he minced to the alcove. "Drink this, dear," he commanded.

Mr Watchet stared upon the glass.

"That's right," said Berry. "Pretend it's a gall and wormwood and toss it off." Somehow Mr Watchet complied. "And that ought to help his vision. In a quarter of an hour or so he'll see all manner of things that we can't see. Blue-based baboons'll be nothing to what he descries."

Boris arranged the cushion and left his disgruntled friend.

"I know you don't mean it," he said; "but Algy cannot appreciate blindness of heart. All he sees is a great, black cloud that is pressing him down. And then he gives way. The other night, at *The Wash-Pot* – "

"Look here, Mr Blurt," said Berry. "An adviser who cannot consider an opinion other than his own is of no use to anyone. He is of no use to me: but, what is more to the point, he is of no use to you. I don't ask you to accept what Mr Basing says: but I do ask you to find someone with whom he can deal. Mr Basing is my expert. Why don't you call in Peruke? He's honest and very well known. And I am prepared to abide by what he says."

"Oh, of course he'll agree with you."

"Why should he? We haven't approached him. You needn't mention our names. Let him see the portraits and tell him the offer you've had."

"But he'll want such a terrible fee, and I'm dreadfully poor. You see, I'm extending my premises. I've taken the place next door. At least, not next door – the one after. The grocer next door is so boorish. He wants to sublet, I know. But he's being contrary, you know. And dreadfully personal. So Algy and I ignore him – I always think that's best. And when he's enfolded in art, I feel that he will respond."

"He'll respond all right," said Berry, "provided, of course, he can breathe. D'you mind if I open a window? Or will that affect his figs?"

"Now you're being naughty," said Boris, wagging a forefinger. He raised his voice. "Can you stand an open window, Algy? Oh, he's asleep. Now isn't that wonderful? You know, I hardly dared hope…"

In silence the window was opened, and Basing cleared his throat.

"If you show him my card, Mr Blurt, Peruke will charge twenty-five guineas – or thereabouts."

"But it's waste of money," screamed Boris. "He'll say the same."

"I think he will," said Basing. "But he will be your adviser – which I am not."

"But Algy is my adviser."

"Is he still asleep?" said Basing.

"I think so."

"Then listen to me. Mr Watchet's opinion is worthless, compared with that of Peruke. Peruke is twice his age and has bought and sold old pictures for many years. You needn't show him that pamphlet which Vandeleur Pleydell produced. Peruke won't have to be told who painted what. The moment he sees those portraits, he'll know who the seven are by. And he'll know that the other five are of no account. And then he'll appraise the lot. And please remember this – that he knows the state of the markets as no one else."

Boris looked furtively round.

"I don't think I can do it," he whispered, fingers to mouth. "Algy would be so terribly, terribly hurt. Besides, he's shown so much interest. And then he's already in touch with a Mr Lemonbaum."

"Of Red Lion Square?"

"That's right" – brightly. "D'you know him?"

But Basing was looking at Berry.

"In that case," he said, "I feel that we're wasting our time." He returned to Boris. "And you will be lucky, young man, if you see ten thousand pounds."

"*What?*"

"Very fortunate," said Basing. "Lemonbaum is one of the biggest blackguards that ever stepped. And you can tell him I said so. He'll only smile.'

Boris was plainly frightened.

"You think," he stammered, "you think I've made a mistake?"

"That depends," said Basing, "on how far you've gone."

251

"He's going to see the pictures on Wednesday next."

"I see. Well, don't let him take them."

"Oh, he's only going to see them," said Boris.

"You'd better be there," said Basing. "I'll lay he comes with a van."

Berry got to his feet.

"Understand this, Mr Blurt. Once those pictures leave Broken Ash, the offer I've made is withdrawn."

Boris was down on his knees by Watchet's side.

"Wake up, Algy, wake up. I've terrible news."

With a fearful grunt, the other propped himself on an arm.

"Wassamarrer?" he said.

"Lemonbaum's going to take my pictures away."

"Thassrigh'. On Wenssy. Bringum up to 's office. 'Sall arrange."

"But I never said – "

Mr Watchet had already relaxed.

Boris was all of a twitter.

"Now he had no right to do that. It's most presumptuous. I never knew anything about it. And now Mr Lemonbaum – Oh, what shall I do?"

Basing replied.

"You'd better go down and stop him."

"How can I?" screamed Boris. "Supposing he's like the grocer. And I can't endure a scene. Any kind of difference upsets me terribly. It's the opposition of wills. I'm all on edge already. And I've had such a tiring day."

Basing shrugged his shoulders.

"It's up to you, Mr Blurt. You have been warned."

Boris was wringing his hands.

"But what can I *do*?"

"You don't want Lemonbaum to take them?"

"Of course I don't."

"And you don't want a scene?"

Boris stifled a scream.

"Oh, I mustn't. It's bad for my heart. The other day, when the grocer was unsympathetic – "

"Then give Major Pleydell permission to take those pictures away. That won't mean that you're selling the pictures to him. It will merely mean that they're safe. I mean, you can trust Major Pleydell to take all care of the portraits he wants to buy. He will take them to White Ladies and lodge them there. If you sell to him, he will keep them. If you sell to somebody else, they will be at your disposal when ever you please."

Boris' face was transfigured.

"Oh, do do that for me, dear. It's a perfectly sweet idea. And we won't tell anyone."

"I'll do it with pleasure," said Berry. "I'm all for taking care of what I hope to possess."

"Well, that's that," said Basing. "But let this be a lesson to you. You see what Watchet's worth. He's damned near let you right down. Cut him right out, Mr Blurt. You've got a perfect excuse. And go to Peruke, as I say. Show him my card, and ask him to go to White Ladies, view the pictures and let you have a report."

"None of us will approach him," said Berry. "The servants will show him in and will show him out."

Boris was savaging his thumb.

"Will you say thirty thousand?" he said.

"No," said Berry, "I won't. Mr Basing has said that my offer is very fair."

"It's more than fair," said Basing. "Peruke will bear me out."

"But Algy – "

" – knows no more than you do," said Basing. "He only pretends that he does. But for the pamphlet he's read he wouldn't dare open his mouth. If you like to put your fortune in the hands of a drunken impostor – "

"Oh, hush. Supposing he hears you."

Basing turned away.

"Listen," said Berry. "Tomorrow afternoon the portraits will be at White Ladies, safe and sound. If you are content for them to stay there, I will write you a cheque for twenty-five thousand pounds. No deductions for commission, insurance or transport fees. But don't forget two things. The first is this – I may withdraw that offer at my time."

"Oh, that's not fair," whined Boris.

"Don't be absurd," said Basing. "D'you expect Major Pleydell to wait – and actually house your pictures, while you metaphorically hawk them, in the hope of improving upon the offer he's made?"

"The second thing's this," said Berry. "That I buy all the portraits, or none at all. Sell one to somebody else, and you can collect the rest the following day."

With that, he picked up his hat.

"Oh, I do wish," whimpered Boris, "I knew what to do."

Basing laid a card upon a table.

"Fire Mr Watchet," he said. "And go to Peruke."

In a somewhat uneasy silence, we made our way to Scotts.

As we took our seats in an alcove –

"I'm much obliged, Basing," said Berry. "Nobody could have done more."

"I don't know about that," said Basing. "I think we've discredited Watchet and I think he will go to Peruke. The most pressing danger is Mr Lemonbaum."

"How so?" said I. "If we take the portraits away..."

"That won't stop him," said Basing. "Lemonbaum is red-hot. And this is right down his street. He won't be deterred by the fact that the portraits are gone. He's got to be broken down, before he'll let go. But I think you're up to his weight. So let him come to White Ladies and butcher him there."

Berry fingered his chin.

"I see," he said slowly. "And how does one discourage a leper like Lemonbaum?"

"Break his heart," said Basing. "Wear him down with misunderstanding. A course of *suppresio veri*: and then *suggestio falsi* with all you've got."

"Aren't you clever?" said Berry.

Such communion was far beyond me, though Berry seemed satisfied. But when, later on, he purchased a second-hand ear-trumpet, I thought I could see the line which he was proposing to take.

As arranged, we collected the portraits the following afternoon. Poor Emma, still in possession, was thankful to see them go. We warned her of Lemonbaum's coming and bade her refer him to us.

We did not hang the portraits – that would have been premature. We put them into a spare room and stood them against the walls. The Holbein and the Van Dyck were laid upon neighbouring beds. As we were leaving the chamber, Berry looked round the improvised gallery. Then he addressed our forbears.

"*Mesdames, Messieurs*," he said, "we shall do our best."

Then he followed me out of the room and locked the door.

The next day, at three o'clock, came Mr Lemonbaum.

All was ready for his coming, for Emma had rung us up when the dealer left Broken Ash. He was to be received in the garden – to be exact, in the heart of the baby maze. Such surroundings, we felt, would be against him. I think they were.

I watched the fellow emerge from the front of his elegant van. His air was confident. But when I saw him again, he had thrown away his cigar and had his hat in his hand.

Berry received him alone, ear-trumpet in hand. Daphne and I were in waiting, two paces away – the hedge of the baby maze was four feet thick.

"This way, if you please," said William. And then, "Mr Lemonbaum, sir."

As the footman turned to withdraw, I strolled into sight.

Before the dealer could speak, Berry had opened fire.

"You're wasting your time," he snapped. "I'm not going to sell."

Mr Lemonbaum started, and a hand went up to his head. Then –

"But the pictureth aren't yourth," he said.

"No, I don't," said Berry. "Besides, he's going abroad."

The dealer stared upon Berry, as though he were not of this world. Then, with a manifest effort, he wreathed his face into a smile.

"I think perhapth," he lisped, "you didn't quite catch what I thaid."

"I never use them," said Berry. "I find the heads come off." He addressed me in French. "This gentleman wants a match."

As I produced a box –

"*Catch*," screamed Lemonbaum. "He didn't *catch* what I thaid."

"Then why didn't you say so?" said Berry. "And it's no good addressing him. He only speaks French."

There was an awkward silence.

Then Lemonbaum pointed to the trumpet.

"Perhapth if you uthed that, thir…"

"Not yet," said Berry. "They don't come out till dusk. D'you want me to use the trumpet? I hear you perfectly well. But I will, if you like."

With that, he put the thing to his ear.

Its mouth was rather too high for Mr Lemonbaum. Twice he put out a hand, as though to lower the horn; but each time his courage failed him, and Berry was looking away. At last he stood a-tiptoe and said his piece.

"I've come for the pictureth," he blared.

"Certainly not," said Berry. "I hate the stuff. Nasty, vulgar habits. And what d'you think this is? A general store?"

The dealer gathered himself. Then he repeated his statement with all his might.

"Mixture?" said Berry. "What mixture?"

"*Pictureth*," screamed the other. "P for Perthy."

"Have you, indeed?" said Berry. "What ever time did you start?"

"No, no, NO. I've come to collect the portraitth. The portraitth from Broken Ath."

" 'Smoking Flax'?" said Berry. "I don't remember the name. It's quite a good title, though. Who is it by?"

"BROKEN ASH," yelled the dealer. "I've come from BROKEN ASH."

"Broken Ash?" said Berry. "I thought there was some mistake. This is White Ladies. Broken Ash is about – "

"The portraitth," howled Lemonbaum, dancing. "I've come to collect the portraitth for Mr Blurt."

"Well, you can go that way," said Berry. "But I always go by Bloodstock. It's more direct."

Mr Lemonbaum wiped the sweat from his face and neck. Then, with bolting eyes, he returned to the charge.

"I am here," he began…

"Of course I can," said Berry. "You don't have to use this trumpet. I told you just now – I can hear you perfectly well."

Mr Lemonbaum turned away and let out a noise which resembled a camel's bark.

"That's the buck toad calling," said Berry. "You're very lucky to hear it. The doe you can hear all the time. But the buck is rare."

The dealer took a deep breath. Then he lugged out a pocketbook and, after peering a moment, plucked a sheet of note-paper out of its folds.

"Give that the oneth over, thir."

Berry took the paper and read the writing aloud.

To Miss Emma Pleydell.
Please allow bearer to take the twelve portraits away.
                                        A Watchet.

Then he handed it back.

"Who's Watchet?" he said.

"Mr Blurtth reprethentative."

"What if he does?" said Berry. "That's his affair."

Mr Lemonbaum choked. Then he seized the trumpet and hooted into its depths.

"But you've got the portraitth," he howled.

"I shouldn't," said Berry. "You'll only get into trouble. And I didn't know Mr Watchet had any pictures there."

"They're Blurt'th," screamed Lemonbaum.

"No, you won't," said Berry. "I have them specially made." With that, he inspected his trumpet and, after inserting his fingers into the horn, drew out about two ounces of cotton-wool. "That's my nephew," he added. "A playful child."

Lemonbaum was making a rattling noise...

"There's the roach-backed warbler," said Berry. "The first time I've heard him this year."

Encouraged by what he had seen, the dealer plainly decided to try again. He had no idea, of course, that the other end of the trumpet was plugged with wax. He poured his soul into the mouth-piece...

"Thith paper...giveth me the right...to take thothe portraitth away."

"Then why d'you wear them?" said Berry. "I mean, it's asking for trouble in weather like this."

"Right," screamed the dealer. "*Right*. I've been to Broken Ath, and they thent me here. You thee, Mr Blurt dethireth to have the portraitth in Town."

"I believe it to be," said Berry, "though I prefer Aberdeen. But what's that to do with Mr Watchet?"

Mr Lemonbaum dabbed at the paper. "He'th thigned it for Blurt," he yelled. "I'm here to take them away."

"I don't remember," said Berry. "I haven't been there for years."

"*He'th thigned for Blurt*," raved the dealer. "THIGNED FOR BLURT."

"Is he, indeed?" said Berry. "How very sad. And that, of course, explains why he's selling. And yet, you know, I'd rather be blind from birth than lose my sight."

Lemonbaum was half-way to frenzy.

"The pictureth," he screamed. "The PORTRAITTH. I'VE COME TO TAKE THEM AWAY."

"I don't think they will," said Berry. "You know what Christie's are."

The name might have been a charm.

With fallen jaw, the dealer stared upon Berry, as a convict regards a Judge who has given him seven years when he had expected six months.

Twice he endeavoured to speak, and twice he failed.

At the third attempt –

"Chrithtieth?" he wailed. "You mean, you've thent them to Chrithtieth?"

"Oh, before then," said Berry. "They advise the end of November, between you and me. And now I think you should go. If you're driving straight back to Perth, you'll get in very late. Besides, I have an appointment. I've promised to go to Dovetail to judge some Edinburgh Rocks. Are you interested in poultry?"

But Mr Lemonbaum was not listening. Protruding a thick underlip, he was staring blindly before him and striking his palm with his fist. Suddenly, as though his most bitter reflection was not to be borne, he made a noise like a cat whose tail has been crushed.

"That," said Berry, "is the copper-bottomed oriole – a very vulgar bird. And no idea of hygiene."

Looking ready to burst, Mr Lemonbaum picked up his hat, which he had let fall, and turned the way he had come.

Daphne, Berry and I retired to the terrace forthwith.

The baby maze is so slight that it scarcely deserves the name. Still, the dealer was not at his best. When he had been yelling for two minutes, we summoned a gardener and told him to lead him out.

Nearly three weeks had gone by, and August was growing old. Jill and Jonah were with us, and the Bishop, Miss Cobbold and the Baldrics were coming to lunch. About Miss Cobbold's presence, there had been an argument. But my sister had been insistent.

"I confess she's Victorian. But that's no reason why we should ask her alone. The Bishop is Edwardian, and Jonathan and Natalie are Georgian. I don't know what we are, but that is beside the point. I believe in mixing the periods. It brings the best out of each."

"The stomacher," said Berry, "is always right."

And so Miss Cobbold had been asked to meet the Bishop of Brooch.

The portraits were still at White Ladies, to our relief. Peruke had come down to see them, to our delight: but we had made a point of being abroad for the day. Ten days after his visit, Berry had written to Boris, renewing our offer and asking him to make up his mind. Boris had replied from Norfolk, declaring that he was awaiting Peruke's report. His letter had reached us that morning – ten minutes ago.

"It's a lie," said Daphne. "Of course he's heard from Peruke."

"That's right," said Berry. "The shy little sweetheart is trying to string us along. Reaching after the shadow, but keeping the substance safe. I'll lay he's got our offer locked up in his make-up box."

"From what you tell me," said Jonah, "I'm much inclined to agree. That type is avaricious."

"Oh, don't talk like that," minced Berry. "I know you don't mean it, dear, but, you see, it always unnerves me." He turned to me. "D'you remember that night at *The Cesspool*, when I was so unnerved? I felt there were great birds all round me. Oh, it was such a nightmare. But you were so wonderful, darling. You lent me your own spittoon."

"He can't," said Jill, "he *can't* be as bad as that."

"It's exactly like him," said I.

"What," said Berry, "I should really have liked to see was the grocer's rejection of his advances, when Boris expressed a desire to rent his shop. Never mind. As you say, he's probably lying. But I don't see what we can do, until Basing comes back. Then he can get in touch with Peruke."

Basing was returning from Paris in three days' time.

Jonah sighed.

"I'm not blaming you,' he said, "but you should have got tough. That is the only way to reduce that type. Of course the man's a fool – he won't get twenty-five thousand anywhere else. But he's a full-marks' knave. What's more to the point, he's a coward. And if you had shown him the whip, he'd have given in."

"What whip, know-all?" said Berry.

"Any whip," said Jonah. "Threatened to bring a gorilla and let it loose in his shop."

Jill and I began to shake with laughter.

"I see," said Berry. "And what about the subsequent proceedings?"

"There wouldn't have been any," said Jonah. "People like Boris never come into Court. And if they do, they go down. If we want to keep those portraits, we'll have to do it yet." He leaned forward. "I'll tell you why. Because, if we don't, the other fellow will. And there'll be the Holbein gone, and Boris crying his eyes out because he forgot the commission of twenty per cent."

There was a painful silence. Jonah was very shrewd.

At length –

"I do wish," said Daphne, "our forbears had had less expensive tastes. Why did they have to go to Holbein and van Dyck?"

261

"My sweet," said Berry, "dishonour where dishonour is due. They wanted the best for us. It never entered their heads that they were laying up treasure for Mr Boris Blurt. The whole affair is enough to make them turn in their graves."

"We've got to have them," cried Jill. "The portraits, I mean. You see, if we let them go, they'll be simply wild. They really will turn in their graves. And we don't want to break our record…"

We knew what she meant. White Ladies had always been an untroubled house. And Basing maintained that ghosts were unhappy beings, haunting the scene of some trouble they could not cure.

"It's a proper swine," said Berry, "and that's the truth. I could put it much more strongly, but let that go. We're ready to beggar ourselves, to get those portraits back – not for ourselves, but because they belong to this house. Nine men out of ten would have jumped at twenty-five thousand pounds. Nine men out of ten would have felt that we had a right to buy them for such a sum. But Boris Blurt is the tenth. That treacherous slice of sob-stuff, that grossly ignorant hybrid is going to do us down – and himself as well. He's damned near done it once. And we had to go out and save him, to save ourselves. And what is our reward – our guerdon? The privilege of housing our pictures, while he does his level best to sell them elsewhere."

"Hush," said Daphne. "I think I hear somebody's car."

"Now if it's dear Jonathan," said Berry, "you're not to take him away. I want him all to myself. We're going to read Dante together in the original tongue. I always think Italian's so piquant. German disturbs me, you know. But – "

"If you go on like that, when anyone's here…"

"That's all right," said Berry. "I'm going to leaven the lunch with a little Lemonbaum." With a hideous leer, he addressed himself to an elegant pillar of bronze. "Itth tho nithe to thee you, Mith Cobbold, and thank you in perthon for thothe delithious medlarth. They're wonderful thingth – I wath up all night, you know."

Before Daphne had time to protest, the door was opened, and the Bishop of Brooch was announced.

Coffee had been served upon the terrace, when the Bishop fingered his chin.

"I'm speaking off the record," he said, "but my opinion is that, before many years have gone by, this civilization of ours is going to come to an end."

"I entirely agree," said Jonah. "But what's to be done?"

"I sincerely believe that the matter is out of our hands."

"Are we so wicked?" said Daphne.

The Bishop shook his head.

"There's room for improvement," he said, "but then there always was. It's simply a question of progress. Once we progressed by crawling. And then we walked. Then we began to hasten. And now we rush. Every year the pace grows hotter. And one day something will go. And don't forget that every year the structure grows more elaborate, and so more vulnerable."

"I quite agree," said Berry. "And now for the date of the deluge."

"No, you don't," said his lordship. "I've said too much, as it is. Besides, I have no idea. I'm not among the prophets."

"Well, you eat strange food," said Berry. "At least, you had that reputation, when we were at Oxford College in 'sixty-four."

"Make it 'fifty-four," said the Bishop. "Then we shall be able to remember the Charge of the Light Brigade."

"What did he eat?" said Natalie.

"His diet," said Berry, "was completely Biblical."

"I regret," said the Bishop, "to have to denounce that report. All I did was to display a discernment denied to and, therefore, misconstrued by my less fortunate colleagues. Where all were *gourmands* – "

"Cries of 'Shame'," said Berry.

" – I was a *gourmet*. I had a weakness for medlars. I have it still."

"Oh, have you?" cried Miss Cobbold. "I'll send you some."

"Do," said Berry. "He can't get locusts here, and I think the Rokesby medlars might take their place."

"There you are," declared Miss Cobbold. "I said that to send them to people was an unfriendly act. But Bursley – that's the butler – was most insistent that they were highly esteemed."

"When was this?" said the Bishop.

"A month ago."

His lordship began to laugh.

"You sent him last year's," he said. "Very few people can enjoy them as old as that."

Miss Cobbold had a hand to her mouth.

"How dreadful of me. Major Pleydell, what can I say?"

"That's all right," said Berry. "After the first two dozen, I felt there was something wrong. So we caught what were left, took them into the meadows and let them go."

"I hope," said the Bishop, "they didn't devour the grass."

"On the contrary," said Berry, "we expect the hay next year to be superfine."

But Miss Cobbold refused to be comforted.

"You're very forgiving," she said, "to have given me lunch."

"Let me absolve you," said the Bishop. "And please let me have a basket of this year's crop."

"No Popery," said Berry. "Indulgences aren't allowed, And how d'you like Rokesby, Miss Cobbold?"

"It suits me very well, thank you. I don't go abroad very much. The grounds are so lovely, you know. But I'm having trouble with servants. I do the best I can, but they find it dull."

"Same here," said Natalie. "How our great-uncle managed, I do not know. We've had to close half the house."

"Progress," murmured the Bishop.

"Uncertainty," said Jonah, "has much to answer for."

"That's very true. The well-known phrase, 'the changes and chances of this mortal life', has come for us all to take on a fearful meaning. Today – we never know. And so all strive to get the most out of our days – which, of course, though natural enough, is a great mistake." The Bishop turned to Jill. "You don't strive, my dear."

"I don't have to," said Jill. "It always seems to be there. I'm very fortunate."

"I think for you it will always seem to be there. But most of us, including our servants, don't want to get left. I deplore, but I can't condemn. The standard of life has risen. We've tasted blood. We take for granted things that our fathers would have gaped at – paid to see. Some of us are sated, and so are glad to throw back. All of us here, I think, set store by the countryside. I'd sooner stroll in my close than sit in a cinema-house. But young men and maidens wouldn't. They want to go out and dance – a very natural impulse, which we have known. All the time, the sand is falling... Can you blame them if Rokesby and Buckram don't suit their book? Jonah's quite right. Uncertainty's Progress' familiar. It marches behind. I don't think we realized that, until the Great War. And then we saw how very small a matter could throw into utter confusion our way of life."

Jonathan Baldric was speaking.

"But what can we do about it? I mean, we look to you."

"Nothing," said the Bishop. "Not even Wycliffe would cut any ice today. The pace is too hot. We can only do our duty...and hope and pray for the best."

"Ah," said Jonathan Baldric, "if everyone did his duty..."

"Precisely. A great many do: but then a great many don't. There are many Gallios going, who 'care for none of these things'. The truth is they haven't time. And so we come back to pace. It's the pace that kills. But I'll tell you one thing I observe, and that is a revival of goodwill. People are growing kinder, one to another. And that is worth everything."

I tried not to think of the portraits – of Vandy, of Boris and Mr Lemonbaum.

"You're perfectly right," said Miss Cobbold. "I've noticed it, too. For the first time since the war that truly English quality, good nature, seems to be coming back. Don't you agree, Major Pleydell ?"

Jill's shoulders were shaking and Daphne had a hand to her mouth.

With a manifest effort –

"Well, I – haven't been knocked down by it," said Berry. "But I think I know what you mean. One, er, notices it on the Bench. The police are more reluctant to give a dog a bad name."

"Oh, come," said the Bishop. "You of all men should put it higher than that. But, whether or no, Miss Cobbold and I are right. We used to be called Merry England, and I shall always think we deserved the name. We have a sense of humour that nothing can ever quench. The blood and slush of the trenches signally failed. But the war was a very great shock. And great shocks have great reactions. We were much more than sobered – nervy, suspicious, fretful for year after year. There was no health in us. But now we are getting better, and our inherent good nature is coming back into its own."

"Well, here's to it," said Berry, raising his glass. "For home consumption only. And the Empire, of course."

Miss Cobbold laughed.

"Isn't that a contradiction in terms?"

But Jonah shook his head.

"In foreign countries, Miss Cobbold, good nature is not understood. It is, therefore, interpreted as weakness. For that I can vouch. Civility – yes, of course. But good nature – no."

The Bishop was looking at Jonah.

"You think we're making mistakes?"

"I'm afraid so. Some very bad ones. We still use the velvet glove, but we find the iron hand *démodé* – not quite nice. And that is a very great pity, for the iron hand is something that foreign nations respect."

"Progress," murmured the Bishop. "We're getting soft."

"You're not, sir," said Jonathan Baldric. "Neither am I. I've been reclaimed, you know. I used to breakfast at ten and retire about three. But my wife has altered all that. I was up at five this morning to – to comfort a cow. I rather fancy the byre. But the lambing season's blank verse. Muckin' about with a lantern all night long. An' a wind like a circular saw, an' the shepherd tight. Mind you, I don't blame him. But if anyone says I'm soft, they've got it wrong."

'It's perfectly true," said Natalie. "He carries calves about."

"Only Ahasuerus," said her husband. "But Ahasuerus has got a crush on me. When I put him under my arm, he licks my face. There's a lot in this livestock racket."

"Would you go back?" said Daphne.

"Not on your life, lady. I don't do the brutes much good, but – they've got me down."

"I give you best," said the Bishop. "Or should I commend your wife?"

Natalie laughed.

"I may have sown the seed, but the soil was terribly good."

"The purest guano," said Berry. "That's why Ahasuerus likes him so much. You don't want a pupil, do you? There's a young man I know called Boris. At the moment he's an interior decorator."

The Bishop threw up his hands.

"Send him to me," said Baldric. "I've got a sow called Sapphira. He shall adorn her sty."

"She won't lay, if he does," said Berry, "or they'll all have three legs or something."

"Her name," said the Bishop, "is suggestive."

"I think," said Baldric, "she's all of the seven sins. And yet I like the old girl. I wink at her, as I pass, and I'll swear she smirks. But she'd enlarge Boris' outlook."

"And he'd enlarge yours," said Berry. "Never mind. Come and see our fountain. After incredible labour, we've got it playing again."

"And then I must be going," said the Bishop...

Before she left, Miss Cobbold was shown the house.

267

As she was leaving, she made us a pretty speech.

"You've been very kind to your neighbour. I won't return evil for good by asking you back. But if some day, when you are passing, you feel like quenching your thirst, please do me the very great pleasure of ringing my bell." She put her hand in Daphne's. "And if my niece should come down, may I really bring her and her husband to see your beautiful home?"

"Certainly," said my sister. "When do you expect them? You see, we may be away at the end of next month."

"Oh, very soon," said Miss Cobbold. She opened her bag. "They're now in Italy. And they were going straight back. He's an American, you know. But now they're coming to England for four or five days." She unfolded and scanned a letter. "Ah, here we are. *We shall arrive on the second and sail on the eighth. We hadn't intended to come to England at all, but Coker has heard of a Holbein which is for sale and you know what he is about old masters.* Such a queer name, I find it. Coker Falk. To tell you the truth, I've never met him, my dear: but I know he collects pictures and he's immensely rich."

I like to think that we said the proper things: but I cannot be sure that we did, for we could think of nothing but the appalling truth, of which our gentle neighbour had made us free. Coker Falk was against us – and he was 'immensely rich'.

Four trying days had gone by, and Berry, Jonah and I were sitting in Basing's flat.

"First, the facts," said Basing. "They're very short. I saw Peruke this morning at ten o'clock. He surveyed the pictures on a Friday: on the following Monday morning his report was in Boris' hands."

"There you are," said Berry.

"That's nothing," said Basing. "You wait…"

"I've seen that report, and it might have been written by me. Boris never mentioned your offer. Had he done so, Peruke would have told him that he was mad to refuse. Not knowing of your offer, Peruke suggested that he (Peruke) should get into touch with Falk, for whom he had acted before, who he knew was in Rome. This, with regard to the Holbein.

"Boris writes back to Peruke, enclosing his fee and saying that, after all, he's decided not to sell. Then he sits down and *writes to Falk himself* – I mean, he must have. How else can Coker know?"

"Oh, give me strength," said Berry.

"I'll say Peruke is angry. We've got a friend there. His one idea is to bring Master Boris down. The question is how to do it…

"And now for Coker Falk. From what you said last night, you met him some years ago. I have never met him, although I know his name. But Peruke knows all about him. He's a very ignorant bloke of the Middle West. Four years ago he was left a very great fortune. Now he lives in state in New York and has started collecting pictures. He knows next to nothing about them, and when he'd been stung once or twice, he drew in his horns. But he found that Peruke was honest, and they have done one or two deals. So Peruke thought they might do another…

"Well, Coker is now in the running. Before he buys, he's sure to consult Peruke – so Boris slipped up there. But Peruke must be fair with Coker. He was going to recommend him to go to sixteen thousand, but that doesn't mean that he won't go higher than that. He's got no rules and he'd like to own a Holbein. So there we are."

"I think," said Berry, "that Coker must be co-opted. Our relation with him was unhappy, but that was not our fault. We must hope that he will see wisdom and wash old enmities out. If Coker comes in – well, if he can't break Boris down, his hand has lost its cunning, and that's the truth."

"And then you toss up?" said Basing. "I mean that's the usual way."

"First things first," said Berry. "Boris has got to be burst. He's a treacherous slab of slime, and he's got to be burst."

"It might be done," said Basing, "if Coker will play."

"That's up to Peruke. Peruke should see him at once. He's due here on Monday next. But I'll lay he stays in Paris a couple of days. Let Peruke ring up *The Crillon* this afternoon."

"At the moment," said Jonah, "we have the Holbein safe. But Boris is going to ask us to send it to Town."

"That's right," said Basing. "He's waiting to hear from Coker. When Coker gives him a date, he'll ask you to send it up."

"And we reply," said Jonah, "that the moment it leaves White Ladies, our offer expires."

"What could be better?" said Basing. "That will shake him badly – and clear the field."

"But he'll have to have it," said Berry. "He daren't ask Coker to go and see it *chez nous*."

"He'll have to have it," said Jonah. "And yet he won't. We'll send up one of the duds. There's one about the size of the Holbein. We'll attach the Holbein's label and send it up. Boris won't know the difference."

"Brilliant," cried Basing. "Brilliant. And while Coker is hesitating, Peruke, who is passing, blows in and denounces the dud as a fraud."

"And here's genius," said Berry. "We'll have the girlie cold. Coker goes off the deep end and threatens to call in the police. We're not there: Peruke is painfully hostile: Coker does his stuff and dictates his terms. 'Nothing said, and the portraits for fifteen thousand pounds.' "

"Make it ten," said Basing. "No good wasting good money on filth like that."

"Oh, I can't believe it," said Berry.

"I don't see why not," said Basing, "if Coker will play."

"And then, what?" said Jonah.

"There's the rub," said Basing. "Unless you can get round Coker, you'll have to toss up. Only for the Holbein, of course. If he wins, he gives you the others. If he loses, you pay him ten thousand pounds."

"That's fair enough," said Berry.

The remnants of our compunction were laid to rest the next day. This office was done by Boris, whose letter shall speak for itself.

August, 1934.

My dear Major Pleydell,

Would you be so dear as to let me have the Holbein for two or three days? A charming friend has offered to photograph the picture, and I feel that, if you are to have it, that should be done. I mean, I should like a memento of what I have lost. He makes such enchanting studies – his values are so fine. Could I have it some time on Monday?

Yours ever sincerely,

Boris Blurt.

PS. You see, I have very nearly made up my mind.

"Gehazi calling," said Berry. "How's that for leprosy?"

"He'll be struck, or something," said Jill.

"He'll be struck all right on Tuesday, if Coker plays. Get on to Basing, someone. He ought to know."

Ten minutes later, perhaps, I took the call.

When I had read the letter –

"Splendid," said Basing. "Send it up by express, will you? Peruke shall take it with him, to round our tale. You see, Major Pleydell was right. Our friend is now in Paris, and Peruke is leaving to join him, at four o'clock."

September was in, and Coker Falk was sitting at ease upon the terrace, sipping 'a high-ball' and smoking a big cigar.

He had mellowed out of all recognition. Though he still spoke fast, the spate of talk had sunk to a decent stream: and, though he took the lead, he was glad to converse. Indeed, he did more than let live, for his manner was now as fair as it had been foul. I found it hard to believe that this was the very man that Berry and I had thrown out some ten years before. That he bore no sort of malice was very clear, and, to our relief and his credit, he had greeted us as old friends. Except that he knew us again, he made no sort of reference to what had passed.

And now, here he was on the terrace, and 'the dud' he had brought in his car was standing against the wall. He had come alone this morning. Mrs Falk and Miss Cobbold were coming to join him for lunch.

"Well, I'd like to say this," said Coker, "before I say anything else. We're a tough lot in New York City, and if we can pull a fast one, that's just too bad for the Willie we leave behind. But my lil girl is English, and I know you're easier folk. But please get this right away – Mercy's not on in this act. She wouldn' be safe. I'll say Arthur made me think, when he spilled the beans: but that was a Bible-reading to yesterday afternoon.

"I made the monkey-house at three o'clock, an' there was the girlfriend waiting, all dressed to kill – with a tie all over his chest, and a cameo-ring on his thumb. And 'the dud' stuck up in an alcove, with velvet draped about it and a spotlight full on the face.

"I'll say I did my stuff with an eye on the clock. I didn't like being alone with a guy like that. But Arthur was due to arrive in half an hour. I was crazy about 'the dud', but when he asked forty thousand I wouldn't play. I said that was much too much and asked if he'd anything else. An' then he produced the pamphlet…

"Well, that was jam for two. I smeared it all over the platter and Goo-goo licked it up and whinnied for more. He'd never dreamed of such luck. He said I could have the lot for fifty thousand pounds… An' then I got asking questions.

" 'How, Mr Blurt,' said I, 'did you get into touch with me?'

"But Judas was ready for that. He'd got a buddy in Rome who knew all about me, an' the moment I'd showed up there, he'd sent him a wire. 'Put yourself in his hands,' he'd said. 'He's an honest man.' Goo-goo said he cried with relief. He didn't care about money. He always felt honour came first… Did I feel sick, or did I? That worm should hire himself out as a stomach-pump.

"Then I go back to the pamphlet.

" 'See here, Mr Blurt,' I said. 'Are you sure these pictures are yours?'

" 'Course they're mine,' he screams, and slobbers about unkindness and how it affects his brain. Prowling beasts crouching about him or some such tripe. Had to leave a theatre once. Darn well refused admission, if you ask me…

" 'That's all right,' I said. 'The pictures are yours. But how did you gather them in? They used to belong to the Pleydells, and they're their family stuff.'

"He said he'd tell me the truth, if I'd swear I'd never repeat it to any living soul. You see, it wasn't his secret. I gave my word an' sat tight. I could see the bomb-trap opening, an' I felt it was going to be big.

"An' this was what Goo-goo told me – an' you mus' pardon me, folk, for not lifting his dirty face. But that would have spoiled the set-up.

"The thing, he said, was this. The Pleydells were poor an' they couldn't keep up their place. And so he had lent them money over a raft of years. But he'd had security – these portraits. That had been written down. And now he couldn't go on. He was poor himself, for all his fortune had gone; and, much against his will, he was forced to foreclose. He'd lent you fifty thousand, and that was the very truth. And he had been very forbearing. But now he was seeking to get his money back."

Coker stopped and looked round. But we said nothing at all. We had no words.

"I guess," said Coker slowly, "I guess I know how you feel. And now you'll see why I said that Mercy's not on in this act.

And I'll say he told a good tale. He broke down and cried once. Real tears, too. They can put on an act, these pansies…

"An' there the shop-door opens, an' in walks Arthur Peruke.

"We'd fixed the reunion all right, and it goes according to plan. We mightn't have seen one another for twenty years.

" 'You wicked old gander,' I says, 'you're just the boyo I want. I'm by way of buying some pictures. I haven't seen the rest, but that's the Holbein there.'

"An' then I looked at the girlfriend…

"I'll say he was terrified. If he'd had any beads to tell, he'd have washed St Vitus' record out of print. He couldn't do his stuff, and he gets behind a couch that'd make a lame guy walk. Then Arthur went in, good and proper, an' I took a stroll up stage. He tore the guts out of Goo-goo, and Goo-goo kept whining an' wailing, 'You don' mean that.' An' then Arthur sees 'the Holbein'…

"He looks at it good and hard; an' then he turns back to Goo-goo. I couldn't see his face, but Goo-goo don't like its shape, an' he gives one hell of a scream an' makes for the door. But I was there first.

" 'Lemme get out,' shrieks Goo-goo. 'I don't like the look in his eyes.'

" 'What's he ask for this – Holbein?' says Arthur, between his teeth.

" 'Forty thousand,' says I. 'Pounds.'

"Arthur sucks in his breath.

" 'Divide by a thousand,' says he. 'An' then it's dear. The blackguard's changed the label. This isn't the Holbein at all.'

"Well, then we all jumped in and trod the grapes. I tried to get at Goo-goo, and Arthur was holding me back, and Goo-goo was making a noise like a couple of baths running out.

"Then I grabbed the phone and tried to get on to Bow Street…

"That broke Goo-goo down. Maybe they know him there, but it broke him down. Before Arthur could stop him, his arms were round my knees and he was begging for mercy with tears all over his face.

" 'I'll tell you the truth,' he sobs, 'but don't do that.'

"This was a new one on me, but I snapped it up.

" 'You mean you'll come clean?' I said.

" 'I will, I will,' he sobs, and so he did.

"What with the breaks for heartache, he took about half an hour; but we boiled it down in the end to half a page." Coker put his hand in his pocket and drew out the cloth-bound pamphlet we knew so well. "I made him write it in this: and on the opposite page you'll find his receipt. You read it out, Major."

Berry took the volume and read the writing aloud.

Mr Vandeleur Pleydell promised my mother that he would leave me something for which his cousins would pay me ten thousand pounds. Until his will was proved, we never dreamed that the portraits were worth any more. I am sure my benefactor did not think so. What he intended was that his cousins should have the portraits, provided they paid me the sum of ten thousand pounds.

Boris Blurt.

Received from Major Pleydell, by Coker Falk, the sum of ten thousand pounds for the portraits described herein.

Boris Blurt.

Before we could speak –

"Well, there you are, folk," said Coker. "I nearly had your Holbein, but what does the poet say? 'Vaulting ambition which o'erleaps itself.' If Goo-goo hadn't been greedy... But what can you do with a bum that eats his dead?"

We had done our best to thank that good-hearted man. We had shaken him by the hand and had drunk his health. Berry had written his cheque and had added one hundred guineas for him to give to Peruke. We had shown him the rest of the portraits and had taken him over the house.

As we came to the head of the stairs, my sister laid a hand on his arm.

"Come and see your present," she said. "It's very slight, and you may not care for it now. But please pretend to like it, because we ask you to take it with all our heart."

With that, she led the way to the picture-clock: and, as she pointed to the picture, the timepiece chimed the half-hour.

In that moment, we had our reward, for Holbein, with all his cunning, could never have set such a light in Coker's eyes.

For fully half a minute, he gazed and gazed.

Then –

"My little love," he said gently. "My little love."

When I went to my bedroom that night, my sister was sitting by the window, looking into the moonlight that graced the lawn and the timber and the sleeping meadows beyond.

As I came in, she stood up.

"Will you ever forgive me, Boy, for giving your present away?"

I put my arm about her.

"I've nothing to forgive, my darling. You'd no alternative."

Daphne laid her head on my shoulder.

"I miss him terribly. He was so comfortable, and he had such a gentle voice. I'd wake in the night and hear it. And when I heard it, I knew that all was well. I used to pretend he was my watchman. 'Half-past two of a windy morning,' he'd cry, 'and all's well.' You can't get away from it, Boy. He'd come to be part of our home."

"I know. I'm terribly sorry. But there was no other way. We had to make some return. And the picture-clock was the only return we could make."

"One shouldn't," said Daphne, "get so attached to things."

"I know. It's a great mistake. 'Lay not up treasure upon earth.' And yet it isn't our fault. Things that have something to them creep into your heart."

"We found him together, Boy. And now we've sent him away."

"To a good home," said I.

"Perhaps. But I think he was happy here. And I sent him away."

It was very childish, of course. We had gained a Holbein and lost a picture-clock. But I must confess that his going had hit me hard.

When I came down to breakfast next morning, a letter lay on my plate.

Dear Mrs Pleydell,
I guess you'll think me crazy, but I'm returning the picture-clock. I couldn't sleep last night for thinking of what I'd done. If I'd gotten it out of the saleroom, well and good. But I'm darned if I'll sack White Ladies to fix my apartment up. I'll always remember the compliment you paid me. And don't you go fretting about my losing your Holbein. Now that I know your home, I'll always be proud to remember I helped to hang it there.

Very sincerely,
Coker Falk.

What could we do? We sent him the best cigarette-case that we could buy, with *Coker Falk from White Ladies* written inside. Feeble enough, I know. But what could we do?

9

In Which Berry Keeps a Diary, and Tells Us a Fairy-Tale

"Can we afford it?" said Daphne.

"No," said Berry, "we can't. But we simply must get away. A change is the only thing. An absolute change. By sea to Lisbon, for instance. It should be nice there just now. And Estoril and Cintra should help us up. And then we can come back here in the middle of May. If we sell out the Collingwood holding…"

"I entirely agree," said I.

"I feel you're right," said my sister. "Only we keep selling out."

"I know," said Berry. "I know. That is the privilege of keeping White Ladies going as it has always gone. But I'm not going to keep the place up and live like a caretaker. And this isn't extravagance. Jill's been magnificent. But she stands in need of two things. Sunshine and pleasant surroundings to which she has never been. To be honest, I think we all need them. Her blow was ours."

So it was.

We had all flown for ages. Piers, Jill's attractive husband, had introduced us to the air. We found the element glorious, and used it whenever we could. Not that we were imprudent. The lines we used were lines that we knew we could trust. And then – Fate stretched out an arm…

What happened will never be known. Enough that an aeroplane crashed, and that passengers, pilot and crew were instantly killed. And Piers and the Fauns among them…

Mercifully Jill was with us, when the news came through. I took the telephone-message – I shall always believe that it took a year from my life: what is quite certain is that from that hour to this day I have never heard with composure the thresh of the telephone-bell.

"The Spensers are in Lisbon," said Jonah. "Rufus is doing some job at the Embassy there."

"Well and good," said Berry. He turned to his wife. "Drop a line to Lettice and ask her to take us some rooms."

Ten days later we landed in Portugal.

"My dears," said Lettice, "I've got you a furnished house. Complete with servants, of course. You'll be very much better there than at any hotel."

"God bless you," said Berry. "Do the servants understand English?"

"Not a word," said Lettice. "But you'll get on all right. I've arranged for an English girl to call twice a day. She'll take and give your orders and make things smooth. This is Senhor Fernandes – he's going to look after you. If you'll give him your passports and checks, he'll get your luggage through and put things straight with the International Police. Oh, and your keys, in case. And now let's be getting along. Rufus couldn't get down, but he's sent his car."

It looked as though we were on velvet, and so it proved.

The house was an Englishman's house and was very well found. The servants were efficient and smiling, and Miss Perowne and Fernandes did more than we could have asked. Before the day was out, we had hired a most excellent car, and Rufus looked in that evening, to pay his respects…

"The idea was this," he said, "that you should be able to be quiet and to go as you please. Nobody knows you're here, and nobody will. By the way, we've a cottage at Cintra we only use for weekends. It's at your disposal for lunch, when ever you like. Just tell Miss Perowne to ring the house-keeper up the evening before."

"A little more," said Daphne, "and I shall begin to cry. You and Lettice have been so wonderfully sweet."

"My dear," said Rufus, "you'd do the same for us." He turned to me. "By the way, you must sample the port. If it suits you, let me know, and I'll get you some more. But it's not on the wine-merchants' lists."

"It was served after lunch," said Berry. "These servants know their job. I think they must drink it in Heaven – it's not of this world."

"Good," said Rufus. "And if you should go away for a night or two, take your ration with you. I mean, it'll travel all right, and you won't get the same."

"He's asking for trouble," said Daphne. "Port always finds him out."

"Oh, this won't hurt him," said Rufus. "It's tawny port. Down in Oporto, they drink two bottles a day."

"We must go to Oporto," said Berry. "I've always wanted to visit that holy town."

"Inform me first," said Rufus, "and I'll tell you where to stay."

Our visit lasted six weeks, and was one of the rare occasions on which Berry kept a diary of any kind. Why he did it, I never knew: but, since it is far more vivid than anything I can write down, I have no hesitation in setting some of it out.

All Fools' Day, 1935.
Lisbon. What a night. Bed and board, synonymous terms. Not that I mind horse-hair, but why compress the stuff till all possibility of resilience has disappeared? Only fly in the grease.

Fly? Stag-beetle. I mean, what about bed-sores? 'By the twitching of my hams. Something wicked this way scrams.' To say that this morning was worthy of the glorious company which today commemorates is nothing. Seldom, if ever, have the time-honoured rites been more handsomely observed. Daphne and Boy, of course. Talk about trumpets sounding. They'll find a clown-band playing when they come to the other side. Even now I can hardly record it. No ink can do it justice, but I'm out of blood and tears. I think perhaps Durer could have drawn it – The Martyrdom of St Bertram…devils with smoking snouts, leering and hailing their prey. The thing was this. Jonah drives us down town in one blinding flash. Said we were late, or something – quite untrue. He drops us three at the Bank and then goes off with Jill, to read the lines of Torres Vedras, wot Arthur did. We'd take a taxi back. Well, there's nothing the matter with Lisbon. I like the place. Never saw the past fit into the present so well. And all is gaiety and vacation of spirit. We strolled about for two hours, forgetting time. I was glad to see Rossio again – I was to have been burned there in 1546: but they hadn't got my size in sanbenitos, so they had a bull-fight, instead. And I had a beer in the Avenida – both superb. If I'd known what was coming, I'd have had two double brandies… Since it was now past noon, we thought we'd go home. So we stopped a taxi – one of what I call 'the forgotten cabs'. Arthur probably forgot it in 1812. But you could still get in. And then the axe fell. My nearest and dearest *couldn't remember our address*. Knew it was Number Six, but didn't know the name of the street. 'Number Six, Lisbon.' I mean, can you beat it? Talk about blue-based baboons – with claw-and-ball feet. No idea of the way: no idea of the district: didn't know the name of the people whose house it is. And there was I, in urgent need of a restorative, confused by the hurly-burly of a strange city and deprived by the criminal negligence of those I love of that right which even the fowls of the air enjoy – that of returning to my own dunghill. When I recovered consciousness, they were endeavouring to appease the driver who was pardonably unable to appreciate why his orders were withheld. Considering that he knew no English and they knew no Portuguese, progress was on the slow side. Then we returned to our street – figuratively, of course. Daphne said that it had a funny name. I offered her *Comic Cut*, but she said that was wrong. Boy said it was a long name and he thought it began with an S. When I said that, when I last saw it, there were two BF's in it, their attitude became hostile. Then the driver returned to the charge. I knew his name was Garlic the moment he opened his mouth. Finally, having yelled 'British Embassy' in every known tongue, except, of course, Portuguese, Garlic made a noise like a sink, added 'OK' and let in what had been his clutch. I pass over the next few moments. I seem to think it was Regulus who was introduced into a barrel which was then allowed to descend a punishing hill. Enough that I am now qualified to appreciate his emotions during that momentous descent. We reached the Embassy, to find that Rufus was out. But the porter was dutiful. Not that we disclosed our dilemma – it was too shame-making. But he told gossip Garlic to drive to the Spensers' flat and said that we'd double his fare if he'd only go slow. Of course we drew blank again – Lettice was lunching out. I said we must do the same – I was feeling faint: but Daphne declared that the servants wouldn't understand. When I ventured to say that I considered my health of more importance than the understanding of my staff, my wife and her brother, omitting no circumstance of calumny, indulged in the foulest abuse. Then we drove back to the Bank, with some half-baked idea of endeavouring to recapture the way by which Jonah had rushed us two hours and a half before. Garlic wasn't in on this, and his efforts to perform a duty, the nature of which was unavoidably suppressed, were not so much distracting as conducive to insanity. Between his outbursts, Daphne said there was a sixteenth-century fountain which she'd know if she saw it again: Boy said we'd passed a house with a Doric portico: when

I asked if it had a Renaissance cesspool, they vouchsafed no reply, and when I actually recognized a dust-cart, they were incredibly offensive. And then, at five minutes to one, we ran into Jonah and Jill... Still, out of evil comes good. My betrayal was infamous; but Jill's blessed laughter was very cheap at the price.

April 3rd.

Midnight. Ought to go to bed, but sofa more considerate. This climate's all right. Estoril – yes. But prefer Cintra. A party of Boches at Estoril throwing their weight about. Enough to defile the Taj Mahal. God, how I hate that race. And I don't like all this German business at all. Find it most sinister. Seems as though we were determined to furnish some future Gibbon with an even finer material than that with which Rome furnished Edward. I can hear the opening sentences rolling out. *True to their traditions, the German people preferred to reject the substance of a friendship which they in no way deserved for the shadow of a dominion for which they were even less qualified. To this end, they chose, for their director, an alien artisan, who was said to have achieved the rank of corporal in the war of 1914, but had failed to distinguish the profession of a painter's labourer.* Oh, hell and all devils, doesn't anyone know the Boche? I haven't set foot in his filthy country since the war: but can the gorilla change his knobs? And what ever would Arthur have said?

April 7th.

Cintra. Lunch at the Spensers' cottage, and very nice, too. With no desire to be sick-making, must confess that Cintra grows on you. This was our third visit: and we shall go again. One leaves the car and strolls in surroundings which are superb. The view from the gallery outside the castle would be more arresting if the drop which immediately confronts you were rather less dire. I went all bugbears at once, and when Daphne and Jill leaned over, my large intestine – well, I couldn't see it on the flags, but the impression that I had lost it was overwhelming. It must have been a very near thing. Before I had recovered, a covey of tourists arrived, in charge of a guide. I was listening to him indicating the lines of Torres Vedras, when a Yank turned to blare in my ear. 'Say, who's this guy, Torres Vedras?' 'The first Portuguese martyr,' I said, 'to be eaten of worms. When the worms were through, they used them as bait. And that's where they put the lines out. They got about four million fish in two hours, so they called it a day and canonized the old boy. There's a painting by Orlando Basusto in the Ministry of Marine. *Torres Vedras and the Worms*. It's not supposed to be shown, but you know what five dollars'll do.' He wrote it all down, but when I looked round the others had disappeared. When I found them again, Daphne said I ought to be prosecuted. But I believe that fools should be fed. And I'll lay Arthur would have laughed. Well, I ought to know. When I was Picton, I saw him four days out of five. I remember the handle came off my umbrella at Badajoz. We floated home, dined early and went to a flick. All in English, God bless them. And then we sat under the trees and drank some beer. Give me the ever-open bar. With the ever-open bar, nobody ever gets tight. And that's a true saying, Sob-Stuff, whether you like it or no.

April 10th.

Showery, so dealt with mail. This includes pompous letter from complete stranger who seems to have fallen foul of the level-crossing keeper at Mockery Dale. Writes to me, as Chairman of the Riding Hood Bench, demanding vengeance. Must be deranged. Know what I should like to reply, but better not. Finally, *Major Pleydell presents his compliments to Mr Groansmith and begs to inform him that he has mistaken the functions of a Justice of the Peace. His confession should be addressed, preferably by word of mouth, to a Clerk in Holy orders, who, provided that he is satisfied that Mr Groansmith's regret is sincere, will indicate the nature of the penance which the latter should perform.* Took Jill to look at the coaches – *Museu dos Coches.* A most entertaining company. That monarchs were monarchs in their day, nobody can deny. Never have I seen gathered together so many gorgeous monuments of pomp and circumstance. And rough and tumble, too. The sluggish liver must have been almost unknown. Delighted to recognize the vehicle in which I used to progress when I was Luisa de Guzman. Parade State – self, two maids of honour, six lap-dogs, two parrots, a monkey and a black page. More than once, I remember, in August, we had to have a window down. And when a linch-pin came out, it was grievous bodily harm. I mean, four hundred pounds of maid of honour *à flot* would make a gorilla think. So to tea in the Rua —. Jill, looking a million ducats, cynosure of all eyes. Tea-shop the last word. Crammed to suffocation and right up to date – tables the size of writing pads and no room to put your hat, umbrella, feet or anything that is yours. Hot chocolate a dream: really worth drinking: guaranteed to make you feel sick as a dog in half an hour. Talking of dogs, charming Irish Terrier at next table displays an embarrassing interest in my shoes. Jill thinks it must be first time he's seen such a good-looking pair. Not so sure. Feel it to be more likely that I've stepped in something. As we're leaving, a wallah rolls up with some roses – exquisite blooms. Jill bows very gracefully and says that there's some mistake – she's ordered no flowers. Wallah explains in French that they're 'from the Management'. Jill smiles and takes them. 'Thank you very much. But you mustn't do this again. Otherwise, I can't come to your café. And I should like to come back.' A clear sky, so we stroll. Encounter Lettice who takes us into her car. Her Sealyham also among the prophets. No room for doubt now. Hope it's only rotten fish.

April 16th.
Here we are at Bussaco, where Arthur stayed. I wish I was at Lisbon, where I reside. I mean, why rush about? Lisbon and its

environs are quite good enough for me. Talk about blue-based baboons. Too many villages on these roads. And dogs. You know. Beat the car, bite the wheel and bark. How Jonah saves their lives, I've no idea. Of course they mean no wrong, but it shortens your life. Of his wisdom Rufus declared that, if we're to visit Oporto, we'd better do so from here. And Coimbra and Vizeu. The way to see this country is to have a private train. The roads leave much to be desired, and if you sleep outside Lisbon, you've got to watch your step. This evening we staggered about the battlefield. I did in a pair of shoes and Daphne fell down. But it all began to come back. Happily able to clear up a puzzling point. Massena knew his onions, so why attack the ridge when he might have turned Arthur's flank? You can say his maps were wrong, but that's no answer, because they always were. Fancy a French map of Portugal. Give me strength. 'I'm inclined to agree,' says Jonah. 'What do you know?' Well, Arthur rode up to me, with his field-glass under his arm. 'Tom,' he said, 'there's Massena…in the carriage with yellow wheels. Now it's most important that he shouldn't get ideas. You've got a carrying voice and you never repeat yourself.' A nod's as good as a wink. By the time my version of his parentage had been translated to Massena, two interpreters were under arrest and the Marshal could think of nothing but getting me down. So he went for the ridge, and Arthur hit him for six. As we got back to the hotel, a car drives up with a bang, and out gets Pony Skene. One of the old school, Pony – without the tie. Up at Magdalen together, a year or two back. Pony was always important, but now he's a very big noise. The seats of the mighty are in his dining-room. But he'd time to thank his chauffeur, before he came up to put his arms round my neck. Diplomats be damned: it's blokes like Pony Skene that make the world go round. He knows why we're here; so he's not going to ask us out: but he thinks, when we visit Oporto, we might see over his lodge. And very nice, too.

April 18th.

Yesterday Coimbra, today Vizeu. Sleepy, little, old town – Vizeu. I liked it well. We left the car in a garage and took to our feet. The greatest courtesy shown us on every side. For all that, I shan't be the same. I mean, the lane was steep, about one in four, and there was a girl walking up, with a bath on her head. A full-size, porcelain-lined bath. And nobody took any notice, except to get out of the way. And it takes two damned strong men to *move* such a thing: and it took six men at White Ladies to get one up the stairs, And there was this girl, with one of the things on her head. And for all she seemed to care, it might have been a box of cigars. You know, if Jill hadn't been with me, I should have suppressed the vision. As it was, I never felt more like a milk and soda in all my life. I suppose they're like that in Vizeu: but I hadn't the slightest desire to meet a child with a steam-roller under his arm. So we repaired to a café and split a bottle of beer. Suddenly Jill gives a squeal – one of her old-time squeals: and it did my heart good. 'What d'you know, sweetheart?' I said – and then I saw. You know, that town's not safe. A tumbril was coming towards us, drawn by a mule. And, as I live, the mule was completely clothed. Two pairs of trousers, a coat and a hell of a hat. But *trousers*. Two pairs, of the best sail-cloth… I suppose the general idea was to thwart the flies. But what about heart failure? I'll say I had a double brandy. I mean, you never know. Supposing Puss-in-Spats had rolled up and asked for a light. Which reminds me of that dear old lay –

A cat went out for a walk one day,
With his hat on the back of his head:
And everyone said,
Oh, look at that cat,
He shouldn't do that,
His head's too fat
And his face too flat,

For a hat on the back of his head, his head,
For a hat on the back of his head.

You know, I think I shall have to do the Alphabet.

A's for Aunt Agatha
All over ants:
They ran up her legs
And into her – vest:
(I thought it was best
To say 'into her vest':)
They gave her no rest:
But this was because
She sat down on their nest.

Well, here we go. Oporto tomorrow.

April 19th.

I forgot to say that Pony told us how to deal with the dogs. 'Believe it or not,' he said, 'they only want to know where you're going. If you're going to Lisbon, shout "Lisbon", and they'll clear out.' You know, it's perfectly true. Yesterday afternoon, one started in, so we all of us yelled 'Vizeu', and off he went, with his tail right over his back. I tell you, it never fails. There's nothing the matter with Oporto. How could there be? First we followed Arthur, saw where he crossed the Douro and put the wind up Soult. What a man. I'll say be deserved to eat Soult's dinner that night. Wasn't it Soult who turned his back on him at the Louvre? And HM apologized. And Arthur said, 'That's all right, Sire. I'm used to that.' But, what a beauty. After lunch we repaired to the lodge. There we were made free of the mystery of how port is done. I can think of many worse jobs. Strolling above the vats, you move in an aroma which has Coty beat to nothing. Clarence was right. Butt of malmsey or pipe of port – that is the perfect way to cross the Styx. And before we went, we each had a glass of nectar. And then we went shopping – and damned near bought the town. As we were going home, 'Whatever's that parcel?' said Daphne. 'Silk stockings,' said I. 'It's all right. I wrote the cheque.' 'But I said six pairs,' she said. 'Six dozen,' I said. 'I heard you.' 'Six dozen pairs,' she screams. 'I must have been out of my mind.' 'No,' said I. 'Just nicely. I give you my word, you looked like the Queen of Sheba. Oporto was your wash-pot this afternoon.' And Jill bought four Persian rugs and slept all the way back. Beginning to see why Pony's so popular.

April 20th.

Arthur used to say there was only one road in Portugal – that from Lisbon to Pombal. Things have improved since then, but I'll lay that much of that stretch has never been touched. Batalha has a fine abbey, but Rolica and Vimeiro are written in letters of gold in the book of Fate. We ate our lunch by Vimiera – cold mutton, of course – where Arthur pushed Junot's face through the back of his head. Yet, he'd only three hundred horse and no transport at all. What a man. Home to tea, thank God. After a bath and a change, felt up to getting my hair trimmed. Taxi a congenital idiot, so couldn't find Rufus' place. Entered another which didn't look too bad. I might have known. Portuguese only spoken – by two dozen butchers in white. And an armoury of clippers – to make the blood run cold. My particular torturer weighed about eighteen stone, and when I waved the clippers away, he fetched a razor with which to shave my neck. When I wouldn't have that, he proposed to cut my eyebrows, while some hanger-on was barking to clean my shoes. In the end they fetched a bloke from over the way. 'Yes, sir?' he says in French. 'Praise God,' I said. 'Will you kindly tell this artist to put all those clippers away? If he can't use a comb and some scissors, I'll go elsewhere. And if that wallah touches my shoes, I'll call the police.' Well, then they came to heel... A blessed evening at home, in front of a slow wood fire, suddenly blown to bits by Jonah's impious suggestion that we should pay a visit to Spain. Oh, I can't bear it. Only just back from a most exacting tour, and we're to leave this haven and fare far worse. 'Stay at Ciudad Rodrigo.' Yes, that's a good one. Rotten fish to eat, and bugs all over the place. Fifteenth-century sanitation – very interesting. But would they have it? No. What was good enough for Arthur was good enough for them. But how romantic. Lot of slobbering pantaloons, if you ask me. I mean, does the body count, or does it? So I pulled out the diapason. 'Look here,' I said. 'Nothing has so ministered to my mind as treading in Arthur's foot-prints and surveying the ground he hallowed by smearing Boney's marshals, one by one. But up to now, it's been in comparative comfort that we have done our stuff. We've had some trying days, but at least we've got in to a bath and a meal that you could consider without feeling physically sick. This latest obscenity ignores these valuable truths. First, we shall have a perfectly poisonous drive: then we shall cross the frontier – an operation which, if I know any-thing of Spain, will be attended by every circumstance of inconvenience, delay, insult and extortion: finally, we shall descend at a fourth-rate Spanish *bodega* – or whatever they call their bestial hostelries. Our rooms will be verminous; the sight and smell of the food will raise the gorge; the offices will be dangerous to health. If you must subdue the flesh, let's do a museum a day, or suck *bacalhao* before breakfast, or – ' 'You filthy brute,' says Daphne, for that got under her skin. I pressed my advantage home. 'My love,' said I, 'if you sleep at Ciudad Rodrigo. before you're through you'll sigh for a hunk of bad cod. And you don't want a smother of warts all over your countenance.' 'Warts?' screams Jill. 'Warts,' said I. 'Evil exhalations corrupt good matter. When I was Oliver Cromwell – ' And there goes the telephone. Rufus. 'Look here, Red Spenser,' says I, 'can we stay at Ciudad Rodrigo?' 'It has been done,' says he, 'but you won't be the same.' 'Hold on,' says I. 'Here's Daphne.' After a minute or so, she asked the Spensers to lunch and put the receiver back. 'Can I have some brandy?' she said. 'I don't feel well. And you can have the game. We're staying in Portugal.'

April 29th.

I like Lisbon more and more. A taxi down to Rossio, and then a stroll. The patterned pavements are delightful. A coarse mosaic of marble, black and white. These things matter. You can say they don't, but they do. Beauty always counts. The proportions of Black Horse Square and the Avenida are really handsome. More mail. Touching letter from a bloke we let down lightly two months ago. *Honoured Sir, Come out last week and done wot you said. No chance of a job not on your life but I sticks around and makes myself useful and after two days the farmer sends for me. Did you strap this mare he says. That's right, sir, I says civil. Good enough he says carry on. I'll start you at twenty-five bob. Easy as that. Had to let you know sir because its all thanks to you. Yours very respectfully, George Bailiwick.* What can one say? *Dear George, What could be better? Well, fifty bob, I suppose. But you'll soon be getting that. The great thing is, it's come off. Good luck and God bless. Yours sincerely, BP.* A very suspicious twinge in my left knee. Gorblime. It can't be the port. Not tawny. Oh, I can't bear it. And Pony drinks a bottle a day. Great argument about *The Times* jigsaw. I mean crossword. Provost of Eton said to do it while he boils his egg. All I can say is he must like his eggs damned hard. Trying to pull a fast one, if you ask me. Why, the anagram's enough to see most people through lunch. And listen to this. Six down – ' Even he had something to eat off.' And Four across – ' I should have said it was aching, but they declined.' You know, that's an obscene libel. I think I'll set one one day. Five across – 'Tell auntie.'

May 7th.

To Cintra by Estoril. Coast road. Reached the Spensers' cottage alive. Lunch quite admirable. Never ate better sardines.

Understand you ought to keep them for five years in box. Later we ventured to prove a private road. Unpardonable, of course: but this one has always beckoned, and we shall soon be gone. Forest at first, and then a most lovely prospect of land and sea. Stopped and got out. Surroundings ideal for meditation. The others strolled on. Woke to find an old fellow sitting beside me, smoking a cigarette, with his hat tipped over his eyes. I pulled myself together and did what I could in French. When I was through, 'Let us speak English,' he said. 'My grandmother was English, but I am Portuguese. My name is —, and you have done me the honour to make me your host.' We would pick a dukedom to gate-crash. 'You're very forgiving,' I said, and gave him my name. 'I'm afraid there are others,' I added. 'They're trespassing, too.' 'Not trespassing,' says the Duke. 'No English can trespass here. I will tell you why. More than once, your great Duke of Wellington stayed here, as my great-grandfather's guest. The old house has gone, so I cannot show you his rooms; but you shall have tea on the terrace on which he used to sit. And you can never trespass where that great gentleman passed.' Would you believe it? And there the others came up. Talk about the Gathering of the Fans... Before five minutes were gone, we were changing hats. What an afternoon. Tea on a lovely terrace, commanding the glorious prospect that Arthur viewed. And the old boy full of the dope that his grandfather handed down. The latter was only ten, when Arthur was here: and Arthur played football with him, down on the lawn below. He remembered Hill very well, and some of the Staff. Years later he stayed at Strathfieldsaye. And there was the musical box which Arthur had sent out from England and had given to him for Christmas, 1810. As good as ever today, it played for us. It was very moving to hear it – as Arthur himself had heard it, a long time ago. Our host's great-grandmother was always concerned, because Arthur would eat so little. But he would only laugh and say most people ate too much. That his officers worshipped him was always clear. Before we left, the old fellow gave us a map. It was a very old map, but Arthur had always said it was very good. The centre of Portugal. And on it Arthur had market the Lines of Torres Vedras with his own hand. This was too precious a possession for us to accept. But our host would have it so. 'That you may remember,' he said, 'this afternoon.' 'How could we forget it?' says Daphne. 'How could we ever forget such kindness as yours?' The old fellow bowed. 'You have made me very happy. Please make me happier still.' And so it will hang at White Ladies, framed in gilt.

May 11th.

Our last day. Lettice and Rufus dined with us last night. Entirely thanks to them, we have been able to relax. Exactly what we needed. All miles better, and – God be praised – Jill is herself again. Pity Adèle couldn't come: though she might have got bored with Arthur, who can't mean the same to her. Packing. Daphne swears she's not going to declare her stockings. There's the woman for you. Actually proposing to smuggle half a gross. Well, a gross, really. I mean it's yelling for trouble. Anything small, of course. But silk in bulk, no thank you. Besides, I don't think it's right. Not a risk like that. A last stroll down the Avenida and round about. A pair of earrings for Daphne, and a little fob watch for Jill. They can wear them. *Au revoir*, Lisbon. You've done us proud.

Nearly six months had gone by, and, after a very quiet summer we were spending a week in Town. People were very kind. 'Dine with us very quietly and say who you'd like to be there. Or, if you would rather not, may we come and see you?' Of such is understanding. That we should take sherry in Charles Street was natural enough. Punch and Athalia Fairfax asked some of our oldest friends.

"Of course I'll come to White Ladies," cried Lady Plague. "For a long weekend this autumn. Soon it will be too late, for, when I become a nuisance, I shall stay put."

"Nuisances," said Berry, "are born. Like fools and bores. You can't become a nuisance."

"I can physically. Dribbling and diets and being helped out of chairs."

"When Lady Plague dribbles," said Berry, "one listens for Drake's Drum. And England will be in peril, when you are helped out of your chair."

"Very specious," said Lady Plague. "But I'm getting on. Mr Forsyth, of course, is ageless. Thirty years ago he looked exactly the same."

"There are times," said Forsyth, "when I feel full of years. I'm growing tired of progress. It was rather fun at first, but now it has gathered speed. Our standard of living is growing absurdly high. But the finer arts are dying. If you are to cultivate them, you get left behind."

"He's right," said Berry. "Who ever found him wrong? We went to a play last night that had run for over a year. I was not only bored, but shocked. Thirty years ago that play would have been shouted down."

"Can't have it both ways," said Jonah. "And England is looking up."

"That's true," said Elizabeth Larch. "Contentment is coming back.'

"I quite agree," said Simon. "I haven't been here for six months, and I notice a very big change."

"The slow belly is less obtrusive?"

"Yes," said Forsyth, "it is. And Lady Larch is right. Contentment is lifting its head. That is beyond all price. I'd sooner see England content than England great. We are great still, of course. But not so great as we were. I think we're less – exacting. Perhaps it's as well."

"We're getting tired," said Berry. "Our reign has been very long. We've taught every other nation how to behave, and, as a result, are hated as no other power has been hated since Time began."

"And trusted," said Lady Plague. "Let's drink our health."

We did so cordially.

"And White Ladies?" said Punch.

"Stands where it did," said Berry. "You must come and see for yourself."

"Some Sunday?" said Athalia.

"Make it a weekend," said Daphne.

"A Sunday would be better," said Punch. "Just now I'm up to the neck."

"Foreign affairs?" said Jonah.

Punch nodded.

"Dear, dear," said Berry. "So much for the Zoo at Geneva. Never mind. Think of the unemployment, if they were to close it down. Thousands of blue-based baboons, all short of a job."

"I knew there was something," said Lady Plague. "What's all this about psychology?"

"The wonder of the age," said Berry. "Like halma and chewing-gum. No more inhibitions, no more hydrophobia, no more surplusage. The elixir of life at three or five guineas a time. It used to be ninepence a bottle at all the principal fairs; but now it's gone up."

"But is there anything in it?"

"There's a lot of money in it," said Berry. "I've a very good mind to have a stab myself. Look in my eyes, Lady Plague."

Lady Plague complied.

"Just as I thought," said Berry. "Your reflexes are turbulent. But that's not all. The chiasmic pollux is fluting, and that we must check. You see, that leads to arthritis. Let me explain. Turbulence is a condition occasioned by failure to relax. If the turbulence is permitted to become constant, the chiasmic pollux balloons, because it is overworked. That affects the diaphragm costive, and, after a little, fluting is bound to set in. Now you don't want arthritis, do you? So I should advise twelve treatments at seven guineas a time."

"And the treatments?"

"You learn to relax," said Berry. "You lie on a couch in a dark room, while I go out and get my hair cut."

"Thank you," said Lady Plague. "Mr Forsyth, what do you say?"

The lawyer raised his eyebrows.

"There are plenty of rogues," he said, "in every walk of life. The practice of psychology, which I have seen defined as the science of the nature of the soul, offers a fair field to the impostor. I mean, he mayn't come off, but he can't be caught out. My personal feeling is that the professional psychologist should be superfluous. The village priest, the family lawyer, the general practitioner – if they are not psychologists, they are no good at their jobs. You can extend the list indefinitely. 'The study of mankind is man.' Of course it's a sign of the times. If we go on like this, we shall have professional sympathizers."

"That's right," said Berry. "Your aunt leaves all she's got to the Barley Water Boys, and you take a course of comfort at two guineas a time."

"My dears," said Daphne, "listen. Elizabeth's got great news. She and Dick are building the perfect house."

"Gorgeous," said Berry. "I've always wanted to build. Something quite slight, you know, with a couple of priest's holes and a hectic tank."

"Tell them, Elizabeth," said Daphne.

"Well, it's down in Wiltshire," said the lady. "The thing is this. Uncle George has sold Bay Morreys for what he could get. But, before he sold, he gave Dick and me five acres – five acres of the park. Now the mansion is being pulled down, and we've bought enough material to build a very small house. Of course we're frightfully lucky. The man who bought it 's a builder and terribly nice. He could easily sting us, but he doesn't. And it does save transport, because we are on the spot. There are times when I feel quite ashamed, but he only laughs. Walls of beautiful stone, flags for the terrace – you never saw such things, a perfectly lovely staircase and parquet floors. The ballroom will easily floor the whole of the house."

"What a dream," said Jonah.

"It's like a dream," said Elizabeth. "Beautiful old stuff for nothing at all. And it's all because we're only five minutes' run. But the builder's a lamb – he picks out the best for us."

"Can't we come and see it?" said Daphne. "It must be wonderful."

"It is rather," said Elizabeth. "I mean, every room is panelled, and so's the hall. It's very tiny, of course: but it's really old. And we've got the stable clock – he made us a present of that,"

"I'm consumed with envy," said Forsyth. "It's often occurred to me that a perfect modern house could be born of one of the monsters of other days."

"Then, why didn't you say so?" said Lady Plague. "I shall write to Valerie to-night. It is the perfect solution. A new Bell Hammer rising out of the old. By Isabella Plantation, facing South."

"Oh, very good," said Berry. "Prejudice apart, Bell Hammer's too big today. Pull it down and build a dower house. Talk about picking and choosing – they'll have a showplace."

"I feel quite old-fashioned," said Athalia.

"Oh, come," said Simon Beaulieu. "Lullaby is superb."

"I know. But a smaller house…"

"You're telling me," said Berry. "But what can one do?"

"The spacious days," said Forsyth, "are over and gone. And I, for one, regret them. They were – magnificent. I know it's the fashion to condemn them; but the men they produced in every walk of life were finer men than those we produce today. But that's by the way. With comparatively few exceptions, the mansions of those great days are now but monuments. Some, like White Ladies, are so lovely that we can only hope that they will see out Time. But many serve no purpose, except to impoverish those who endeavour to keep them up. It would be so very much better if these were taken down and smaller, modern houses were built in their stead. As in Lady Larch's case, much of their stuff could be used to great effect; and the park would become a recognized building estate."

"There's a big chance there," said Simon.

"If," said Jonah, "the work was carefully done, the country would not be spoiled and England would be enriched."

"Homes worth having," said Berry. "Perhaps we shall see it yet." He turned to Elizabeth. "When may we come and see Bay Morreys' son?"

"Whenever you like, of course. But don't expect too much. I suppose you couldn't think of a name."

"*The Minor House*," said Berry. "No, that won't do. And somebody's got *Clovelly*. What about *Renaissance*?"

"Too grand," said Elizabeth.

"I must think it over," said Berry. "What's Bay Morreys mean?"

"We can't find out. Years and years ago it used to be called Hare Hall."

"Well, there you are," said Berry. "Leveret Lodge."

"Full marks," said everyone.

Athalia Fairfax was speaking.

"You're terribly lucky, Simon, to live in France."

"You are indeed," said Berry. "Not that I'm mad about the French. Certain of their shortcomings are painfully short. And I wouldn't reside in Paris for thirty thousand a year. But much of the country offers what England has lost today – the spirit and manner of an old-fashioned age. Of course they're behind the times – but that's what's so valuable. Take any French market: it might be a market in England sixty years ago. And Husbandry is still Husbandry. It mayn't be economic, but it's devilish picturesque. Then again, look at the service you get in France."

"We are very lucky," said Simon. "I realize that. And all Berry says is true. Our staff is proud of being part of our home. Our interests are theirs. If a tradesman puts a foot wrong, they're more angry than we. They work very well and they clearly enjoy their work. In their eyes it isn't degrading to run our home. Their one idea is to have their parents to tea and show them round. Pat, of course, always sees them before they go, and they always thank her for taking such care of their girl. It's the old outlook, you know; and good or bad, it makes for happiness."

"Company?" said Forsyth.

"We live our own lives," said Simon. "With certain exceptions, the French upper classes don't appeal to us. Our doctor, in fact, is a perfectly charming man: speaks perfect English, of course, and holds two English degrees. He dines with us and we go to lunch with him. But 'his betters' won't have him at their table. He's worth ten of them any day; but, because he works for his living, he is outside their pale. But lots of English people are round about, and we're not very far from Biarritz – for what that is worth."

"Unemployment?" said Punch.

Simon shook his head.

"None that I know of," he said.

"Of course there's none," said Berry. "Because they're behind the times. Unemployment goes with progress. Are a scythe and a yoke of oxen such false economy?"

"Taxation?" said Lady Plague.

"Largely indirect and half the rest evaded. How the country goes on, I do not know."

"Paradise," said Berry. "But…in a foreign field."

"There's the rub," said Jonah.

"I quite agree," said Simon. "Many a time we've thought of coming back. But when we go into the matter… I mean, it isn't one thing: it's one thing after another." He touched his cuff. "This shirt is five years old. Linen lasts in France, because it is properly washed."

"Exactly," said Berry. "By hand. 'As it was in the beginning.' What's France compared with us? As copper is to gold. But we have refined our gold. '*Gold* is good: but if the *gold* have lost his *virtue…*' But the copper's not lost its virtue, for France is behind the times."

"And now cheer us up," said Athalia. "You promised once to tell me a fairy-tale."

"Oh, dear," said Berry. "I'm sure I must have been tight."

"Off you go," said Punch, refilling his glass.

"There was once," said Berry, "a king, who was full of beans. Everything possible was done about it, without result: and at last his physicians declared that magic alone could relieve his unfortunate state. So a Council was held.

" 'Well, what about it?' said the King. 'I mean, these blasted beans are getting me down.'

"There was an awkward silence.

"Then the Comptroller swallowed.

" 'I told you not to,' he said. 'I remember it perfectly.'

" 'Of course,' said the King, 'there's something coming to you. I didn't summon you to remember my shortcomings. What I want is a reliable witch.'

" 'Exactly,' said the Comptroller. 'And eighteen months ago you fired all the witches out. Twenty-four hours to leave the kingdom.'

" 'If you ask me,' said the Chancellor, 'that's why you're full of beans.'

"The King frowned.

" 'We all make mistakes,' he said. 'Besides, I had every right. What about that invisible cloak? That I got for the servants' ball? Invisible, my foot. I never felt such a fool in all my life.'

" 'I know of one,' said the Master of the Horse. 'As a matter of fact, she's my aunt. She isn't really a witch, but she does a bit of sorcery on the side.'

" 'Is she any good?' said the King.

" 'On her day,' said the Master of the Horse, 'she's not too bad. I've seen her change my uncle into a jug of milk.'

" 'Have you, indeed?' said the King, wiping his face. 'Is the marriage still a success?'

" 'Dissolved,' said the Master of the Horse. 'She forgot to tell the maids, and they gave him to the cat.'

"The King looked round uneasily.

" 'We don't want any mistakes,' he said. 'All I want her to do is to spill my beans. Supposing you sounded her?'

" 'OK,' said the Master of the Horse; and so it was left.

"The next day, at another Council, the King received his report.

" 'My aunt will do it,' he said, 'but she wants a very long price.'

" 'That's absurd,' said the King. 'As one of my subjects – . Besides, I shall, er, recognize her services in the usual way. After all, I'm the fountain of honour.'

" 'And a widower,' said the other. 'She wants to be Queen.'

"As soon as he could speak –

" 'Are you being funny?' said the King.

"The Master of the Horse shook his head.

" 'That's treason,' said the Comptroller, who didn't like the idea.

" 'That's right,' said the King. 'High Treason. You'd better make out a warrant and serve it yourself.'

" 'That,' said the Comptroller, 'is the Chancellor's job.'

"The Chancellor swallowed.

" 'We don't want to be precipitate,' he said.

" 'I do,' said the King. 'Very precipitate.'

" 'And what price your beans?' said the Chancellor. 'Besides, she's well preserved.'

" 'Well preserved!' said a voice.

"The King looked round.

" 'Was that an echo?' he said.

" 'I don't think so,' said the Master of the Horse. 'I mean...'

"The King's eyes followed his gaze. Where the Chancellor had been sitting, was standing a jug of milk.

"The King thought very fast.

"Then –

301

" 'Serve him right,' he said. 'Talking like that about a beautiful girl. Why, if I were twenty years younger…'

" 'Are you sure you're not?' said the voice. 'I mean, I've heard it said that a man is as young as he feels.'

"The King clapped his hands to his stomach.

"Then a seraphic smile illumined his face.

" 'She's done it,' he cried. 'She's spilled them. My beans are gone.'

" 'Not gone,' said the voice. 'They're in that chest over there. You've only to say the word, and I'll put them back.'

"There was a pregnant silence.

"Then the King walked to the chest and lifted its lid…

"His physicians said it was cardiac failure. In any event, his funeral was very grand. The Master of the Horse was not present. He was sharing a very small hutch with two other toads. You see, he had exceeded his instructions. His aunt had told him to put a quart of beans in the chest. As she reminded him *ad nauseam*, she had said nothing about giant marrows."

The deserved applause subsided.

"And the moral?" said Lady Plague.

"I wouldn't know," said Berry. "But the title is obvious."

"Not to me," said Forsyth.

"*Psychology Reinforced.*"

10

In Which Berry Dispenses Justice, and I Attend Fallow Hill Fair

Only ten days had gone by, when out of a drunken frolic arose 'The Vision Case'. Millions of readers devoured the full reports: a certain firm of solicitors must have done very well: but for Berry, as Chairman of the Justices before whom Vision appeared, the episode was most trying from first to last.

For some years now, Berry had, so to speak, carried the Riding Hood Bench. He was scrupulous, level-headed, kindly and very shrewd. No doubt he made mistakes. The fact remains that his colleagues depended upon him and looked to him for guidance more than they should have done. Be sure they backed him. But the weight of the business was always upon his shoulders, and 'The Vision Case' was a burden he would have been glad to share. The Clerk was a sound lawyer, but that was all: he looked to Berry, just as the others did.

It had been a full day, for we had been to Bay Morreys and had visited Leveret Lodge. We had enjoyed every minute; but such inspections are tiring, say what you will. The girls had retired, and Berry and I were about to follow them up at a quarter to twelve, when, as I got to my feet, the telephone went.

Berry picked up the receiver – calls were put through to the rooms, when the servants had gone to bed.

303

"Yes... Oh, that you, Superintendent? Good evening. No, I was just going up... Yes, Curlew Corner. I know where you mean... Yes... Yes... I see. No, no alternative, clearly... That's up to you, Superintendent... Well, we shall see... At two o'clock tomorrow... No, that's all right. Good night."

Berry replaced the receiver, sat back and closed his eyes.

"And here's trouble," he said. "One of the Bluecoat school."

The phrase must not be misinterpreted. It had nothing to do with Horsham or with that most honourable foundation which enriched the City of London till 1902. The pleasant manor of Bluecoat had changed hands more than once since Withyham's day; and now it was owned by a man whose wife was not young, but immensely rich, whose record was not too good. The parties they threw were said to be very fierce: though the bright, young things that stayed there probably meant no harm, they certainly did no good: the place had become a byword for careless revelry.

Berry continued slowly.

"A smash at Curlew Corner. I'm not surprised. In a way, it's a dangerous place. Constable George was very nearly killed. In fact, there's nobody hurt, but the driver, a lad called Vision, was palpably tight. Dr Fawcett was going that way and arrived on the scene. Vision was very violent and has been charged. His host is expected to come and bail him out."

"Vision?" I said.

"That's right. The Honourable Edward Vision. White's wouldn't have him about six months ago."

"What a rotten show."

Berry shrugged his shoulders.

"Let's hope he pleads. But I have an uneasy feeling that one of that crowd will fight."

" 'Double, double toil and trouble.' "

"Precisely. He's money to burn, and the Press will eat it up. Of course he mayn't have been tight. I mustn't prejudge the case. But Fawcett says he was, and Fawcett's no fool."

At noon the next day we had a visitor. A Mr Baal arrived and sent in his card. This did not say that he was the junior partner of Messrs. Mosaic and Baal, Solicitors, of Furbelow Court, EC. He desired to see Major Pleydell – urgently.

"Act One, Scene Two," said Berry. "All right. Show him in."

Baal came in softly, after the way of a cat – a tall, sallow-faced fellow, with an eternal smile.

"Could I see you alone, Major Pleydell?"

"This is my cousin," said Berry. "I have no secrets from him."

Baal bowed and took his seat.

"I think I'm addressing the Chairman of the Riding Hood Bench."

"Yes," said Berry, "you are."

"I have reason to believe that you'll shortly make the acquaintance of a young friend of mine."

"And who may that be?" said Berry.

"The Honourable Edward Vision."

Berry raised his eyebrows.

"You say he is your young friend. Does he happen to be your client?"

"I have that honour, Major Pleydell."

"I see. Now tell me this, Mr Baal. Had the accident which happened last night occurred in the Strand, would you have approached the Bow Street Magistrate at his private house?"

Baal's smile looked a little forced.

"I – might have."

"Allow me to correct you," said Berry. "You would have done no such thing. I'll tell you why, Mr Baal. Because you wouldn't have dared." As I touched the bell, the solicitor rose to his feet. "The court you will presently enter is little known. But its justices are not to be corrupted, or bluffed, or diverted in any way from the duty they seek to do. You will make what observations you please in open court. But please remember this – that to the Riding Hood Bench, there are no back-stairs."

There Falcon opened the door, and Baal passed out.

305

With his eyes on the ceiling, Berry fingered his chin.

"There's a poisonous blackguard," he said. "And after that interview, I am expected to approach this blasted case with an open mind. I'd better speak to Evesham. Baal's quite capable of trying to get at Gorse."

One minute later, perhaps, the connection was made.

"Oh, is that you, Superintendent? Major Pleydell here. The Vision case. Mr Baal, of Mosaic and Baal, is appearing for the accused. I think he may try to see Gorse, but I don't think he should… Did he, indeed? Well, just see he doesn't, will you? And you might ring up the doctor. You never know."

Berry replaced the receiver and looked at me.

"He's tried already," he said: "but Gorse was out."

Scene Three was the little court I had come to know so well.

When I entered it, just before two, there was next to no room; but I found a place at the back, from which I could watch the proceedings unobserved.

Baal, with a clerk in attendance, was plainly pleased with life. For the moment he was the lion of 'the Bluecoat school'. This was well represented – by Mr de Rasen, host, and seven guests. Four of the latter were girls. Had they been asked, they would have declared that they 'took their fun where they found it'. And now they were ready and waiting and hoping to find it here. All eight were hanging upon the solicitor's lips. But Riding Hood was his dunghill. Encountering him in Mayfair, they would cut him dead. Their conversation was sprightly and meant to be audible. A reporter, clearly excited, was alternately looking about him and taking notes. Superintendent Evesham was whispering with the Clerk, and Constable Bush was standing beside the door.

Old Gammon appeared on the Bench and leaned down to speak to the Clerk.

The latter lifted his voice and spoke to Baal.

"Are you ready, Mr Baal?"

"Ready for anything," said Baal.

A burst of Bluecoat laughter acclaimed the *riposte*. Then Baal took his seat at the table between the Clerk and the dock, the door to the Bench was opened, and Berry appeared.

"Silence in Court," cried Bush, and most of us rose.

"D'you mean we've got to stand up?" said a high-pitched voice.

"Silence," snapped Bush, as John Lefevre and Colonel Lawson of Merry Down took their seats.

Shepherded by the jailer, the prisoner entered the court.

As he stepped into the dock, the Bluecoat contingent applauded violently.

When order had been restored, Berry looked round.

"One more demonstration like that, and the Court will be cleared."

There was no mistaking his tone, and a pregnant silence succeeded the simple words.

The Clerk addressed the prisoner, reciting the three offences with which he was charged – that of driving to the common danger, that of being drunk while in charge of a car and that of obstructing the police.

Baal rose to his feet.

"I appear for the accused and I plead not guilty to all charges. I also ask for an adjournment, that counsel may be instructed on the accused's behalf."

Berry consulted his colleagues.

Then –

"Very well, Mr Baal. We will hear the constable's evidence, and then a remand will be ordered for seven days."

Vision might have been good-looking, if heavy drinking had not disfigured his face. His age, I believe, was given as thirty-two. His air was resentful and haughty. Who was be to stand in the dock? If these people knew how to behave, they would give him a seat on the Bench.

Constable Gorse was sworn.

"At ten-fifteen on the seventh of November, I was approaching Curlew Corner from the direction of Mockery Dale. When I was close to the corner, I heard a car – "

"Is all this necessary?" said Baal.

"Be good enough to rise," said Berry, "when you address the Court."

After a long look, the solicitor got to his feet.

"Yes?"

"I was venturing to inquire, when I was interrupted, whether it was necessary that the constable should give his evidence in full."

"Before ordering a remand," said Berry, "it is the practice of this Court to hear evidence of arrest. As the arrest was made by the present witness, it would be out of all order for him to select from his testimony such particulars as he may think proper to lay before the Court." He turned to the witness. "Go on."

Approaching Curlew Corner from the East, Gorse, who was on his bicycle, had heard a car coming up very fast from the North. Once it reached the corner, the car must turn East or West, for there was no road to the South. Gorse dismounted and stood waiting, as close to the wall as he could. He was on his left side. The car turned to the East, but was going too fast to take the right-angled turn. As he saw it coming, Gorse let his bicycle go and leaped for the top of the wall. The car struck the wall below him a glancing blow and, running over his bicycle, came to rest. The car had a left-hand drive: otherwise the driver must have been seriously hurt, for all the right side of the car was badly crushed. Gorse got down from the wall and the accused got out. He was alone in the car. He was using very bad language and staggered about the road. He was drunk. He refused to give his name and address. Here Dr Fawcett arrived. After some conversation, Gorse asked the doctor to drive them to Riding Hood. When the doctor assented, the accused became very violent and went for Gorse. Between them, the doctor and

Gorse had got him into the car. At Riding Hood he had been charged…

Baal rose to his feet.

"Tell me this, Constable. If…"

"Mr Baal," said Berry, "the Bench has no objection to your questioning the constable now. But if you do so, Counsel cannot question him on Wednesday next."

"I've only one question to ask."

"Either you cross-examine, or Counsel. It is for you to choose."

Baal hesitated. His hands were working: I could not see his face.

Then –

"The Bench is determined to embarrass the defendant," he said.

"As you and I know," said Berry, "that observation is beneath contempt. The prisoner will be remanded for seven days."

"On the same bail," said Baal.

Berry looked at the Superintendent.

"Are you content with the bail?"

"Yes, sir."

"The same bail," said Berry. "Call the next case."

I think Baal felt that something had to be done. Before the Bluecoat contingent, he had been put in his place. And that was not 'according to plan'.

"I should like to enter a protest against the treatment I have been accorded today. I have been ordered about, interrupted and, finally, refused permission to question a witness for the Crown. I confess that my practice lies chiefly in the High Court, but on those occasions when I have appeared before Justices, I have always received the courtesy to which my profession is entitled."

"Your statement," said Berry, "that you have been refused permission to cross-examine is, to your knowledge, untrue. For the rest, you have received from the Bench a better treatment than your manner to the Bench has deserved."

Here the next case was called, and Baal and the Bluecoat contingent made their way out of the court.

As we were driving home –

"Did I go too far?" said Berry.

"Certainly not," said I. "The swine was out to smear you in front of 'the Bluecoat school'. But Counsel will have more sense."

"That's right. Baal is out of his depth in open court. His field is behind the curtain. Nice show we shall have next Wednesday. Evesham will keep you a seat."

"Will the police be represented?"

"I think they should be, and Evesham is going to apply. I mean, they'll have to put Vision in the box. And they may call evidence."

"To say he drank nothing but water all day long?"

"It's a wicked world," said Berry. "Did you see Fawcett at all?"

"I did," I said. "Counsel may shake Gorse, but he won't shake him. He followed the car, because he knew it would crash. And Vision couldn't stand up."

"Who'd be a Magistrate?" sighed Berry.

"You've been one now for more than twenty-five years."

"I know. And I'm glad to be one, when I can do some good. But here I can do no good. Vision is a law to himself. And now he has fallen foul of a law that is greater than he. I represent that law and am, therefore, his deadly foe. Though I let him go with a caution, Vision would hate my guts. D'you remember Lewis, the poacher – that came to a sticky end? He was the same. He knew no law but that of his own desires. In cases like these, the Magistrate is simply a hangman. My God, what a farce it is. I've got to sit there on Wednesday and probably Thursday as well, listening to Counsel misrepresenting the facts and to men and women committing perjury. And against them are Fawcett, who's nothing whatever to gain by telling the truth, and Vision's face. And Baal. Does anyone go to Baal, if his hands are clean?"

"What you want," said I, "is a drink. And you must keep an open mind."

"I stand corrected," said Berry. "But no man can have it both ways. To be any good at his job, a JP must be able to size up his fellow men – to tell a fool from a knave and a sheep from a goat, no matter what clothing they wear when they are in Court. Say that I have acquired that curious faculty. Well, you can't turn it on and off, as you can the spigot that graces a barrel of beer. So how can I help being struck by the pageant this afternoon? Fawcett, grave and keen-faced, a dutiful, clean-living man. Vision, as wilful a drunkard as ever I saw. (I'm not throwing any rocks. But for the grace of God, there go you and I.) The Bluecoat contingent, an idle, worthless bunch, actually cheering their crony when he is degraded by stepping into the dock. And Baal, the embodiment of evil... Don't be alarmed, gossip. If Fawcett goes back on his proof, the drunkard will leave the Court, an unconvicted man. The run he will have will be absolutely fair. But pity the poor JP, whose bogey is prejudice, who sees the truth sticking out, because he has eyes to see."

Half an hour later, perhaps –

"Was it very unpleasant?" said Daphne. "You look so tired."

"Not too bad," said her husband. "I had to put Baal in his place."

"I suppose half Bluecoat was there."

"They were bound to come," said Berry. "They couldn't let the side down."

"And Vision?"

"A very ordinary bloke. May or may not be guilty. We'll have to see what he says."

"Oh, you're no good," said Daphne. "I'll have to talk to Boy. Wait a minute. Look in my eyes." And then she was down on her knees, with her cheek against his. "My blessed darling, why will you take things so hard?"

"Because I'm a fool," said Berry. "Motley's my wear. I can strut in the counsellor's gown: but the executioner's tunic chafes me under the ribs."

The next day the London papers were full of 'The Vision Case'. The headlines were naturally arresting – EARL'S BROTHER CHARGED…DUEL BETWEEN CHAIRMAN AND SOLICITOR… SHARP PASSAGES IN COURT. Reporters arrived at White Ladies before midday. I gave them a photograph of Berry – I thought it best. We were drinking beer in the hall, when Berry appeared.

"Ah," he said, "a party," and poured some beer. "Here's to Contempt of Court." There was a roar of laughter. "And if you say I said that, the Vision case will be heard *in camera*."

"Won't you give us something, sir?"

"Have a heart," said Berry. "How can I? I know it'd be a scoop, but what about me? I don't want to be impeached, or what ever the procedure is."

"Just something, sir."

"I will, on one condition – that you don't say you got it from me."

"That's all right, sir."

"I mean that."

"We'll promise."

"That's good enough."

For a quarter of an hour he spoke of Riding Hood – of Justices he could remember, of famous counsel defending the motorcar, of how a Lord Chancellor had been summoned and had appeared by counsel and paid his fine.

"Who was that, sir?"

"No, you don't," said Berry. "I don't want to lose my job. But he was very angry – I'll give you that. 'Biting the hand that fed us,' was what he said. So in fear and trembling we fined him thirty shillings… As you may believe, the case was not reported."

And then, at last, Wednesday came.

312

If the court had been full before, that day it was crammed. But for Evesham, I should not have reached my seat. Mr Romeo, of Counsel, was sitting with Baal: small and dark, be looked extremely efficient. The police were represented by Arthur Leech, a very pleasant solicitor, not up to Romeo's weight. The Bluecoat contingent was stronger – I counted ten. They were making a lot of noise, when Romeo shot them a glance and whispered to Baal. Baal got up and went over to where they sat. And then they quietened down. The Press was present in force – I recognized three reporters, and they saw me.

The Magistrates took their seats and Vision appeared. Romeo's demeanour left nothing to be desired. The man knew how to behave. But I was pretty sure that be had a whip in his boot.

He had – and he hit Gorse hard. But Gorse was hardly fair game. And he could do nothing with Fawcett, try as he would.

" 'Drunk' is a loose expression?"

" 'Drunk' is a wide expression, loosely used."

"D'you ever use it loosely?"

"Off the record – yes."

And later on –

"You're an experienced doctor. Have you ever known a case in which a man appeared to be drunk, but was really ill?"

"I have known three such cases."

"In which a mistake was made?"

"Yes."

"Excusably?"

"Yes. In every case the man appeared to be drunk."

"But he wasn't?"

"No. He was very seriously ill. Two of them died, and the third was discharged from hospital after six months."

Shock went the same way. Nothing could shake Fawcett. Vision was drunk.

Finally –

313

"You are determined, doctor, to send this young man down?"
Berry leaned forward.

"Please reconsider that question, Mr Romeo."

"As you please, sir," said Counsel, and took his seat.

Then the accused was called, and put up a dreadful show. He made extravagant statements, none of which, I feel sure, appeared in his proof. Even I could have torn him in pieces. Leech was more lenient; but he tied him up more than once. His manner was atrocious.

Whilst he was being cross-examined, he went too far.

"Do you usually 'blind' by night along roads that you do not know?"

"Of course I don't. I'm not such a — fool."

Berry looked up.

"You will immediately withdraw that epithet and apologize to the Court for using it."

For a moment there was dead silence.

Then Baal left his seat, to approach the witness-box.

"Leave him alone, Mr Baal."

There was another silence.

Then –

"I beg your pardon," said Vision, sullenly.

"Go on, Mr Leech."

When he had returned to the dock, Romeo rose.

"I have four more witnesses, sir, and it is half-past five."

"Then we'd better adjourn," said Berry. "If tomorrow will be convenient, the Bench is prepared to sit at eleven o'clock."

Romeo consulted with Baal.

Then –

"Thank you, sir. That will suit us very well."

"And you, Mr Leech?"

"It's all right for me, sir, thank you."

"Very well. The accused is remanded till tomorrow at eleven o'clock."

We were on our way back.

"I'm sorry for Romeo," said Berry. "You couldn't see his face, when Vision was in the box.'

"I can imagine it," said I.

Berry expired.

"The whole thing's so damned unpleasant. Every soul in that court knows that Vision has done the things he is said to have done. And there he is, a gentleman born, telling lie after lie upon oath and flaunting his contempt and resentment of a system which has presumed to embarrass his way of life. And now say your piece about not prejudging the case."

"I can't," I said. "Not after Fawcett and Vision. The words won't come."

"Is it possible," said Berry, "that Romeo will persuade him to withdraw his plea of 'Not guilty' and plead, instead?"

"If I know anything of Counsel, he'll have a damned good try."

"Let's hope to God he succeeds. I should feel so much better about it – everyone would. It would be a redeeming feature, and that is what this case needs – and has not got."

But Vision must have hardened his heart, for when the morrow came, the case went on.

The witnesses from Bluecoat were called. They spoke to the quality and quantity of the liquor which Vision had consumed. They swore that he was not drunk when he left the house. Under cross-examination, one of them went to bits and made an awkward admission, which plainly shook Romeo up.

Still, he made an excellent speech. Few men could have made such bricks without any straw. It might have shaken a jury, drawn from the countryside. But Berry, Lefevre and Lawson were not jurymen.

"Before I sit down, I should like to thank the Bench for the latitude I have been given, for the patience and courtesy shown me from first to last. You will please believe, sir, that I am very grateful."

"As a man sows, Mr Romeo, so shall be reap."

Counsel smiled and bowed, and the Magistrates retired.

No one in court, I think, can have had any doubt that on two, at least, of the charges they would convict the accused. The only question was, would they be content with a fine? Reviewing the circumstances of the case, I could not believe that they would. Vision had no excuse. No harm had been done, of course: but that was not Vision's fault. And the public had to be protected against such selfishness. The way to protect it was to show prospective transgressors how hard might be their way. For Lefevre, I could not answer: Lawson believed in discipline – that I knew: Berry was very human – his bark was worse than his bite.

Five and twenty minutes went by, before they returned.

Then the accused was brought in, and Berry looked round.

"The accused," he said, "stands charged with three offences, far the most serious of which is that of being drunk while in charge of a car. It is to that charge that most of my observations will relate.

"It is the bounden duty of every Judge, Juryman or Magistrate to weigh the evidence given before him on oath. If the testimony of each of the witnesses in this case is separately weighed, no man of average intelligence can deny that the evidence of Dr Fawcett is very much more weighty than that of anyone else. In the first place, he is the only completely independent witness that has been called. He is not the Police Surgeon, and, until that unhappy evening, he had never so much as set eyes upon the accused, So far, therefore, as Dr Fawcett is concerned, there can be no question of bias, for or against. In the second place, he is a General Practitioner of fifteen years' standing, has been House Surgeon at St Bartholomew's and served with a combatant unit throughout the War. With such a record, he is far better qualified to decide whether or no a man is drunk than is any other of the witnesses that have been called before us. In the third place, according to the evidence of the constable, which has not been disputed, Dr Fawcett arrived upon the scene little more than one minute after the accident had occurred. And so, in his person, we have the only independent witness, the best qualified witness, and a witness who was, to all intents and purposes, on the spot. Now, for his evidence. He was about a mile from Curlew Corner, when he was met and passed by the accused's car. So high was its speed and so erratic was its course that, although he was on his way home, he turned his car round and followed, in case his services should be needed, when the accident, which he felt to be inevitable, had taken place. He arrived, to find the accused out in the road. He immediately examined him, and this is his report. 'He was unhurt: he was not suffering from shock: he was drunk.' Counsel, in the execution of his duty, did his best to shake those conclusions. In the opinion of the Bench, he failed. Pressed in cross-examination, the doctor used these words. 'In my time I have seen a great many intoxicated men. They may be divided into three classes – those who are under the influence of drink, those who are drunk, and those who are dead drunk. When I saw the accused, he belonged to the second class.' And a little later, in re-examination, 'He might have been suffering from shock, had he not been drunk. But he was not in a condition to appreciate how narrow had been his escape.' So much for Dr Fawcett. The constable, whose evidence is less weighty, bears out what the doctor says. Four witnesses have come from Bluecoat, and each of them has sworn that, when the accused left the house, he could not be said to be under the influence of drink. But from the cross-examination of one of them, a significant fact emerged. And that was that, as soon as it was realized that the accused had left the mansion, two cars were at once turned out to find out which way he had taken and follow him up. The witness in question declared that this action was not inspired by apprehension; but we cannot ignore the strong resemblance it bears to that which the doctor took. Finally, there is the evidence of the accused. He has sworn that he was perfectly sober, that the constable was on his wrong side and that it was in an endeavour to avoid the latter that he took his car into the wall. Upon that statement, he was asked two questions. The first was, 'How did you see the constable, if he was on his wrong side?' The accused replied, 'I saw the glow of his bicycle lamp.' The second was, 'In that case how do you account for the bicycle's being found beneath the car?' To this the accused made no answer. For this and other reasons, the Bench is quite unable to accept his evidence.

"The charge of obstructing the police will be dismissed. On each of the other charges, the Bench has decided to convict. On the charge of driving to the common danger, the accused will be fined twenty pounds, and his licence will be suspended for a period of six months. I cannot pretend to minimize the gravity of the third charge. For a man to be drunk while in charge of an automobile is always serious. One can well conceive such a case in which there are, what are called, mitigating circumstances. Take that of a man who drives a lorry for his living, and has been on the road all night, in winter weather. His conduct cannot be defended, if he succumbs. He is putting in peril life and limb. But we should not be human, if we did not remember that he has been bred in a rough school, that his life is a hard life, that weariness, strain and cold have called for more resistance than he is able to show. In the present case, there are no mitigating circumstances. The accused is a man of education, of no occupation, and he was doing no duty when the accident occurred. We do not attach more than due importance to the fact that, but for his presence of mind, the constable must have been killed: we regard it, rather, as a vivid illustration of the havoc which may be caused by a powerful car in the hands of a man who is drunk.

"The Bench has considered very carefully what punishment it is its duty to inflict upon this charge. And it has come, with reluctance, to the conclusion that no fine will meet the case. The accused and all who read the reports of this widely reported case must be shown that such wanton misconduct does not pay; that a law which was made to protect His Majesty's subjects cannot be set at nought; that no man's self-indulgence can be allowed to imperil with comparative impunity the well-being of his fellow men."

Berry surveyed Vision.

"Upon the remaining charge, the sentence of the Court is that you be imprisoned for six weeks with hard labour."

Amid the buzz of excitement, Counsel got to his feet.

"I beg to give notice of Appeal, sir, to the Quarter Sessions."

Berry smiled and nodded, and the prisoner was taken away.

Then the Justices rose. They acknowledged the bows of Counsel and the solicitor for the police. The next moment they had withdrawn.

"Was it all right?" said Berry.

"Terribly good," said I, and so it was.

"I don't know about that; but I do think justice has been done. If the Sessions vary the sentence, I shall retire."

(I did not tell him what I knew Baal would do. On the ground of the prisoner's ill health, he would get the appeal postponed until the Spring. And then he would bring in his doctors... That was exactly what happened. And a powerful silk was instructed, to lead Mr Romeo. So the Sessions quashed the conviction upon the third charge – and six months later Berry retired from the Bench.)

"I won't go," said Berry.

"You must," said Daphne. "After all, it's the Dean's daughter."

"I don't care if it's the Archbishop's morganatic wife. Which reminds me – I dreamed last night that I was an exceptionally hansom cab. Pleased with my appearance, his Grace climbed into my recesses and took his seat upon mine. After a rum shrub at *The Elephant and Castle* – "

"That'll do," said Daphne. "I promised that you would be there."

Berry expired.

"At this stage of our union," he said, "it should be superfluous for me to remind you that for a mammal to engage her lord is not only nugatory, but provocative. Besides, strange as it may seem, a sale of work is among those undertakings whose allurement, so far as I am concerned, defies detection."

"My darling," said Daphne, "this is no sale of work. Diana Cigale is opening a luxury shop – the kind of shop you see in South Molton Street. Brooch has nothing like it, and she ought to do very well."

"All the more reason," said her husband, "why we should keep away. We have no money to spend upon luxury goods. I want a new cummerbund, but I'm making the old one do,"

"Don't you want a backgammon board?"

"She won't have that," said Berry. "Nothing useful belongs to the luxury shop. She'll have nests of looking-glass tables and leather cocktail sets: pewter book-ends and cigarette-lighters about ten inches by eight."

"She's having three boards for us to choose from. Is that any good?"

(Our board had not been improved by the addition, in a moment of excitement, of half a pint of beer. It was Berry's beer, it was Berry's cuff that upset it; and when, because his chances were good, he proposed to postpone its removal, until the game had been won, even Jill had condemned his outlook in scathing terms.)

"Oh, the siren," said Berry. "I ought to have plugged my nose. Don't say they've got cork bottoms?"

"They'll be lined with cork," said his wife, "if that's what you mean. But don't you worry. I'll choose one."

"Oh, the vixen," said Berry. "And what do you know about that venerable game? Why, you can't even set the board out, without my help. When I was Bung-si-Hole in the Gong dynasty, my boards were specially made – of ivory, fretted with gold and floored with ambergris. No, this a different matter. If she can produce to me a board, at once discreet, sumptuous and inexpensive…"

"She's promised," said Daphne, "to give us a special discount."

Her husband fingered his chin.

"When do the shambles open?"

"On Thursday afternoon."

"Well, we can't go," said Berry. "We're lunching at Maintenance."

"That's tomorrow," said Jill.

Berry swallowed.

"I decline to promise," he said. "My attendance will depend upon my health. How would you like to dream that a dignitary of the Church had dropped his fare in your straw. Roked it about with his feet, causing me the greatest discomfort. And he never found his gaiter-button. I suppose it'll be all right."

Seven months had passed since the Hon. Edward Vision had faced the Riding Hood Bench, and another Midsummer Eve was only a week away. Jenny Chandos' husband was not at home, and when we had lunched at Maintenance, she would return with us, to spend a week at White Ladies, to our content. To her content, too, I think, for between her and Jill was a bond which was stronger than understanding: both belonged to Nature, heart and soul, and where others swam or struggled, the two of them seemed to walk upon the waters of Life.

We were always happy to visit Maintenance. The William-and-Mary mansion, the ancient rookery, the blowing meadows that ran right up to the house, a leisure of cows, suspending mastication, the better to watch the car, and now a pride of hunters cropping the shadows of immemorial trees: these things made up a picture, to warm the heart.

On this particular Wednesday, the expedition seemed fairer than ever before. The weather was brilliant, the countryside superb. And goodwill seemed to be rampant. We found a char-à-banc in trouble, and Fitch and I were able to help the driver to put it right. When we had done, the occupants crowded about us, shaking our hands and clapping us on the back. Yet, there was the Rolls waiting... It was more than an echo of the old days. Something more precious than gold was once again current coin.

"This," said Jenny, "is Cyclops. He's only one eye, you see: but he doesn't miss much. He's always about the stables. The horses love him so."

The goat considered us severally, licking his lips.

"An acquired taste," said Berry, "look at it how you will."

"He's very friendly," said Jenny.

"Yes," said Berry. "I wasn't thinking of that. Their quality, like that of mercy, is not strained. I sometimes feel that's a pity."

Here Cyclops advanced upon him, rose upon his hind legs and, to our infinite mirth, removed his button-hole.

"Cyclops!" cried Jenny.

"That's all right," said Berry. "The sk-goat is always downright. And his need is greater than mine."

"It isn't all right," said Jenny. "He ought to be ashamed of himself. Go and say you're sorry at once."

"Oh, er, don't bother him," said Berry. "I mean, his idea of sorrow..."

"Go and say you're sorry," said Jenny.

Cyclops let fall the rose and advanced upon Berry again. After eyeing him carefully, he rose again upon his hind legs and, placing a hoof upon his breast, approached his muzzle to my brother-in-law's chin.

With starting eyes –

"Okey doke, Cyclops," said Berry. "Remorse is better than sacrifice, as I feel sure you'll agree. And now shall we break away? I mean, you've purged your contempt."

Cyclops looked at him very hard. Then he withdrew, taking Berry's silk handkerchief with him, before its owner could think...

The next few moments were crowded.

Arrested, reviled and threatened, Cyclops rendered to his mistress a sodden rag, while Berry gave his head to the air and spoke of the cloven hoof.

As we returned to the house –

"But I can't understand it," wailed Jenny.

"My love," said Berry, "between the goat and me there is a great gulf fixed. Any attempt to bridge it has always failed. To begin with, as you have seen, our respective outlooks upon the rights of property are poles apart. I should never attempt to dispossess a goat of the piece of refuse adhering to its beard. I mean, it wouldn't enter my mind. On the other hand, the goat has only to see me to be filled with a burning desire to despoil me of what I have. A year or two back, it was a pearl-grey Homburg: by the time it had been recovered, its hue was, er, less fashionable and its general condition not to be mentioned by those of the Christian faith. Then again, our respective body odours do not, I fear, find favour, the one in the other's sight. It's the old story – 'The reason why, I cannot tell, I do not like thy filthy smell.' Indeed, to be perfectly frank, if I offend the goat as much as the goat offends me, then Cyclops has shown great restraint. Mark you, I bear him no malice. Possibly, in his eyes – eye, I was overdressed. And I should like him to have that handkerchief in memory of today. Soak it in asafoetida first, and then perhaps he'll revise his opinion of me."

"Shall I tell you what I think?" said Jenny.

"Of course."

"Well, he's terribly wise, Cyclops. And when he heard what you were saying – "

"That's right," said Jill. "About his being an acquired taste. Of course he got cross."

"Wait a minute," said Berry. "Let's get this straight. Is it your solemn belief that that most attractive ruminant understood all I said?"

"Perhaps not all," said Jenny. "But I think he got the general idea."

"I'm much obliged," said Berry. "If he could be put in a loose-box, I'll have another word with him after lunch."

We came home by Dovetail and Gamecock: the latter had seen sore changes, since Big James' day. Shops were flanking a garage on the site of that master's forge: Mulberry Corner was gone, and a block of hideous cottages stood in its place. As a matter of fact, few villages had been spared: not all had been so much corrupted, but few had been spared. This seemed to us a pity, for beauty should cost no more than ugliness.

The next day we visited Brooch – and the luxury shop.

I was sure, from the moment I saw it, that its lease would be very short. Brooch was too small and old-fashioned to digest so lordly a dish. In the window was standing a modern tallcase clock, with a dial of black and silver, most easy to read: I could see its pendulum swinging: but it did not tell you the time: it told you the day of the week and the day of the month. I confess I should have liked to possess it. I later learned that its price was one hundred pounds. At its foot was a glass ashtray, at least twelve inches square. Such is my outlook, I should have liked that, too.

"There you are," said Berry. "What did I say? Is shambles singular or plural?"

"Do be quiet," said Daphne, and led the way in.

Several people we knew were there, all looking something subdued. Mrs Cigale was waiting upon Miss Cobbold, who was looking very hard at a demijohn full of water, turned into a table-lamp.

"It's marked eleven guineas. I'll let you have it for ten. They're getting so scarce, you know. In another year or so…

Good afternoon, Mrs Pleydell. Will you go through? Your boards are on a table right at the back."

As we made our way down, my eye was caught by a snowstorm – one of those little glass balls, with a baby cottage inside. And when you shake it, snow-flakes begin to fall. I had not seen one for years; but I had found one in my stocking, when I was a little child. I decided to buy it for Jenny... But when I had looked at its ticket, I hardened my heart. Twenty-two shillings and sixpence. And I very much doubt if mine had cost eighteenpence.

The backgammon boards were the finest I ever saw. One was of Russia leather and had a table to match. The *ensemble* was marked thirty-five guineas. I supposed there were people who could afford such things. Another was of crocodile skin, with retractable, chromium legs. Its price was nineteen pounds ten. The third was of scarlet morocco – I must say I liked it well. It was a 'travelling' board: that is to say, its cups and dice and counters reposed in a leather case that fitted within the board, and the board could be closed and locked, and boasted a little handle, to carry it by. I do not have to say that it was lined with cork, so that the dice when falling would make no sound. But its price was ten guineas.

"Better not," said Berry. "Perhaps Baal'll send us one next Christmas, and then what fools we shall feel."

Mrs Cigale arrived.

"That's my favourite," she said. "I know it's a lot of money, but it will always look as it looks today. And it's very pleasant to play on a good-looking board. Miss Rocket."

Her assistant glided to her side.

"Yes, Mrs Cigale."

"This board is marked ten guineas. Can we possibly do it for nine?"

Miss Rocket looked rather rueful.

"Oh, I think we can," said her mistress. "It's nine guineas to you, Mrs Pleydell. But please don't think you must have one, because I have got them down." She turned to me. "How d'you like that clock in the window? It strikes at midnight, you know, just to ring the old day out."

"I covet it," I said; "but I haven't a hundred pounds."

"I know. It's a lot of money. But what an almanac. Ten per cent. discount for cash."

"Sorry," I said, "and I mean it. But I'm not a millionaire."

Of course we bought the board, and I got the snowstorm for Jenny for twelve and six.

As we were driving home –

"The thing," said Berry, "is this. If we'd liked to go to the Stores, we could have got a board for two pounds ten. A first-class, cork-bottomed board, that would see out Time. But the moment you step inside the luxury pale – well, your entrance fee is added to what you pay. And a superfine board like this is behind the bars. If you want it, you've got to go in and pay the entrance-fee. We were mugs to do it, of course: but we don't often splurge like this, and it's rather fun."

"That almanac clock," I sighed. "I can't get it out of my mind. I've never seen one before, but they must make them cheaper than that."

"Not very much," said Berry. "They're also within the pale. If you want a black bath, you can have it – at twice the price of a white."

My sister's arm was in his.

"Aren't you glad you decided to come?"

Yes, I suppose so," said Berry. "I'm deriving a guilty pleasure from what we've done – savouring that monstrous relish which only an unwarrantable extravagance can ever generate. But no drinks on the table with this one."

As soon as she could speak –

"Is that observation," said Daphne, "directed to me?"

"To all present," said Berry, piously. "We have seen the horrid waste which liquor, improperly quartered, may commit upon its lodging. It would be a great shock to me if this very beautiful board were to be likewise debauched."

"I have heard," said his wife, "of Satan rebuking sin: but Satan admonishing the good is a new one on me."

Berry sighed.

"I don't see why it should be," he said. "St Francis addressed the birds: why shouldn't the Prince of Darkness exhort the goats?"

"I said 'good', not 'goats'."

"This speculative theology," said Berry, "is beyond me. I think, perhaps, it's because of the mote in my eye."

Twelve days had gone by, and Adèle and I were staying deep in Scotland, at Castle Ruth. The Cullodens made perfect hosts and the lovely weather was that of the golden world. Susan Culloden was also American-born, and I had known her husband for thirty years. They could not afford to entertain house-parties, but if an old friend was willing to share what they had, they made him very happy day in day out. It was immensely refreshing to stay at their pleasant home, and though they had little money, I found them absurdly rich.

It was while we were there that a letter from Berry arrived.

Brooks' Club,
St James's Street.
25th June, 1936.

Dear Brother,

Repugnant as I find it to address you, it is meet that I should share the surfeit of gall and wormwood, which now is mine. It will be bitter drinking, and the taste will linger in your mouth: but that is no more than you deserve and is, indeed, the condign portion of the slow belly. That I, who have done no wrong, should be penalized is of course monstrous: and when it is remembered that it was I who protested with vigour against a policy which, if followed, could only lead to our damnation – well, from where I sit, I can hear the stones crying out. But that is always the way. The wicked triumph, and the godly go down the drain. I mean, you find it in the Psalms.

Let me begin at the beginning, for I have an evening to spare and the notepaper here is free.

It will be within your knowledge that, during your absence from home – an event, I may say, which has afforded me the utmost relief – I had arranged to spend three nights in the metropolis. Amongst other charitable duties, I desired to see Forsyth and to quell the suspicions of Coutts. One of those nights has passed, for I came up yesterday. To my great inconvenience, the appointment I had this morning was altered to two o'clock, and I found myself at eleven with nothing to do. I, therefore, strolled forth, to see the sights of the town. I found them inspiriting. The volume of traffic is prodigious, and the tortoise outstrips the hare. Indeed, the condition of the thoroughfares provides a startling illustration of that inexpressibly sad proverb which records the inability of man to introduce a quart into a pint tot. Virgil Pardoner declares that whoso shall walk from Charing Cross to Knightsbridge will be there before the fool that engages a cab. I suspect that this statement is tinged with exaggeration: but I must confess that the dimensions of some of the traffic-blocks are preposterous. Still, everyone seemed in good fettle, every shop seemed busy, and I could snuff prosperity in the air. Believe me, I captured something which has eluded my senses for nearly twenty-two years. I had the definite feeling that the last of the lean-fleshed line had disappeared in the river from which they came, and that others, fat-fleshed and well-favoured, were, so to speak, surfacing and moving towards the bank. I stopped to look into the shops. Quality and quantity are rising – a steady rise this time, and prices are going down. They're not what they were, of course: I doubt if they'll ever be that: but you do get your money's worth and the very deuce of a choice.

I was honouring Jermyn Street, when I encountered Fernandes – that energetic courier who kept our conscience in Lisbon a year ago. If he wasn't ravished to see me, he covered it up very well; and a crowd was beginning to form, when I stopped a hackney-carriage and pushed him inside. Not knowing where else to direct him, I told the driver to make his way to the Mall, and the journey gave me nice time to hear Fernandes' news. It had been his first visit to London, and he was to leave for Lisbon the following day: but he had seen more in ten days than I had in twenty years. When I could get in a word, I naturally asked if I could do anything for him, and it's Grosvenor Square to a gum-boil you'll never guess what he said. There was one sight he hadn't seen: and he didn't think he could see it, unless he could find a member, to take him in. But a friend of his had told him that he must on no account miss this remarkable thing. I thought of the Commons dining-room and the Pavilion at Lord's. But I was quite wrong. What he was mad to see was the Army and Navy Stores. By then we had reached the Mall, so I let the taxi go, and we walked to Victoria Street.

I think it was the abundance that hit him under the chin. Every conceivable grocery, tinned and untinned. Sides of bacon and hams: cheese by the stone: tons of jams and biscuits and farinaceous foods: sauces, figs, foie gras – everything you can think of, and thirty kinds of each. And customers swarming, like ants, all over the place. Fernandes turned to me. 'With all these purchasers, sir, even these great deposits will soon be gone.' 'My dear Senhor Fernandes,' I said, 'it is now a quarter past twelve. If I bought the lot here and now, and took it away, there would be another lot here before a quarter to one.' It seemed simpler to put it that way. Then I led him into the 'Drugs'. Crates of sponges and

every known make of soap: bath-salts of every description:
cosmetics and miles of tooth-paste: combs by the gross:
everything in bulk that the most exacting toilet could ever
require. So to the 'China and Glass'. Shelf after shelf of
services – dinner and tea: all shapes and sizes of glasses: fine
crystal and kitchen ware: eggshell china and vases half an
inch thick. The Tobacco Department shook him. Walls of
cigars and tobacco and cigarettes: tens of thousands of pipes:
tray after tray of smokers' requisites. And all being sold –
and, as they were sold, replaced. He could not get over the
abundance – which we have taken for granted all our lives.
Then I took him upstairs… By a lucky chance, I divined that
he needed a suitcase. When he saw five hundred to choose
from, he went and sat down. But I kept him up to the bit,
and we finally settled on one that will last him for twenty
years. He was lunching with friends at one, so we couldn't
complete our tour: but, as we made for a lift, I SAW
OUR BACKGAMMON BOARD. I give you my word, it was
exactly the same. Cork-bottomed, scarlet morocco, and self-
contained. I examined it carefully. And then, with bulging
eyes, I desired to be told the price. Four pounds, seven
shillings and six pence… And we had paid nine guineas to
Mrs Cigale.

How I got out of the place, I do not know. I vaguely
remember saying goodbye to Fernandes and waving away his
thanks. I'm not sure we didn't embrace in Birdcage Walk. But
I found myself back in the Club at five minutes past one. Yes,
I had a still lemonade.

If you can beat it, I can't. But there you are. Next time,
perhaps, you will be guided by me. If, indeed, there is a next
time, for no man, born of woman, can suffer a shock like that
and be the same. As I have so often reminded you. most
lepers would count themselves blessed to number a saint
among their relatives. They would hang upon his lips and

fight to wash his feet. They would mouth the hem of his garment and feel refreshed. Above all, his counsel would be received with veneration. But my inherent meekness has been the undoing of us all. For years I have accepted abuse, often obscene, in the hope that my gentle answers would wear indecency down: for years I have couched my protests in studiedly temperate terms, making every possible allowance for the verminous slabs of sewage you call your souls. And what is my latest reward? The privilege of being betrayed and despoiled by a vile and malignant harpy, wearing the habit and semblance of a lady born. And she knocked a guinea off, and let us have it for nine. But what self-sacrifice! What an oblation to lay on the altar of peace and goodwill! My God, the treachery of women! You know, they leave us standing, and that's the truth. Which reminds me, they're charging Fernandes' suitcase to your account. I think it was seven pounds ten, but it may have been more. I felt that you would wish him to have the best.

Give their Graces my love. I was, I remember, the first to commend their engagement some years ago. Which accounts, of course, for the fact that their marriage has been a success. Indeed I sometimes feel that my translation is at hand. Should I become air-borne before your return, there must be no cheese-paring about the stained-glass window. I had better be portrayed in a hair shirt, with an orb in one hand and a beer-opener in the other. My legs should be crossed, to show that I have been ejected at closing-time.

Well, here we go,
Berry.

PS. Must Adèle sail so soon? 'Are not Abana and Pharpar, rivers of Damascus, better than all the waters of Israel?'

I shall never know what took me to Fallow Hill Fair. But, just at that time – the late summer – my occupation was gone, and I did what my fancy dictated, because I was seeking distraction at any price. (Adèle had sent me a letter, to say she was not coming back.) And so I took Fitch and drove to Fallow Hill Fair.

For all the good that it did me, I might have stayed where I was, and, after strolling about for a quarter of an hour, I had just decided to make my way back to the car, when a lad of about seventeen came up to my side.

"Will you please to speak to my mother?"

"Who is your mother?" I said.

"Deborah Crane."

"Oh, the fortune-teller," I said. "And what does she want with me?"

"She knew you before I was born. Her name was not always Crane."

"Very well," I said. "Where is she?"

He led me behind a booth and lifted the flap of a tent; and there was the gypsy standing, with one of her hands to her breast.

I knew at once that I had seen her before. It was – yes, it was in the greenwood: and…

"That is right," she said. "By Gamecock. I was Sam Lewis' wife. I have seen you sometimes since then, though you have never seen me."

"I remember," I said. "I have good cause to remember. You did us a very good turn."

"I know. You are kindly people. I am sorry to see you troubled; but you shall sleep to-night."

"Thank you," I said.

"Come here and look into my eyes."

I did as she said.

"Do you see the flecks of hazel upon the grey?"

"Yes, I see them," I said.

"Think of them, when you would slumber, and I will see that you sleep."

"You're very good," I said. "I will do as you say."

She pointed to a chair, and I turned.

As I took my seat –

"So many come to me and, though they do not know it, go empty away. But that is not my fault. And others, whose lines are manifest, pass me by. And you were passing... And so I sent for you."

"Are mine so clear?" I said.

"They are clear to me. Shall I tell them?"

"Yes, if you please."

"I speak for the five," said the gypsy. "I know but three, but I can see there are five. You are set together, as stones are set in a ring. I think there were seven, but two of the stones are gone."

"That is true," I said. "And what of the five?"

"You have suffered two losses, and you will suffer two more."

I bit my lip.

Then –

"Death?" I said quietly.

The gypsy shook her head.

"Death has taken his toll and has gone his way. But the losses will be very sore. And the second will be the greater, although it will be the less."

"How can that be?" said I.

"I cannot tell. As I say, so you will find it."

"And then?"

The gypsy knitted her brows.

"It is strange," she said, as though she spoke to herself. "You will not be unhappy, and yet you will be denied your heart's desire."

I made no comment, and presently she went on.

"I find it strange. I would not have said that you would cry for the moon."

"That's not like us," I said.

"And yet you will. Your heart's desire will be that which no man can have."

"I see. Yet we shall be happy?"

"In one another. Always, always, the four will comfort the one." She put her hands to her eyes. "That is all," she said. "But, as I am standing here, it will come to pass."

I got to my feet, took a note from my case and held it out.

"That is much more than my fee: and I would have asked you nothing, for you are a friend."

"That is why I offer it you."

"And that is why I take it. I wish you well."

"My sister," I said, "would wish to be remembered to you."

"Please give her my best respects."

"Won't you send her your love?" I said.

Deborah's face lighted.

"Indeed, I will," she said. "And say that I have her picture fast in my heart."

Then I took my leave and went home. And I slept for eight hours that night – a dreamless sleep.

As I have shown elsewhere, within four years the half of her words came true. And now her bitter-sweet prediction is being fulfilled. I could not read it – they say that you never can. But now the riddle is answered…

We are not unhappy, because we are five in one. Indeed, I think we resemble a half-hoop ring. Berry is set in the centre, and Daphne and Jill support him on either side: and Jonah and I are the flank-guards, for what they are worth. And if one is dull, the others lend it their virtue… And yet it is true that we lack our heart's desire. But that is verily something that no man can have. I confess I never thought that we should cry for the moon. We don't cry aloud, of course. But now and again we fall silent, and Berry, who is reading, forgets to turn over a page. He is looking over his book, at the smoulder and glow of the logs.

And Daphne's needle is still: and Jill's grey eyes are sightless: and Jonah is frowning upon the bowl of his pipe. We have, I know, so much to be thankful for: we are, I know, properly grateful. But we should not, I think, be human, if now and again we did not remember the old days and wish them back. 'O, call back yesterday, bid time return.' Then Berry puts out a hand, and Daphne's fingers take it; and Jill sets her cheek against mine, and Jonah is smiling again, as he feels for his pouch. The *mauvais moment* is over.

After all, the past is ours. Let the morrow bring forth what it will, the past is ours. Lordly year and season, and handsome month...gay weekend and exquisite summer evening...care-free hour and the flash of a laughing minute... Of these things we have the fee-simple: and no one and nothing can ever take them away.

Epilogue

...And so I wrote to Sir Edward, as you always said to do. He came down on the Wednesday, and Fitch and I said how we felt. He's very understanding, Sir Edward. I told him that Fitch and I didn't care what work we did and neither had Mr Falcon – he was cleaning the gallery casements the day he caught his chill: but we had to have men and maids as would do as we said. After all, we know White Ladies. But the young won't take it from us, because Fitch and I are servants. It's not like it used to be. Sir Edward saw at once, and he said he thought the best thing would be to have an ex-officer and him to hold a position like the Secretary of a Club. He knows a very nice gentleman that used to have his own place down Tewkesbury way. He used to be in the Scots Guards and he's lost a leg. And he'd staff the house with ex-soldiers who'd do as he said. And then Fitch and I could retire as arranged, he said. He said that he'd write to you and see the other Trustees; but as he was sure you'd approve, he'd get in touch with the Colonel without delay. And now he's coming tomorrow, to talk to me and Fitch and have a look round.

I seem to feel, Madam, that this will go through. And I hope and pray it will, for, no matter what we do, Fitch and I can't keep White Ladies alone. We did the Royal Chamber this morning – it hadn't been touched for days. I tell you, Madam, you're better off with no one. And if it does go through, then our place is with you. We both of us feel that way, and if you would care to have us, we'll come wherever

337

you are. I can keep house and maid you and keep your things in order – you know I can. And I always did like sewing. And Fitch, as you know, can turn to anything. And if we can't be at White Ladies, we'd rather go right away. After all, we've had the best, and things aren't the same.

    Hoping to have your decision very soon,

Yours very respectfully,
Bridget Ightham.

PS. I kept this open to tell you about the Colonel. I'm sure you'd like him, Madam, and he does know. Mr Falcon would have liked to hear him on how to keep the floors. And if the arrangement is made, he'll come to be with us a fortnight and learn what we know. Not that we can teach him, but we do know White Ladies and all Mr Falcon did. Fitch took him to see the panel to Mr Falcon over the White Ladies pew.

Daphne's reply went pelting.

1946.

My very dear Bridget,
Of course you must both come to us as soon as ever you can. Major Pleydell is making all arrangements and is writing to you himself. As I told you, we can't go back to our home in France just yet. And so we are moving about – not an existence we like, but there you are. We have the house we are in for the next nine months. There is plenty of room, and I think you and Fitch will like it. It's old-fashioned and very quiet, twenty miles from the town. Of course it's inconvenient in many ways, but we are lucky to have it, and that's the truth. All our stuff is in France, and we can't get it out: but a friend has lent us some silver, and we have bought some rugs. There's a pleasant room, which opens on to a courtyard, where you and my lady and I can sit and work –

and talk about other days. Captain Pleydell is writing again, and Major Pleydell is building a dry stone-wall. He learned how to do it in France – they can't do it here so well. He has a man to help him and lift the stones. The man can't talk any English, and the Major can't talk Portuguese; and to hear them conversing together would make you die.

Colonel Mansel and Carson are due next week. I hope they will bring a car, for ours is on its last legs. Major Pleydell usually drives it, for Captain Pleydell's knee still gives him a lot of trouble – I fear it always will. But we are very happy in this quiet life. We've so much to be thankful for, Bridget. They've good English films in Lisbon, and sometimes we go a bust and drive into Town for the night. And we dine at a restaurant and my lady wears her pearls. But mostly we live very quietly day after day. So long as we can be quiet – you know what I mean. All that has happened – the changes – has driven us into ourselves. We can't do anything about it, and so we have just retired. But it will be heaven to have you and Fitch again. How very nice of you both to want to be with us once more. And I know you're right about White Ladies. Ever since your last letter, we had been worried to death. With a man like Colonel Scarlett, it should have a new lease of life. It mayn't be a very long lease, for things that are old aren't granted long leases today: but we have all done our best, and now we can't do any more. We have, all of us, played our parts as well as we could. And now our play is over, for 'period' actors can't do the modern stuff. It's a new technique, Bridget, that you and I've never learned. So come and 'pretend' with us – like children playing 'houses'… It doesn't hurt anyone else, and it's rather fun. I sometimes feel that we ought to do more than that. I've tried, and so have the others – more than once. But we're out of our depth, Bridget, in this new world. So come and share what we have. It'll be like old times to have you and Fitch about us…

Jill leaned over my shoulder, to set her cheek against mine.

"It's half-past twelve, darling, and you promised to stop at twelve. Come out and get Berry in."

An obedient husband, I rose and looked round for my stick.

"Take my arm," said Jill.

We passed downstairs and into the shady courtyard, hung on our heel by the fountain of old, grey stone, and turned to climb the path that led to the pocket meadow where Berry was building his wall.

Unobserved by the operatives, we stood beneath a mimosa, watching the busy scene.

"You son of Belial," said Berry. "You bull-nosed – "

A roar of delight cut short the apostrophe.

"*Sim, sim, senhor.*" Annibal's eyes were upon a very round stone. "*A nossa bola.*"

"I'm glad you concur," said Berry. "But I see no occasion for mirth. For mortification, perhaps."

"*Gangrena?*"

"I shouldn't be surprised," said Berry. "Mock the sage and meet the wart-hog, you know. And now remove that vile body and put in its place that very beautiful rock. Yes, that one. *Esse*, you blue-based serpent. What d'you think I've fashioned it for? *Inutilizar* be damned. It's a work of art."

"*Muita bem.*"

"I should hope so."

In silence one stone was discarded, and another was laid in its place. Berry adjusted this, grunting. Then he stood back.

"You see?" be said. "Fits like a blasted glove."

"*Sim, sim, senhor. Muito elegante.*"

"You've said it, brother," said Berry. "The great Benvenuto himself – "

"*Sim, sim. Bem venusto.*"

"You shut your head," said Berry. "I was talking about a fellow craftsman. A most entertaining wallah, rather before my time. Oh, you know that word, do you? Wonderful how the b-brain'll work for the b-belly, isn't it? All right. Get to your flesh-pots, Annibal. *Artistico ressumpcao a tres horas.* And bring some crags when you come. We're running short."

"*Sim, sim, senhor.*" Annibal turned, to see us a little way off. "*Boas tardes, senhor, senhora.*"

We gave him good day.

"Well, there we are," said Berry. "Gorge-like, the wall is rising, a sober monument. I glean a queer satisfaction from shaping and piling these stones. They're big with sermons, you know, as Shakespeare says. And they need a wall of sorts here, and the one I'm building will last. It isn't very lovely to look at, but – "

"I find it lovely," said Jill. "And the lizards will, too. Years after our time, the lizards will make their homes there and sun themselves on its top."

Berry nodded.

"History repeats itself. 'They say the Lion and the Lizard keep the Courts where Jamshyd gloried and drank deep.' Come, my sweet coz. Let us complete the prophecy. A glass and a half of sherry will suit me down to the socks."

As we turned to go back to the quinta –

"I'll say you've earned it," said I.

But Berry shook his head.

"Such increment," he said, "is unearned. There have been times, in the past, when I have pulled my weight. But this here wall is a vanity."

"So is my work," said I, "for the matter of that."

"I don't understand," said Jill.

"Let me put it like this," said Berry. "Some animals, when aggrieved, put forth an offensive odour. Others, such as the skunk, are still more downright. Reluctant to employ methods so crude, your husband and I turn to labour – in self-defence. Such work is vanity, for it is inspired not by the lust for achievement, but by the urge to avoid vexation of spirit."

"I don't agree," said Jill, taking his arm. "Good work's never vanity. Just now you rejected the stone that Annibal chose. I thought it looked all right; but it wouldn't do for you, because it was not the best. And Boy's the same. He'll spend half an hour on one sentence – until he's satisfied. Well, that's not vanity."

"That's *amour propre*," said Berry. "Once you're afflicted with that, you can't shake it off. It used to be common enough. but I'm told the percentage of sufferers is very much lower today. Wonderful thing, progress."

"I don't care," said Jill. "And *amour propre* and vanity don't agree. We can't compete today – I'll give you that. And so we're marking time. If we were standing easy, that would be vanity."

Berry took her small hand and put it up to his lips. "You win – as always," he said. "*Omnia vincit amor* – and always will."

And there was my sister by the fountain, with a basket of grain on her arm and pigeons strutting and fretting about her feet.

When she heard us, she looked up, smiling.

Then she addressed her husband.

"You're looking tired, darling. You ought to have stopped before."

"You're not – you're looking lovely. But that's your way."

Daphne's lips framed a kiss.

"Will you promise to rest till three?"

"Till five minutes to. The master must keep the disciple up to the bit."

Daphne scattered the last of the grain. Then she took Berry's arm and turned to the house. And Jill and I followed after.

"What were you discussing?" said my sister. "I thought I heard Latin used."

"We were being very highbrow," said Berry. "I furnished the feast of reason, and Jill the flow of soul. And then I repeated an adage, the truth of which you two darlings have never failed to shew forth."

"Spare me the Latin," said Daphne, "but what was that?"

"Women and children first. Ovid puts it better, but – "

"You wicked liar," shrieked Jill. "Boy, what was it he quoted?"

"Virgil," I said, laughing. "A very pretty saying."

"I forbid you," said Berry, "to repeat it. I will not wear my heart on my seat – sleeve." Daphne winked at me over his shoulder. "Yes, I saw you, you witch. And while I'm washing my hands – "

" – we shall do our best," said Daphne.

Her husband protruded his tongue.

Dornford Yates

As Berry and I Were Saying

Reprinted four times in three months, this semi-autobiographical novel takes the form of a conversation between members of the Pleydell family; in particular Berry, recalling his childhood and Oxford days, and Boy, who describes his time at the Bar. Darker and less frivolous than some of Yates' earlier books, he described it as 'my own memoir put into the mouths of Berry and Boy', and at the time of publication it already had a nostalgic feel. A hit with the public and a 'scrapbook of the Edwardian age as it was seen by the upper-middle classes'.

Berry and Co.

This collection of short stories featuring 'Berry' Pleydell and his chaotic entourage established Dornford Yates' reputation as one of the best comic writers of his generation and made him hugely popular. The German caricatures in the book carried such a sting that when France was invaded in 1939 Yates, who was living near the Pyrenees, was put on the wanted list and had to flee.

Dornford Yates

Blind Corner

This is Yates' first thriller: a tautly plotted page-turner featuring the crime-busting adventures of suave Richard Chandos. Chandos is thrown out of Oxford for 'beating up some Communists', and on return from vacation in Biarritz he witnesses a murder. Teaming up at his London club with friend Jonathan Mansel, a stratagem is devised to catch the killer.

The novel has equally compelling sequels: *Blood Royal, An Eye For a Tooth, Fire Below* and *Perishable Goods*.

Blood Royal

At his chivalrous, rakish best in a story of mistaken identity, kidnapping and old-world romance, Richard Chandos takes us on a romp through Europe in the company of a host of unforgettable characters.

This fine thriller can be read alone or as part of a series with *Blind Corner, An Eye For a Tooth, Fire Below* and *Perishable Goods*.

DORNFORD YATES

AN EYE FOR A TOOTH

On the way home from Germany after having captured Axel the Red's treasure, dapper Jonathan Mansel happens upon a corpse in the road, that of an Englishman. There ensues a gripping tale of adventure and vengeance of a rather gentlemanly kind. On publication this novel was such a hit that it was reprinted six times in its first year, and assured Yates' huge popularity. A classic Richard Chandos thriller, which can be read alone or as part of a series including *Blind Corner, Blood Royal, Fire Below* and *Perishable Goods*.

FIRE BELOW

Richard Chandos makes a welcome return in this classic adventure story. Suave and decadent, he leads his friends into forbidden territory to rescue a kidnapped (and very attractive) young widow. Yates gives us a highly dramatic, almost operatic, plot and unforgettably vivid characters.

A tale in the traditional mould, and a companion novel to *Blind Corner, Blood Royal, Perishable Goods* and *An Eye For a Tooth*.